DEFINING *the* AGE

DEFINING *the* AGE

DANIEL BELL,
HIS TIME AND OURS

EDITED BY

PAUL STARR AND JULIAN E. ZELIZER

Columbia University Press   *New York*

Columbia University Press
Publishers Since 1893
New York   Chichester, West Sussex
cup.columbia.edu

Library of Congress Cataloging-in-Publication Data

Names: Starr, Paul, editor. | Zelizer, Julian E., editor.
Title: Defining the age : Daniel Bell, his time and ours /
edited by Paul Starr and Julian E. Zelizer.
Description: New York : Columbia University Press, [2022] |
Includes bibliographical references and index.
Identifiers: LCCN 2021027095 (print) | LCCN 2021027096 (ebook) |
ISBN 9780231203661 (hardback) | ISBN 9780231203678
(trade paperback) | ISBN 9780231555173 (ebook)
Subjects: LCSH: Bell, Daniel, 1919–2011. | Sociologists—
United States—Biography. | Sociology—United States—History. |
Social sciences—United States--History.
Classification: LCC HM479.B445 A3 2022 (print) | LCC HM479.B445
(ebook) | DDC 301.092 [B]—dc23
LC record available at https://lccn.loc.gov/2021027095
LC ebook record available at https://lccn.loc.gov/2021027096

Cover design: Lisa Hamm
Cover photo: Courtesy of David A. Bell

To the next generation of intellectuals who take an ethics
of public responsibility seriously

CONTENTS

PREFACE AND ACKNOWLEDGMENTS

Every generation of intellectuals periodically needs to revisit its predecessors to decide how much of their thought belongs to the past and how much is still alive. This book is a contribution to that work. Our subject, Daniel Bell, was a major figure in American intellectual life, who played two distinct roles from the mid-to-late twentieth century. He was a journalist and critic, centrally involved in the controversies of his time. And he was a sociologist and social theorist who sought to develop ideas that would have durable value in understanding post-industrial society and the relationship of the economy, culture, and politics.

In September 2019, on the one-hundredth anniversary of Bell's birth, we brought together a group of historians and social scientists for a conference at Princeton University to reconsider his work. Some of the participants focused on Bell in his historical moment, while others were more concerned with evaluating the merit of his ideas in light of subsequent developments. The chapters in this book are the outgrowth of that conference.

We are grateful to all the participants, as well as to Princeton's Department of History, School of Public and International Affairs, and Center for Human Values for the financial support they provided for this enterprise. Throughout the process, we have especially benefited from the insights and counsel of our colleague, David A. Bell, who started us off on the project and helped keep it on course. We also thank our editor at Columbia University Press, Eric Schwartz, for his work in bringing this project to fruition.

DEFINING *the* AGE

INTRODUCTION

PAUL STARR AND JULIAN E. ZELIZER

The sociologist Daniel Bell had a singular ability to put his finger on critical changes in the United States and other Western societies in the twentieth century. The ideas summed up in the titles of his major books—*The End of Ideology* (1960), *The Coming of Post-Industrial Society* (1973), and *The Cultural Contradictions of Capitalism* (1976)—became some of the most hotly debated frameworks for understanding the era when they were published. As a social theorist, Bell also sought to identify the structural forces and long-term direction of the United States and other technologically advanced societies. *Defining the Age: Daniel Bell, His Time and Ours* is about Bell's legacy: how well his ideas capture their historical moment and have continued to provide insight into the contemporary world.

We would not have brought together a group of distinguished historians and social scientists to explore Bell's contributions if we did not think they had durable interest. Bell has often been cast as a representative and influential public intellectual of his time. But he was also a distinctive figure who stands out from his contemporaries as an original interpreter of American society and as a theorist of the great transformations of the modern world. His work holds interest from both of these perspectives—as a representative intellectual of the mid-twentieth century, and as a critic and theorist with ideas of continuing interest.

As a representative intellectual, Bell exemplifies the story of a generation that rose to influence after World War II. He was an important figure among a group known as the "New York intellectuals," most of them the children of Jewish immigrants who came of age during the Great Depression, were active in left-wing circles opposed to Stalinism in the 1930s and 1940s, and played a central role in American intellectual life and literary culture over the next several decades.[1] He was also one of an international group of social democratic intellectuals in the 1950s who defended liberal principles, opposed the extension of the Soviet Union's influence in Europe and elsewhere, and were denounced by their critics as "Cold War liberals" and "NATO intellectuals."[2] From the 1970s on, he was lumped together with the neoconservatives, an identity that has trailed after him even though he rejected it.[3] That label has probably done more than anything else to diminish and distort the historical understanding of his thought and politics.

Bell's substantive interests have put him in other company. As a result of his pioneering history of American socialism and his studies of work and unions, he ranks among the foremost analysts of the development of the American left and labor movement.[4] The interpretation that he and his colleagues introduced to account for McCarthyism in the 1950s remains one of the most influential accounts of the "radical right" in the United States.[5] His formulation of the theory of postindustrial society puts him among the principal thinkers about the information revolution and social forecasting.[6] His work on capitalism's "cultural contradictions" puts him among the leading theorists of capitalism and modernity.[7]

The various ways of grouping or labeling Bell locate him within broader intellectual and political currents and help explain the attention that his work has received. Bell's work opens a window into the political culture of the United States and the history of ideas in Western societies in the twentieth century. But to reduce him to any of the usual labels or categories or to confine him to the postwar American moment would be a mistake. Readers who get beyond the titles and secondhand descriptions of his books discover that his work is more complicated and far-ranging than they expect. That is partly why it also has held more continuing interest than much other writing of his era.

Bell stands out from his generation in part because of how he both maintained and revised his early left-wing commitments. Many others who began as socialists or communists in the 1930s became liberals in the postwar decades and ended up as conservatives by the 1970s. In contrast, Bell came to say that he was "a socialist in economics, a liberal in politics, and a conservative in culture."[8] He continued to adhere to the social democratic values he had stood for in his twenties as a socialist journalist, even after he turned to liberal politics and to a more conservative understanding of literature, the arts, and religion. Today, with the revival of interest in socialism in the United States, Bell's writing on the subject should have a new audience.

Bell was also distinctive in how he combined different intellectual roles. He moved from journalism to the academy, but throughout his career, he was concerned with both contemporary social criticism and social theory. During the 1960s, he gravitated toward more practical issues as he became a leading policy intellectual, and in 1965, with Irving Kristol, he cofounded and for eight years coedited an influential policy journal, *The Public Interest*. But, as Kristol moved to the right, Bell parted ways with him, and instead of becoming immersed in policy research, Bell turned more squarely to theoretical concerns in his two books of the 1970s, *The Coming of Post-Industrial Society* and *The Cultural*

Contradictions of Capitalism. Together with *The End of Ideology*, these volumes give Bell's account of how the European tradition in social theory, originating in the nineteenth and early twentieth centuries, needed to be revised in light of contemporary, largely American developments. Few scholars have left as formidable a body of work to be reckoned with by those who want to understand the trajectory of the modern era.

Bell's work commands attention for another reason as well. The United States and the world changed in fundamental ways from the 1930s through the turn of the twenty-first century. Anyone who lived as long as Bell did—ninety-one years, from 1919 to 2011, sharp until the end—was entitled to change his views, and his views did evolve. Nonetheless, his work shows a remarkable constancy of moral judgment and temperament. In an interview for a 1998 documentary on the New York intellectuals, he said, "I think I've been consistent all the way through. It's not that my politics haven't changed. Politics is basically a response to particular situations. I think my fundamental values have remained."[9] To understand what that moral framework was, we have to start where Bell started.

BELL'S BEGINNINGS

Daniel Bell grew up in poverty on the Lower East Side of New York City, the son of Jewish immigrants from what is now Belarus. Like most other children of immigrant families, he had no elite pedigree or patronage. His father died when he was an infant, and as a child he was often left at what was then called a "day orphanage" while his mother worked in a garment factory. The city's public educational system, including Stuyvesant High School and the tuition-free City College of New York, made it possible for him to get an education. But he later recalled two other institutions as framing his early years: his *shul* (synagogue) and the socialist movement, which opened up the wider world of ideas to him.[10] It was through the socialist movement that he had a precocious introduction to politics and a quick ascent that launched him into a key role in political journalism by his early twenties.

Bell started out at an early age as both antifascist and anti-communist. In fact, he was just thirteen years old in 1932 when he became a member of the anti-Stalinist Young People's Socialist League (YPSL) and stood on street corners campaigning for the Socialist Party's presidential candidate, Norman Thomas. During the following two years, he was attracted to the communists but turned sharply away from them after reading about an event that came to symbolize the brutalities of the Soviet regime: the Bolsheviks' savage repression of a rebellion by sailors at the Kronstadt naval base in 1921. The Moscow trials and purges that began in 1936, in which Stalin had many of his fellow revolutionaries executed, and the Nazi-Soviet Pact in 1939 later reinforced Bell's choice. From his teenage years on, in the internecine battles in the socialist movement, he stood with the social democrats, who were committed to democratic methods.[11]

Bell entered City College in the fall of 1935 and became active in a circle of radicals who ferociously debated the relevance of Marx's ideas to the events of their time. As a social democrat, he was to the right of two of his contemporaries, Irving Kristol and Irving Howe, who were both Trotskyists (followers of Leon Trotsky, the Russian revolutionary, then in exile, who advocated "permanent revolution"). In 1936, when the American Socialist Party split over the rising influence of a militant faction that called for seizing power in a revolutionary crisis, Bell supported the moderates who broke away to establish the Social Democratic Federation. The federation took control of several socialist institutions in New York, including the party's weekly paper *The New Leader*.

Leaving college after three years in 1938, Bell attended law school at Columbia University for the fall term and then transferred into the graduate program in sociology, where he was a full-time student for a year and a half. He had already been writing occasional articles for *The New Leader*, and he joined its staff in the summer of 1940 and, by his own account, was soon turning out 5,000 words a week under several invented bylines besides his own. When the managing editor left the next year, Bell assumed the position by default while the business manager looked for a replacement. But by 1942, Bell had become the managing editor in his own right, at a time when *The New Leader* was a platform for left-wing writers who opposed both the Communist Party's Popular Front and the Socialist Party's unwillingness to support the entry of the United States into World War II.[12]

During the war, Bell took on other editorial duties as well. When a group led by the theologian Reinhold Niebuhr left the Socialist Party to support the war, Bell for a time edited the bulletin of the new organization, the Union for Democratic Action (forerunner of the liberal Americans for Democratic Action). He also delivered a weekly commentary on radio station WEVD (the initials stood for Eugene Victor Debs, the longtime Socialist leader). "In 1942," Bell later recalled, "I even wrote the state platform for the American Labor Party," a third party established by the Social Democratic Federation and limited largely to New York. When Bell left *The New Leader* in 1944, he took a better-paying job with another socialist publication, *Common Sense*.[13]

As the war went on, Bell's expectations about its political implications changed. At first optimistic that the war would advance socialism and the labor movement domestically, he became increasingly concerned about the power of big business. By 1944, he was arguing that the United States was on its way to a kind of "democratic corporativism" that he called the "Monopoly

State . . . a system whereby industry and labor are locked together under contractual compulsion by the State and forced along a line of ill-defined national interest."[14] But though he had a contract for a book on the Monopoly State, he never finished it. Describing his decision to abandon the project, he later said that after writing several hundred pages, he "suddenly realized" that he had been "very badly educated . . . in a vulgar Marxist framework." He had imagined "American business as somehow coming together in a central web with a small, controlling clique dominating society," but he became convinced that it was an oversimplification.[15]

The late 1940s were an intellectual and political turning point for Bell. From 1945 to 1948, he served as an instructor in the undergraduate social science program at the University of Chicago, a period he later credited as affording him an opportunity to do more reading and acquire a more thorough education than he had before. He benefited especially from his fellow instructors—David Riesman, Edward Shils, Robert Redfield, Barrington Moore, Phillip Rieff, and Morris Janowitz—who would go on to become major figures in the social sciences. It was during this period, he said, that he became "much more of a Weberian than a Marxist" (some of Max Weber's most important work had just been published in English for the first time). The war and the Holocaust had shaken his earlier optimistic and progressive view of human nature and society, and he now looked at the Marxism that he had learned as "mechanical and sterile." In Chicago, though, he still maintained his commitment to socialist politics and became involved in a failed Midwestern effort with union activists to start a new social democratic third party.[16]

The breaking point for Bell was the Socialist Party's crushing electoral defeat in 1948. Years later, the socialist Michael Harrington would describe 1948 as "the last year of the thirties" because it marked the end of radical hopes.[17] Returning from Chicago to New York that year, Bell initially edited a new social democratic review, where he argued that socialists could wield their greatest influence by working through the Democratic Party. But that venture soon folded, and he instead took a job writing on labor for *Fortune*, the nation's leading business magazine, where he remained for most of the next decade.

So began the most intellectually productive period of Bell's career, from the end of the 1940s to the mid-1970s. It was at the end of the 1940s that he wrote his first book, *Marxian Socialism in the United States* (1952), in which he sought to come to terms with the failure of American socialism. Between 1951 and 1959, he wrote the essays that went into *The End of Ideology*. In 1955, he published an edited volume, *The New American Right*, an inquiry into McCarthyism that grew out of a faculty seminar at Columbia (and was expanded and reissued as *The Radical Right* in 1962). In 1956, he came out with *Work and Its Discontents*, a concise, probing examination of how work, and thinking about work, had changed in the industrial era. By the early 1960s, he was circulating the first of his papers on postindustrial society; he also took a year to study and reflect on the state of liberal arts education at Columbia, and the resulting report, *The Reforming of General Education*, was published as a book for a wider audience. *The Coming of Post-Industrial Society* and *The Cultural Contradictions of Capitalism* came out in relatively quick succession between 1973 and 1976, the fruit of the work that he had been doing during the 1960s and, in some respects, a response to the changes of that decade.

These were also the years when Bell switched careers from journalism to academia. Even while at *Fortune*, he had kept a foot in sociology, serving from 1952 to 1956 as an adjunct lecturer at Columbia. He then spent the 1956–57 year in Paris as the director of seminars for the Congress for Cultural Freedom, an international organization of liberal intellectuals formed in opposition to Soviet influence. (A decade later, in 1966, disclosures revealed that the group had received funds from the Central Intelligence Agency—an enormous embarrassment to Bell and others who had been associated with the organization.[18]) Returning from Paris, Bell resumed writing for *Fortune* for a year before becoming a full-time professor at Columbia. At that point, he still did not have a doctorate. "After everything had gone through and I was already appointed with tenure," he later recalled, "[the university provost Jacques Barzun] asked, 'Does Dan have a PhD?' " But Bell had never handed in a dissertation. Following a precedent that the university had set in another case, it awarded him a doctorate for a published book. *The End of Ideology* became his dissertation.[19]

Bell became deeply engaged in national policy during the 1960s as postwar liberalism was reaching its peak. From 1962 to 1964, he served on a presidential commission investigating technology, automation, and the economy, and then on a second federal panel that sought to develop social indicators parallel to the indicators of economic performance that the government routinely produces. When the American Academy of Arts and Sciences organized the Commission on the Year 2000 in 1964, it asked Bell to chair the group; the founding of *The Public Interest* came a year later. Bell's 1966 report on general education at Columbia involved him in debates about the future of the university, and in 1968, he was closely involved in a failed effort by Columbia's faculty to settle a student rebellion on campus.[20] The conflicts of the late 1960s created rising tensions not only on campus, but also among the circles in New York that had been so important to Bell personally and intellectually. Bitterly divided over the Vietnam War, the youth revolt, and other issues, the old community of New York intellectuals broke up and began dispersing. Bell himself was one of those to leave the city. In 1970, he moved to Cambridge, Massachusetts, taking up a professorship in Harvard's sociology department, where he continued to teach until his retirement.

BELL IN HISTORICAL CONTEXT

Beginning in the early 1960s, Bell occupied a position of unusual influence. A survey of writers for leading publications in the early 1970s identified him as one of the ten most influential American intellectuals, along with such figures as Noam Chomsky, Susan Sontag, and John Kenneth Galbraith.[21] (The term "public intellectual" came later; "intellectual" used to imply an orientation to the public and didn't need a modifier.) A much-discussed 1987 book even called Bell one of the "last intellectuals," as though the species was dying out.[22] In 1995, when Britain's leading review, the *Times Literary Supplement*, chose the 100 most influential books since World War II, two of Bell's works—*The End of Ideology* and *The Cultural Contradictions of Capitalism*—made the list.[23]

The intellectual and political world where Bell had begun his career was altogether different from the one where he achieved international influence. Professional opportunities for an aspiring left-wing Jewish intellectual were limited in the late 1930s; anti-Semitism in the universities and other elite institutions blocked careers for Jews at the higher reaches of the world of ideas. Bell was lucky to get a job in journalism in 1940, when few of his contemporaries with intellectual ambitions had jobs that paid them to write.[24] Besides *The New Leader*, the publications where he got his start during the war were "little magazines" of the left, all edited by radicals who had turned against the Communist Party: *Partisan Review* (Phillip Rahv and William Phillips), *Common Sense* (Lewis Corey), and *Politics* (Dwight MacDonald). Bell also wrote for *Commentary* after it was established by the American Jewish Committee in 1945 (a decade later, he was offered the opportunity to edit the magazine, a job that went to Norman Podhoretz after Bell turned it down).

Despite his marginal beginnings, Bell built up an extraordinary network of contacts through his role in a series of editorial positions and his time at the University of Chicago. By the time he was thirty years old, he already knew many of the people who would go on to become leading figures in postwar intellectual life.

The postwar decades brought about a change in the relationship of intellectuals and academics, who until then had largely been two separate groups. University appointments had been a rarity among intellectuals before the late 1940s. But when universities expanded as a result of the GI Bill and increased state spending on higher education, new opportunities developed for intellectuals to teach, write, and earn a good living as well. Social barriers that Jews had long confronted in American society were also falling, a change that particularly affected the New York intellectuals and their relation to universities. And so, like many other Americans, they began enjoying middle-class affluence for the first time.

In this new context, Bell's generation became more approving of American society, though not without some ambivalence. As Bell wrote in 1959, "The American intellectuals found new virtues in the United States because of its pluralism, the acceptance of the Welfare State, the spread of education, and the expanding opportunities for intellectual employment. And in the growing Cold War, they accepted the fact that Soviet Russia was the principal threat to freedom."[25] But tensions and divisions emerged among them over "selling out," settling into middle-class comforts, and especially over anticommunism and the Cold War. Jewish intellectuals experienced a particular form of ambivalence, which Bell described in an article in 1946:

> In Jewish life the cradle of love is the family. . . . It is also, in our time, the most painful. For the heritage of each Jew is the loss of

home and the destiny of footsore wandering. The story of the Prodigal Son, thus, is ever alive. But it is more meaningful and real today, for the Prodigal Son's return can rarely be realized. The Jew values the quality of sacrifice which characterized that home, yet he knows that two languages, not one, are spoken, and the sons cannot speak to the elders. . . .

The young Jew is left helpless, and aware. He is aware of a distance both from the Jewish culture from which he came and the Gentile culture into which he cannot or will not enter. He is helpless, for he cannot find his roots in either. Yet out of this tension of understanding and inhibition has been bred a new kind of Jew, the Jew of alienation, a Jew who consciously accepts this situation and utilizes his alienation to see, as if through a double set of glasses, each blending their perspective into one, the nature of the tragedy of our times.[26]

This sense of loss and sadness permeated much of Bell's work. His book on Marxian socialism, he said, addressed the "melancholy" question as to why there was no socialism in the United States. But he also claimed that alienation was a strength. "Alienation over the years," he said in a 1971 interview, "became such a cant word that anyone who had a bellyache suddenly became alienated. For us alienation had the sense of double consciousness, the sense of distancing oneself from events to allow a degree of detachment and involvement, yet never a complete involvement. Now if there is an intellectual and emotional source to the theme of the end-of-ideology, it would be in this very particular conception of alienation."[27]

The idea of double consciousness, of being one step removed from full involvement, affected Bell's conception of his own vocation as a critic. "Alienation," he wrote in *The End of Ideology*, "is not nihilism but a positive role, a detachment, which guards one against being submerged in any cause." Ideology was surrender. "The claims of doubt are prior to the claims of faith. One's commitment is to one's vocation"—in other words, not to an ideology or a movement. But this commitment to the vocation of social criticism did not require a denial of "one's roots or country," for it was possible to be "a critic of one's country without being an enemy of its promise."[28]

Throughout Bell's career, he was suspicious of fanaticism. "An intellectual," Bell liked to say, "is a person who knows how to make relevant distinctions."[29] No distinction may have been more important to him than one that Weber made between "an ethic of ultimate ends" and an "ethic of responsibility."[30] An ethic of ultimate ends requires total devotion to those ends, to the disregard of the human cost, whereas an ethic of responsibility requires a weighing of consequences. Bell's choice was the ethic of responsibility, and how he interpreted that ethic critically affected how he responded to the major intellectual and political issues of the postwar decades.

The 1950s are remembered as the decade of the "quiet generation," the 1960s as a decade of renewed political activism. During the 1950s, Bell wrote, the terms that dominated intellectual discourse were "irony, paradox, ambiguity, and complexity," whereas the 1960s saw a return of passionate commitments drawn in sharp contrast.[31] But both decades were roiled by bitter conflicts on the left—in the 1950s, about communism and McCarthyism, and in the 1960s, about liberalism and the New Left.

Bell, as we have already mentioned, opposed communism from an early age, and as a social democrat, he regarded the communists and their methods as inimical to democracy. The Communist Party, in Bell's view, was more of a conspiracy than a legitimate political party because it acted at the behest of a foreign power (a point on which no doubt can possibly remain since the opening of the Soviet archives), and because it operated through "front groups," in which its members concealed their party connections, beliefs, and motives. But while Bell viewed the Soviet Union internationally as a threat to freedom, he had no sympathy with Senator Joseph McCarthy and others on the right who were conjuring up a vast communist menace in the United States. Bell argued that when the "communist issue" became central to American politics in the early 1950s, McCarthy was grotesquely exaggerating the influence of the Communist Party and recklessly damaging American democracy with unfounded accusations and suspicions.[32]

But how had McCarthy been able to gain so much power and wreak so much damage? Unlike earlier Marxist and Progressive historians, who typically saw the political right as the creature of reactionary elites, Bell and the other authors he assembled in *The New American Right* granted that McCarthyism had genuine popular support. They interpreted that support as originating not from economic suffering, but from the "status anxieties" of groups who saw themselves as being victimized by social change and denied their rightful place of honor by disloyal elites. By the time the book appeared in 1955, the fever of McCarthyism had already broken, but Bell argued that the forces that he and the other contributors identified were deep rooted.[33] Today, when analysts explain right-wing populism as originating from the anxieties of white conservatives about demographic and cultural change, they are basically invoking the same theory of frustrated privilege that Bell and his colleagues developed for the radical right of the mid-twentieth century.

During the second half of the 1950s, with both the radical left and the radical right marginalized, ideological politics was at a low ebb, and Bell's book *The End of Ideology* captured that mood—what he referred to in the subtitle as "The Exhaustion of Political Ideas in the Fifties." He was using "ideology" in a restricted sense, only to refer to "all-inclusive" systems of thought that were "infused with passion" and sought "to transform the whole of a way of life."[34] At least in the United States and Western Europe, the old arguments between Marxism and free-market liberalism appeared to have given way to consensus on a compromise—a modified form of capitalism with a strong role for government in managing the economy and protecting workers and consumers. This was the main sense in which the French sociologist Raymond Aron and others had discussed an end to the "age of ideologies" at a meeting of the Congress for Cultural Freedom in Milan in 1955.[35] Although some critics interpreted the "end of ideology" to imply support for the status quo, Bell was an advocate of further liberal reforms. For example, the presidential commission on which he served under John F. Kennedy and Lyndon B. Johnson recommended that the government guarantee a job to anyone who exhausted unemployment benefits, assure a minimum income to every family, and provide free public education for fourteen years (through the second year of college). Although President Johnson shelved the report, Bell believed that its proposals would eventually be adopted.[36]

But Bell was skeptical about the demand for quick solutions in Johnson's War on Poverty. In 1967, he wrote that he had been "appalled by the fact that the Kennedy and Johnson Administrations had 'discovered' the problems of poverty, education, urban renewal, and air pollution as if they were completely new." What was needed was long-range and rational planning. The purpose of the Commission on the Year 2000, as Bell saw it, was to lay out "the future consequences of present public policy decisions, to anticipate future problems, and to begin the design of alternative solutions so that our society has more options and can make a moral choice, rather than be constrained, as is so often the case when problems descend upon us unnoticed and demand an immediate response."[37]

By 1967, Bell was laying out the main lines of his own think-ing in a series of articles about the future of "post-industrial soci-ety." At the core of his argument were a number of interconnected trends. The economy was shifting from the production of goods to the production of services, particularly more complex ser-vices such as education, research, and health care; innovation was becoming more dependent on advances in science and theoreti-cal knowledge. Consequently, the professional-technical class was on its way to becoming the most important occupational group, and universities were becoming the key institution for economic development. Certain new technologies, particularly computers, would play an important role (in later versions of the argument, Bell emphasized the convergence of computers and telecommuni-cations). The postindustrial society, Bell believed, raised problems that would have to be addressed collectively: "In the 'Great Soci-ety' more and more goods necessarily have to be purchased com-munally. The planning of cities and the rationalization of transit, the maintenance of open spaces and the extension of recreational areas, the elimination of air pollution and the cleaning up of the rivers, the underwriting of education and the organization of ade-quate medical care, all of these are now necessarily the concern of 'public institutions.' "[38]

Although he was criticized as "technocratic," Bell always empha-sized that policies reflect moral values and that political leaders would continue to be the pivotal decision-makers. In fact, because decisions were shifting from the market to the political arena, postindustrial society would aggravate political conflicts: "The political arena is an open cockpit where decision points are more visible than they are in the impersonal market; different groups will clash more directly as they contend for advantage or seek to resist change in society." To be sure, Bell insisted that good deci-sions required more exact knowledge and that technical experts would play a larger role, but he never saw technical expertise as superseding moral and political judgment. The more telling criticism is that despite Bell's liberal political sympathies, he was overly optimistic about the consequences of the postindustrial shift for industrial workers, and he paid relatively little attention to the implications for racial minorities and women. The Commission on the Year 2000 illustrated in an extreme form the elite biases typical of the period—its membership consisted entirely of white men.[39]

In a speech to a social democratic labor group in 1964, Bell called upon Black leaders to follow the example of the industrial unions, which in the 1930s turned from sit-ins and other protests to bargaining over concrete gains. He also cited as a model the communal, self-help institutions that white immigrant groups had created, while recognizing that the "legitimate political demands" of the civil rights movement had to be met.[40] On the whole, though, race was a blind spot in Bell's work; he tended to subsume race under the general heading of "ethnicity" and to see the challenges facing Blacks from the standpoint of an analogy with white immigrants that made sense to many in his generation of social scientists because of their own heritage and experience. That analogy, however, had great limitations as a way of understanding the racism that Blacks confronted.[41]

Bell was only one of a number of social scientists and popular writers in the late 1960s and early 1970s trying to anticipate how the technologically advanced societies would evolve. But even with his blind spots and other limitations, he offered a clearer analysis of how change in the "techno-economic" realm was likely to alter social structure, reorder institutions, and create new political challenges. One advantage of his approach, paradoxically, was that it was cautious and open-ended. Rather than try to forecast how the political decisions would come out, Bell argued that postindustrial change would create a "new agenda" for politics.

Bell also argued that the changes in technology, the economy, and social structure did not determine cultural life. Quite the opposite: there was an emerging disjuncture of culture and social structure. As he put it in 1967, "Society becomes more functionally organized, geared to knowledge and the mastery of complex bodies of learning. The culture becomes more hedonistic, permissive, expressive, distrustful of authority and of the purposive, delayed-gratification of a bourgeois, achievement-oriented technological world."[42] This argument would become central to the book that he published nearly a decade later, *The Cultural Contradictions of Capitalism*.

Cultural Contradictions had an immediate relevance in a period when Western societies seemed to be coming apart. The idea that Bell proposed of a disjuncture between culture, on the one hand, and the economy and social structure, on the other, suggested a more deep-seated explanation for contemporary conflict than the proximate events of the mid-1970s. And if the book still has power, this is where it lies: not in Bell's reaction to the New Left and the 1960s counterculture, but rather in his general theoretical framework. Bell was arguing against the traditions that sought holistically to account for the long-term evolution of societies. The two major contending traditions in sociology, Marxism and structural functionalism, both sought to give a unified account of society. Marxism saw that unity as rooted in material conditions, whereas structural functionalism saw it as stemming from dominant values.

Against both of those views (and other variants of holism such as Michel Foucault's conception of epistemic ordering), Bell argued that culture and politics were decoupled from the economy and social structure. That was not to say that they were entirely separate, nor was it to deny long-term patterns of development. Rather, the different realms of society were not reducible to one overriding force, however that might be conceived. Much thinking about American history and society in the mid-twentieth century had assumed consensus or harmony; Bell's approach rejected those assumptions but conceptualized the sources of conflict and contradiction in a distinctive way.

Although Bell was sometimes described as a "futurist," that was not how he saw himself. The whole purpose of trying to anticipate the future implications of developments in the making or on the horizon was to get a better grasp of the deeper forces at work in society and the moral and political choices that needed to be made. No one could try to peer into the future without making mistakes. In a 2011 book about financialization that begins and ends with quotations from Bell, the sociologist Greta Krippner remarks, "Bell's special brilliance was that he was prescient even when his predictions missed their mark."[43]

A mistake that Bell made himself in one of his papers in 1967 for the Commission on the Year 2000 is revealing. He recalled a 1924 book about science and the future by the biologist J. B. S. Haldane, which had many remarkable and accurate predictions. But Haldane, Bell said, had made one mistake: lacking "foreknowledge of nuclear energy," he had predicted that future sources of energy would come from "wind or sun."[44] Sometimes what seems like an error—in this case, Haldane's energy forecast—remains worth taking seriously regardless of history's apparent verdict, and sometimes it turns out to be right.

ORGANIZATION AND THEMES OF THE BOOK

The essays in *Defining the Age* attempt to provide a fresh perspective on Daniel Bell's work. Most of the scholarship on Bell dates from the 1980s and was concerned with his early career and ideas, particularly in the context of the "end of ideology" debate and the history of the New York intellectuals.[45] It is now roughly a half century since Bell's major work, and a decade since his death, and it is time for a broad reconsideration of his thought. This is what the contributors to this volume have sought to do: some as historians, others as social scientists, variously concerned with Bell's historical significance and the continuing merits and limitations of his ideas.

Two general interpretative essays follow this introduction. The historian David A. Bell approaches his father's career and ideas from two perspectives. The first concerns the tension in his father's temperament and thought between Yiddish radicalism and Hebrew conservatism—the first born of the Jewish history of humiliation and expressed in his father's socialism; and the second born of the fear of the collapse of order and expressed in his father's understanding of culture. Drawing on work in his own field on the social history of ideas, Bell then turns to the intellectual circles where his father flourished, particularly the circles outside the university where intense conversation inspired him to write.

In "Daniel Bell's Three-Dimensional Puzzle," the sociologist Paul Starr, cofounder and coeditor of the *American Prospect*, who was first a student of Bell and then a colleague of his, examines Bell's account of himself and his theory of society. Bell claimed that the three parts of his self-description fit together; he could be a "socialist in economics" while also a "liberal in politics" and a "conservative in culture." But in contemporary society, Bell argued, the economy, politics, and culture were driven by conflicting principles—efficiency in the economy, equality in politics, self-realization in culture. Starr explores how, from his early to his mature work, Bell arrived at his cross-cutting normative views and antiholistic social theory.

The next three sections of the book look specifically at the various phases of Bell's intellectual development. Part II, on ideology and politics, focuses on three books that Bell published between 1952 and 1960: *Marxian Socialism in the United States*, *The New American Right*, and *The End of Ideology*. In an essay that is both personal and analytical, the historian and *Dissent* editor Michael Kazin—Bell's nephew—continues a lifelong argument he had with his uncle. He writes that Bell's book on socialism marked the beginning of historical scholarship about the American left, and that much of Bell's acerbic criticism of radicals from the 1930s to the 1960s was justified. But, in Kazin's view, he also failed to see what was of lasting value in both the Old and the New Left.

Julian E. Zelizer takes up the ideas about McCarthyism and right-wing groups that Bell and his circle offered in *The New American Right* (retitled *The Radical Right* in later editions). Like Kazin, Zelizer finds continuing relevance in Bell's ideas—in this case, about the sources of support for right-wing extremism. But the far right has proved far more significant than Bell and others in the postwar era imagined.

The third essay in part II, by the political theorist and intellectual historian Jan-Werner Müller, concerns the connection between Bell's ideas about the "end of ideology" and political thought since the 1990s. During the decade after Bell's book was published in 1960, the resurgence of protest movements on the left seemed to contradict the "end of ideology" thesis. But in the 1990s, the collapse of Soviet communism gave rise to a debate that paralleled the earlier discussion about the "end of ideology." In a 1989 article and 1992 book on "the end of history," Francis Fukuyama claimed that the grand alternatives to liberalism were finished. Although Bell used the term "ideology" in more than one sense, Müller suggests that in at least one respect, the 1990s recapitulated Bell's diagnosis of the 1950s: "there were no new comprehensive belief systems comparable to what had emerged in the nineteenth century." Comprehensive belief systems, Müller argues, have also played little role in the rise of populism and authoritarianism. Identity has certainly mattered a great deal, but that is fundamentally different from a politics framed around ideologies of universal and comprehensive ambitions.

Part III focuses on Bell's 1973 book *The Coming of Post-Industrial Society* and related writings of his on social forecasting and higher education in the 1960s and early 1970s. Since that time, the concept of a postindustrial or information society has framed much of the thinking about social change, but now many people argue that we are living in a "neoliberal" era. Starr's essay in this part contrasts postindustrialism and neoliberalism as rival definitions of our age. Starr argues that partly because Bell took for granted an expansive government role, he failed to anticipate the brutal aspects of the postindustrial transformation that the neoliberal turn has exacerbated. But much of the core of Bell's argument holds up and has been fruitfully extended.

In parallel fashion, the historian Margaret O'Mara also finds renewed relevance in Bell's ideas about postindustrialism. She pits Bell against Alvin Toffler, exploring why Silicon Valley entrepreneurs were attracted to Toffler. But O'Mara argues that Bell's work provides a better account of how Silicon Valley actually developed. The sociologist Steven Brint explores the critical role that universities have come to play in postindustrial societies, although he argues that they have fallen short of the dominant position that Bell anticipated. He also lays out the institutional reasons why colleges have not followed the approach that Bell called for in *The Reforming of General Education*. The historian Jenny Andersson puts Bell's work in a more international context, examining his role and influence in trans-Atlantic efforts to develop new means of social forecasting.

Part IV addresses the themes that were the focus of Bell's last major book, *The Cultural Contradictions of Capitalism* (1976), and some of his later social commentary. Fred Turner, a historian of culture and technology, argues that there was no contradiction; on the contrary, the cultural tendencies of the 1960s and 1970s—expressed among a group he calls the "New Communalists"—led directly to the practices of the leading Silicon Valley firms and to other changes in the corporate economy. Taking up another theme from *Cultural Contradictions*, the political theorist Stefan Eich suggests that Bell was right that the "double bind" of contemporary capitalism would express itself in growing conflict over the "public household." Eich points out that although Bell himself did not call for or favor a shift in policy toward markets and financialization, his analysis identified the reasons that turn was about to occur: "Market-based interventions could serve as a convenient tool for hiding the all-too-visible hand of the state."

The contributors to *Defining the Age* reach varying judgments about the merits of Daniel Bell's work. But taken together, these essays reveal a substantial thinker who crystallized key ideas in the mid-twentieth century that are still relevant to today's world. To inquire into the defining ideas of that era is implicitly to ask what ideas define ours. We hope, therefore, that this volume sheds light and provokes reflection on both past and present—Bell's time, and our own.

NOTES

1. Irving Howe, "The New York Intellectuals: A Chronicle and a Critique," *Commentary* 46, no. 4 (October 1968): 29–51; Alexander Bloom, *Prodigal Sons: The New York Intellectuals and Their World* (New York: Oxford University Press, 1986); Alan M. Wald, *The New York Intellectuals: The Rise and Decline of the Anti-Stalinist Left from the 1930s to the 1980s* (Chapel Hill: University of North Carolina Press, 1987); Neil Jumonville, *Critical Crossings:*

The New York Intellectuals in Postwar America (Berkeley: University of California Press, 1991); Joseph Dorman, *Arguing the World: The New York Intellectuals in Their Own Words* (New York: Free Press, 2000). For Bell's own discussion of these issues (including a genealogical chart), see "The 'Intelligentsia' in American Society," in *The Winding Passage: Essays and Sociological Journeys, 1960–1980* (Cambridge, MA: Abt Books, 1980), 119–37.

2. The major attack was in Christopher Lasch, *The Agony of the American Left* (New York: Knopf, 1969), 63–114. For historical analyses, see Bloom, *Prodigal Sons*, 259–73; Peter Coleman, *The Liberal Conspiracy: The Congress for Cultural Freedom and the Struggle for the Mind of Postwar Europe* (New York: Free Press, 1989); and Frances Stonor Saunders, *The Cultural Cold War: The CIA and the World of Arts and Letters* (New York: New Press, 2000). For a sensible verdict on the controversy over the funding of the Congress for Cultural Freedom by the Central Intelligence Agency (CIA), see Tony Judt, *Postwar: A History of Europe since 1945* (New York: Penguin, 2005), 223–24.

3. Peter Steinfels, *The Neoconservatives: The Men Who Are Changing America's Politics* (New York: Simon and Schuster, 1979). In later books on the subject, which reflect the turn of neoconservatism to a hawkish foreign policy and Reaganite economic views, Bell drops out of the story. See, e.g., John Ehrman, *The Rise of Neoconservatism: Intellectuals and Foreign Affairs, 1945–1994* (New Haven, CT: Yale University Press, 1995). But the mistaken identification of Bell as a neoconservative lingers; see, e.g., Douglas Martin, "Gertrude Himmelfarb, Historian of Ideas, Dies at 98," *New York Times*, December 31, 2019.

4. Michael Kazin, "The Agony and Romance of the American Left," *American Historical Review* 100, no. 5 (1995): 1488–1512. He writes that nearly every historian writing on the history of socialism has found it necessary to take a position on Bell's interpretation. See also his essay in this volume.

5. Cas Mudde describes the book as "the classic study of the postwar radical right," which laid "the groundwork for much of the European scholarship of the late twentieth century (even if this is rarely acknowledged explicitly)." Cas Mudde, *The Far Right in America* (New York: Routledge, 2018), 88, 123. For a strong, detailed defense of Bell's volume against its critics, see David Plotke, "Introduction to the Transaction Edition (2001): The

Success and Anger of the Modern American Right," in *The Radical Right*, 3rd ed., ed. Daniel Bell (New Brunswick, NJ: Transaction, 2002 [1955, 1963]), xi–lxxvi.

6. Krishan Kumar, *Prophecy and Progress: The Sociology of Industrial and Post-Industrial Society* (London: Allen Lane, 1978); Jenny Andersson, *The Future of the World: Futurology, Futurists, and the Struggle for the Post–Cold War Imagination* (New York: Oxford University Press, 2018).

7. In his "Key Sociologists" volume on Bell, Malcolm Waters writes that "Bell's work is a central element in the sociological canon." Malcolm Waters, *Daniel Bell* (New York: Routledge, 1996), 9; also see Krishan Kumar, *From Post-Industrial to Post-Modern Society: New Theories of the Contemporary World*, 2nd ed. (Malden, MA: Blackwell, 2005).

8. Daniel Bell, "Foreword: 1978," in *The Cultural Contradictions of Capitalism*, 20th Anniversary ed. (New York: Basic Books, 1996 [1976]), xi.

9. Dorman, *Arguing the World*, 174.

10. Dorman, *Arguing the World*, 33.

11. Daniel Bell, "First Love and Early Sorrows," *Partisan Review* 48, no. 4 (1981): 532–551.

12. "Interview with Daniel Bell, May 1972," in Job Leonard Dittberner, *The End of Ideology and American Social Thought: 1930–1960* (Ann Arbor, MI: UMI Research Press, 1979), 309–36. Hereafter referred to as "Dittberner interview."

13. Dittberner interview, 313.

14. Daniel Bell, "Word Surrealism," *Partisan Review* 11, no. 4 (1944): 486–88.

15. Dittberner interview, 319.

16. Dittberner interview, 319; Howard Brick, *Daniel Bell and the Decline of Intellectual Radicalism: Social Theory and Political Reconstruction in the 1940s* (Madison: University of Wisconsin Press, 1986), 101–19.

17. Cited in Brick, *Daniel Bell and the Decline of Intellectual Radicalism*, 102.

18. In response to an interviewer's question, Bell insisted, "One has to distinguish between being CIA funded, which it was, and being a CIA front, which it was not. . . . You couldn't tell [the intellectuals associated with the Congress for Cultural Freedom] what to do. . . . There was never any direction of the Congress, never any effort to control it." Dittberner interview, 325.

19. Bloom, *Prodigal Sons*, 430, n. 112.

20. On Bell's role, see Jerry L. Avorn et al., *Up Against the Ivy Wall: A History of the Columbia Crisis* (New York: Atheneum, 1968), 76–79; for Bell's own account, see Daniel Bell, "Columbia and the New Left," in *Confrontation: The Student Rebellion and the Universities*, ed. Daniel Bell and Irving Kristol (New York: Basic Books, 1969), 67–107.

21. Charles Kadushin, *The American Intellectual Elite* (Boston: Little, Brown, 1974).

22. Russell Jacoby, *The Last Intellectuals: American Culture in the Age of Academe* (New York: Basic Books, 1987).

23. "The Hundred Most Influential Books Since the War," *TLS, the Times Literary Supplement* (October 6, 1995), 39.

24. Bloom, *Prodigal Sons*, 134.

25. Daniel Bell, "The Mood of Three Generations," in *The End of Ideology: On the Exhaustion of Political Ideas in the Fifties* (Cambridge, MA: Harvard University Press, 1988 [1960]), 311.

26. Daniel Bell, "A Parable of Alienation," *The Jewish Frontier*, November 1946, as cited in "The 'Intelligentsia' in American Society," 133–34.

27. Dittberner interview, 315.

28. Bell, *The End of Ideology*, 17.

29. David A. Bell, "Daniel Bell's Relevant Distinctions," in *For Daniel Bell*, ed. Mark Lilla and Leon Wieseltier (privately published, 2005), pp. 9–16.

30. Max Weber, "Politics as a Vocation," in *From Max Weber: Essays in Sociology*, tr. and ed by H. H. Gerth and C. Wright Mills (New York: Oxford University Press, 1958 [1946]), 77–128.

31. Bell, "The Mood of Three Generations," 300.

32. Daniel Bell, "Interpretations of American Politics" (1955), in Bell, *The Radical Right*, 47–73.

33. Daniel Bell, "The Dispossessed" (1962), in Bell, *The Radical Right*, 1–45.

34. Bell, *The End of Ideology*, 400.

35. Howard Brick, "The End of Ideology Thesis," in *The Oxford Handbook of Political Ideologies*, ed. Michael Freeden and Marc Stears (Oxford: Oxford University Press, 2013), 90–114.

36. Daniel Bell, "Government by Commission," *The Public Interest*, no. 3 (Spring 1966): 3–9.

37. Daniel Bell, "The Year 2000: The Trajectory of an Idea," in "Toward the Year 2000: Work in Progress," *Daedalus* 96 (Summer 1967): 639–51.

38. Daniel Bell, "Notes on Post-Industrial Society (II)," *The Public Interest* (Spring 1967), 102–18. For a later version framed around the concept of the information society, see Daniel Bell, "The Social Framework of the Information Society," in *The Microelectronics Revolution*, ed. Tom Forester (Cambridge, MA: MIT Press, 1981), 500–549.

39. "Members of the Commission on the Year 2000," *Daedalus* 96 (Summer 1967): 978.

40. Daniel Bell, "Plea for a 'New Phase in Negro Leadership'; The civil rights movement has reached a point of crisis, says an observer. Here are his suggestions for what should be done beyond protest," *New York Times*, May 31, 1964. For more discussion of this speech, see Paul Starr, "Daniel Bell's Three-Dimensional Puzzle," in this volume.

41. Daniel Bell, "Ethnicity and Social Change" (1975), in Bell, *The Winding Passage*, 184–209; on the general tendencies of Bell's generation to marginalize race and subsume it under the categories of ethnicity and class, see Michael Omi and Howard Winant, *Racial Formation in the United States: From the 1960s to the 1990s* (New York: Routledge & Kegan Paul, 1994).

42. Daniel Bell, "The Year 2000: The Trajectory of an Idea," 645.

43. Greta R. Krippner, *Capitalizing on Crisis: The Political Origins of the Rise of Finance* (Cambridge, MA: Harvard University Press, 2011), 138.

44. Daniel Bell, "Coda: Work in Further Progress," *Daedalus* 96 (Summer 1967): 985–988; J. B. S. Haldane, *Daedalus or Science and the Future* (London: Kegan Paul, Trench, Trubner, 1924).

45. The books include Brick, *Daniel Bell and the Decline of Intellectual Radicalism*; Waters, *Daniel Bell*; Dittberner, *The End of Ideology and American Social Thought*; Nathan Liebowitz, *Daniel Bell and the Agony of Modern Liberalism* (Westport, CT: Greenwood, 1985); and the books on the New York intellectuals cited in note 1.

PART I

OVERVIEW

1

REMEMBERING DANIEL BELL

Two Perspectives

DAVID A. BELL

A s a historian of early modern Europe, I am accustomed to writing in a relatively detached manner about men and women who passed out of living memory a long time ago, and to whom I have no personal connection. But I cannot adopt this manner in an essay about Daniel Bell. I do not think it has ever been easy for sons to write about fathers, and it certainly has not been easy for me to write about him. He has loomed over me all my life, of course. He passed away in 2011, the year I turned fifty, but scarcely a day goes by that I do not think of him. Many nights, I dream about him. So what follows is inescapably intimate.

This is not my first attempt to write about him. During his lifetime, I wrote a short essay for the privately published *Festschrift*, compiled by two of his protégés in 2005.[1] Looking back on that essay now, it strikes me as almost deliberately detached and unsentimental. After my father passed away, I made several attempts to write a more personal essay. But the emotions were too raw, too overwhelming. It was only as the hundredth anniversary of his birth approached, in 2019, that I felt capable of trying again. In addition, by this point, I felt that my reflections might serve some small purpose. Memories, inevitably, were fading. It had been more than forty years since the appearance of his last major work, *The Cultural Contradictions of Capitalism*. Leading American sociology departments, including those in which he had taught, had in large part turned away from the sort of issues that had principally concerned him.

It was increasingly clear (as several of the contributions to this volume remind us) that many of the most important forecasts he had made—especially about the "end of ideology" and the nature of postindustrial society—had not come to pass in anything like the way he expected. I did not want to mount a defense of his work: that is not my role, and in any case, I do not have the necessary expertise. But I did think that a personal reminiscence that also situated him in his various historical contexts might contribute to our understanding of what shaped him, what drove him, and what moved him—and could help recall him not just as a thinker, but as a historical person in the fullest sense.

What follows are two reminiscences in which I also offer some reflections on Daniel Bell's life, on the worlds in which he lived, and how these worlds shaped his thought. Both are personal, but they offer different perspectives. The first reflects, above all, on the creative tension between two aspects of his Jewish background and the ways that it contributed to both his personality and his work.[2] The second offers some thoughts about the milieu of the so-called New York intellectuals and the ways that it shaped his intellectual style and academic career.

HEBREW CONSERVATISM AND YIDDISH RADICALISM

I always regret that my father did not write memoirs. In the early 1990s, I spent a long time trying to persuade him to do so. He was then in his early seventies and had just retired, very much against his will, from his professorship at Harvard (they still had mandatory retirement for academics in those days!). For over a decade, books about the New York intellectuals had been appearing at a steady clip, and they usually devoted considerable attention to him: his early years in the socialist movement and at the City College of New York, his career as a prolific intellectual journalist, and his development into one of the great modern sociologists. Most of the authors treated him quite favorably. Some had done extensive interviews with him.

Nonetheless, every time a new book arrived at his house in Cambridge, he would call me, fulminating about the inevitable misrepresentations and mistakes. Sometimes he would go so far as to send long letters on the subject to the unfortunate author, typed on his old Smith Corona electric, with shaky, handwritten corrections. If the book had treated him unfairly, as some did, the letter would turn distinctly dyspeptic. "You should write memoirs," I would tell him on the phone. Get your own story out. Make sure future historians have your side of it. He was particularly annoyed when the authors called him a "neoconservative," as journalists had done since Peter Steinfels had published *The Neoconservatives* in 1979.[3] My father insisted that he remained a man of the left, a "socialist in economics," a "Menshevik." Don't tell this to me, I would say. I know it already. Write it.

But he would always demur. He couldn't write honest memoirs, he insisted, without revealing certain secrets that would hurt people he had known, or their families. This seemed like a transparently false excuse. When I pressed him about the secrets in question, they either involved quite minor peccadilloes or were entirely tangential to his own life story and could easily have been left out.

More important, I think, was the entirely human and understandable reason that memoir-writing seemed too much of a last chapter—to a career, to a life. My father was a man who almost never exercised after graduating from high school at age sixteen, generally ate red meat at least twice a day (especially bacon and salami), and developed diabetes in his forties. When he was just fifty-four, he told my mother that he didn't think he would live another decade. I think he was as surprised as anyone that he made it to ninety-one.

In the end, he did leave some shards of memoirs. One is a brilliant essay called "First Love and Early Sorrows," which he published in *Partisan Review* in 1981.[4] It begins with a tender and vivid account of the way he became, at age thirteen, what he called a right-wing socialist. The other is in Joseph Dorman's wonderful 1998 documentary *Arguing the World*, about him, Irving Kristol, Nathan Glazer, and Irving Howe. There, he told stories about his childhood and about the fabled days in "Alcove 1" in the cafeteria at City College, where these four poor Jewish boys, the sons of Yiddish-speaking immigrants, became friends. Dorman also beautifully traced their subsequent careers, the way they dealt with McCarthyism and the New Left, and their political parting of ways: Howe the democratic socialist (and *Dissent* founder) on one side, Kristol the unabashed neoconservative and Reaganite on the other; and Glazer and my father somewhere in between, with my father eventually tending more toward the left.

The essay and the film help make up for the lack of memoirs. So do the various histories of the New York intellectuals, not to mention three biographical studies. But much inevitably is missing. A son's perspective may be anything but impartial and unfiltered, but it does help me see what has been left out.

He himself left a lot out, even when he did not seem to be doing so. "First Love and Early Sorrows," for instance, is beautifully, touchingly written, but it says little about his inner life. Except for a brief, affecting vignette about his shock at the pervasive poverty in New York City during the Depression, which he credits with making him a sociologist, the most personal section deals with how he reacted, at age thirteen, to the diary of the anarchist Alexander Berkman, which recounted Trotsky's brutal suppression of the sailors' mutiny in 1921 at the Kronstadt naval base, outside what is now St. Petersburg. One passage of the essay has become deservedly famous: "Every radical generation, it is said, has its Kronstadt. For some it was the Moscow Trials, for others the Nazi-Soviet Pact, for still others Hungary (the Raik Trial or 1956), Czechoslovakia (the defenestration of Masaryk in 1948 or the Prague Spring of 1968), the Gulag, Cambodia, Poland (and there will be more to come). My Kronstadt was Kronstadt."[5]

Arguing the World seems to offer a much more personal, unrehearsed portrait. Personal, yes; unrehearsed, no. As everyone who knew my father could testify, he was a well-practiced and experienced raconteur. He had a huge stock of stories, jokes, and quips that he could sprinkle into his talk with perfect timing and delivery. "What do I specialize in?" he would ask. The answer: "I am a specialist in generalizations."

"Why did I give up a career in journalism for academia? Three reasons: June, July, and August."

"What is an intellectual? Someone who asks, if something works in practice, does it also work in theory?"

By the time I went off to college, I could almost always predict which of these bon mots was coming several sentences in advance (and, in good adolescent fashion, start rolling my eyes at it). They were a performance. But they were also a shield of sorts, allowing him to deflect the conversation away from areas where he felt uncomfortable.

The shield was there, in part, to cover some very deep-seated vulnerabilities and pain, some of which he readily acknowledged and some of which he did not. When he was less than a year old, in early 1920, his father had died of the Spanish flu. He, his older brother Leo, and his mother Annie, a poor immigrant garment worker, spent the next few years squeezing into the already-overcrowded apartments of other family members and relying on Jewish charities for support. His mother regularly took him and his brother on the long subway ride from the Lower East Side into deepest Queens to visit their father's grave.

As a toddler, he spent his days in a so-called Jewish day orphanage, and if his mother could not pick him up early enough, he would have to spend the night there as well. He could describe in heartrending terms the fear he felt every day, standing at the door of the day orphanage, waiting for his mother to come, and not knowing if she would make it on time. It was one of his well-rehearsed stories. He was more reluctant to discuss his feelings toward the stepfather his mother married when he was thirteen, and with whom he never got along (I never met his two stepsiblings). Only late in life did he talk to me about the agonizing breakup of his second marriage in the early 1950s, which sent him tumbling into depression and intensive Freudian psychoanalysis.

Still, he made his way out of that labyrinth, thanks in large part, as he always said, to his analyst. In my own lifetime, while I could see my father sad, or frustrated, I rarely saw him in the grips of something worse, and I remember many moments of real joy (especially of him beaming uncontrollably at my own children). There was emotional scar tissue aplenty, but it was mostly old, settled, and overgrown with healthier material. At least this was the case until my mother, Pearl Kazin Bell, had a terrible fall and suffered serious brain damage in the spring of 2002. The accident crushed his spirit for a long time and left him bereft. But he did eventually recover, somewhat, and struggled heroically to take care of her, building an extension onto their house in Cambridge so that she could stay at home with twenty-four-hour nursing care. I am sure one reason he lived as long as he did was because of his need to take care of her.

The performances were not just a shield, of course. The sport of the New York intellectuals was competitive talking, and they all needed their stories, their performances, to be contenders. Cocktail and dinner parties tended to turn into intellectual jousting matches, and while loud male voices usually dominated, Diana Trilling and Bea Himmelfarb Kristol easily held their own in this company (my mother was somewhat—but not always—more reserved). Like any child who has heard his parents' stories a thousand times, I groaned at the repetition, but I also grasped that his stories were, in fact, very good ones: entertaining, witty, and also thought-provoking. One of the best ones made its way into *Arguing the World*. It recounts the moment when my father, with his orthodox Jewish background (his paternal grandfather was a cantor), told his rabbi that after his bar mitzvah, he would no longer attend *shul* because he did not believe in God. "Tell me," the rabbi replied. "Do you think God cares?"

As with this story, the performances always centrally involved Jewish humor. My father liked to tell the story of a Jew who had a conversation with God. "Lord, is it true," the Jew asked, "that in your scale of reckoning, a thousand years is like a minute?" God said: Yes. "And is it true that in your weights and measures, a thousand dollars is like a penny?" The Lord again said: Yes. So the man continued: "Lord, I am poor—can you give me a penny?" The Lord replied: "All right. Just wait a minute." Then there was the story of the Jew who volunteered to serve in the Israeli navy. "Do you know how to swim?" the recruiter asked him. "I know the theory of it," the man replied. There were many, many other such stories.

It would be easy to see this humor as incidental to understanding a man who was, of course, a deeply serious thinker, author of long tomes of often difficult social analysis. In fact, it is absolutely central. Humor is, of course, a classic kind of emotional shield, a way to deflect from hurt and vulnerability. But there was also much more to the stories my father told, which he always insisted could never just be reduced to mere "jokes," to Borscht Belt comedy.

He thought deeply about Jewish humor, bringing to bear the considerable Jewish learning that this nonbelieving and largely nonobservant Jew nonetheless managed to acquire over the course of his life. One of the loveliest things he ever wrote, too often neglected by his biographers, was the commencement address he delivered at Brandeis in 1991, titled "Serious Thoughts on Jewish Humor." In it, he called Jewish humor "a wisdom literature that draws upon a thousand years of experience and gives one a sense of human yearning, and its limits." And he explained the way in which it is deeply, inescapably political:

> Jewish humor is the tension of two contradictory elements in its makeup: a Hebrew theology, which is deeply conservative, and a Yiddish experience, which was intensely radicalizing. Hebrew theology reads the nature of man in the histories of Sodom and Gomorrah, of Babylon and Rome. It has witnessed the sweeping, unrestrained impulses to break the law, to unloose murder and pillage on populations, to inflict cruelty and suffering on victims, such as have occurred—and will repeatedly recur—throughout the millennia. But Yiddish experience has been radicalizing, because it has been an experience of humiliation. The humiliation of Jewish students in prewar Poland who had to sit on ghetto benches in the lecture room and chose to stand, rather than accept the condition; the humiliation of being barred from positions in universities despite their evident abilities; to the humiliations of being either pariah or parvenu, a stranger often in a land that could not be their own, when entering the modern age.[6]

This was one of the most revealing things my father ever wrote about himself, because he was a mix of the conservative and the radical in exactly the way he described here. The humor may have been a shield, and a performance, but it also offers a glimpse into some of the most important impulses behind both his writings and his politics.

Start with the conservatism. My father was fortunate to have been born in New York rather than in his parents' shtetls in present-day Belarus, so he never had personal experience of the horrific violence of the twentieth century (he did not serve in World War II). But the death of his own father, his childhood experiences at the Jewish day orphanage, and his battles with depression in the 1950s all left him with a deep fear of abandonment—of the abyss, whether physical or mental, that could sometimes seem all too close.

After he died, I found among his papers a long journal of sorts, written after his second wife, Elaine Graham, left him, that breathes with utter, piercing anguish at the loss and suggests psychological wounds that went very deep. The phrases repeat: "always in despair"; "anxiety attack"; "I always begin in sadness." After reading it, I could only think of the lines of Gerard Manley Hopkins: "O the mind, mind has mountains; cliffs of fall / Frightful, sheer, no-man-fathomed. Hold them cheap / May who ne'er hung there."

He often said that what mattered most in politics was temperament, and his own temperament was undoubtedly conservative, precisely because of his painful sense, born out of his own childhood experience and his memories of the Depression, of how fragile the structures of ordinary, civilized life could be. I think he reacted so strongly, at age thirteen, to Berkman's description of Kronstadt, and continued to recoil against political extremism throughout his life, because of a deeply personal revulsion at the violence and cruelty that could so easily overwhelm civilization's weak defenses. A person of a different temperament might have been more ready, as so many communists were in the 1920s and 1930s, to accept Trotsky's actions as necessary and perhaps even to take a certain savage pleasure in the crushing of the Revolution's enemies. That kind of pleasure did not exist in my father's emotional repertoire.

Of course, my father's political experiences after 1932 only seemed to confirm what he had first felt upon reading Berkman. There was the unfathomable degree of murder, pillage, cruelty, and suffering of Stalin's purges, and the show trials, and the Great Terror, followed by the war and the Holocaust. And even after the Holocaust ended and the war was won, a threat remained. Stalinists took power in Eastern Europe, with more purges, more show trials, more terror, and even, at the end of Stalin's life, the threat of renewed persecution of the Jews.

Defeating this threat mattered more than anything. This is why, in the 1950s, he devoted so much time to the Congress for Cultural Freedom, which was striving to counter communist influence, especially in Western Europe. A decade later, he sensed something of the same temperamental excess, the same "sweeping, unrestrained impulses to break the law" in 1960s student radicalism, and he turned away from that in revulsion as well. But he was no happier with the self-consciously "tough guy" poses adopted by some of his fellow Jewish intellectuals, especially when they became the sort of neoconservatives who never stopped beating the drum for American military action (he often referred to one of the most prominent of them using the German word *Grobian*, meaning a coarse and vulgar person).

Yet another of his well-known remarks was his definition of himself as a socialist in economics, a liberal in politics, and a conservative in culture. That cultural conservatism expressed itself abundantly in his personal life. He detested most popular culture, especially television and rock music (although, oddly, he had a taste for televised football). He was horrified by the love of comic books that I developed as a small child, and when he saw that it was a losing battle, he did everything he could to steer me from the garish American variety to the more sophisticated European sort, especially Astérix and Tintin (thereby setting me on the road to my PhD in French history). Although he enthusiastically promoted women students and colleagues and took enormous pride in my mother's literary criticism, their marriage was entirely too traditional when it came to the division of household labor. He adored a certain aristocratic sort of Englishness and often said that the year that he and my mother spent at King's College, Cambridge, in 1988–1989, was one of the happiest of his life. He had just as deep an attraction to Japan, which he adored for the elegant simplicity of its art and manners. He was not a connoisseur of radical, flamboyant artistic experimentation.

This conservatism found its way into his work, above all in *The Cultural Contradictions of Capitalism*. From its very first paragraphs, he warned about "the unraveling of the threads which had once held the culture and the economy together," and about the destructive effects of the "hedonism" he saw embodied in popular culture. He warned of a world dominated by "impulse and pleasure alone."[7] While he may have been referring most immediately to the youth culture of the 1960s, it is hard for me not to hear in the words an echo of the "sweeping, unrestrained impulses to break the law" that he saw Jewish theology as struggling to contain. The law mattered. Order mattered. He was not a frequent reader of Shakespeare, but the play that always spoke most deeply to him was *King Lear*, where the collapse of order in the realm is matched by its collapse in the family, in the natural world, and ultimately in the mind of its title character.

At the same time, there was also, still, much Yiddish radicalism in him. He did not himself encounter the sort of fierce, radicalizing humiliation that his Jewish counterparts had faced earlier in Poland and Russia. Again, he was fortunate to have been born in New York, at a time when anti-Semitic barriers were dropping and he could make his way through institutions like Stuyvesant High School, the City College of New York, and Columbia University to become an editor at *Fortune*, and then a professor at Columbia and Harvard. Another of his favorite remarks, humorous but as always bearing a deeper wisdom, was: "Between Rome and Jerusalem, I choose . . . New York!"

Even so, especially when he traveled outside New York, he encountered his share of genteel anti-Semitic humiliation. He didn't like to talk about these moments, but they were certainly there, and they stung. As late as 1985, the British historian Hugh Trevor-Roper wrote a particularly nasty letter about him. "As for Bell," he sneered, "whose real name is, I think, much longer, I made up my mind about him at a conference in Venice a few years ago. He pomped away on 'futurology' and gave himself great airs. . . . I have a full (illustrated) private record of that conference: most of the illustrations are of D. Bell, in various animal forms."[8]

My father may have been Anglophilic, but he never tried to make himself into an Englishman, as some of his American Jewish academic contemporaries did. His accent and manners remained proudly those of a New York Jew. And he often spoke, with a certain mischievous pride, of the time he and a friend broke out into a loud chorus of "The Internationale," in Yiddish, in that inner sanctum of Englishness, the Reform Club in London. For him, the response to humiliation was to force the people who wanted to exclude him to accept him.

It was this stubborn Yiddish radicalism which, as much as anything, kept him from following his friend Irving Kristol into neoconservatism. The defining moment was the 1972 presidential election. He had no love for George McGovern, whom he saw as having given in too easily to the spirit of the 1960s, and what he saw as the antinomian ethos of the youth movement. From his time editing *The Public Interest* magazine (which he had founded with Kristol), he had developed a distinct skepticism about the effectiveness of Great Society social programs, worrying about what he saw as their ideological dogmatism and overreach. But he could not stand Richard Nixon (another *Grobian*), and, more important, could not bring himself to break with the political tradition that he had first embraced as a very young teenager, in the Depression.

It was always a matter of pride with him that he had cast his first presidential vote for Norman Thomas. The poverty and despair he remembered from the 1930s also amounted to a form of humiliation, and that stuck with him. He remained, always, a great reader of Karl Marx, whom he often described to me as the most profound social analyst he had ever encountered. One of my own prize possessions is the complete set of Marx and Engels in fifty volumes, published in the Soviet Union, that I inherited from him.

Throughout his life, the conservatism and the radicalism wrestled within him. But the moment that best encapsulates that wrestling for me had nothing at all humorous about it. It is one of my sharpest early memories of him, in fact, from the spring of 1968. He was still teaching at Columbia, and it was being torn apart by the student protests. In late April, radical students occupied various university offices, including the president's. A standoff ensued, and my father was one of the faculty members who tried to negotiate between the protesters and the university administration. He worried about the student movement, feared its wildness, and looked askance at the hedonism associated with it, but he still could not help sympathizing with its political radicalism.

But on the night of April 29, the negotiations broke down, and the police moved in with nightsticks and tear gas. Many of the students were badly beaten, and hundreds were arrested. I remember waking up early on the morning of April 30—I was six years old at the time—and finding my father, fully dressed, on the couch. He had been up all night, and he was weeping uncontrollably.

Perhaps this is another reason why he never wrote memoirs. He could never quite reconcile the Jewish conservative and the Yiddish radical within him—never quite decide from what perspective to judge and interpret the times he had lived through. In other ways, though, this same tension (the cultural contradictions of Daniel Bell?) fortunately did not matter so much. In his writing, it helped generate some of his most important and creative insights. In his politics, it kept him sensitive to the dangers of extremism, but also to the dangers of injustice. And in his life, it did not just drive the Jewish humor, but also the endless hours of warm, brilliant, wonderful talk that I remember so keenly. I miss that talk.

ENLIGHTENMENT

I am by training a historian of Enlightenment and revolutionary France, and when I try to think of my father and his work in a systematic way, I inevitably bring this perspective to bear. At first glance, it may seem like an odd, idiosyncratic perspective from which to view an American intellectual born in 1919. The Paris of the *Lumières* was quite far removed from the New York of the twentieth century, and the concerns of its *philosophes* quite different from those of the New York intellectuals. In fact, one reason I chose the subject was precisely its distance from my father's concerns and expertise. He was naturally interested in my work and could rarely keep himself from commenting on what I wrote. To establish my independence, I wanted to be in a field where the psychological weight of paternal commentary could be at least somewhat counterbalanced by my own particular expertise.

Yet the path to an academic specialty is inevitably more mysterious than it first appears and can twist through some surprising territories of the subconscious mind. For in fact, the Paris of the *philosophes* and the New York of the twentieth-century intellectuals have a surprising amount in common, as I may well have been subconsciously aware all along. Indeed, my father in some ways came about as close as twentieth-century America got to a *philosophe*. Like the *philosophes*—and very much unlike most contemporary academic sociologists—he was intellectually omnivorous. Like the *philosophes*, he wrote not for academic specialists but for an educated general public. Like the *philosophes*, he was politically engaged, commenting frequently on matters of public interest. And like the *philosophes*, he knew how to deploy humor to get his points across. His well-known quip about being a specialist in generalizations is one that Voltaire would have appreciated (and probably stolen).

The field of French Enlightenment studies also happens to be one where historians have developed intellectual tools that are peculiarly appropriate for studying the twentieth-century New York intellectuals. My own thesis advisor, Robert Darnton, described these tools as the "social history of ideas."[9] By this, he was not just referring to the social background of authors, but to the larger social world in which they operated and its relation to the ideas generated within it. The social history of ideas extends to literary institutions, both formal and informal. It extends to systems of censorship, the structures of the publishing business, the legal framework of authorship, practices of intellectual sociability, and much else. Darnton famously argued that while the *philosophes* of the Enlightenment first emerged as a classic group of outsiders mounting a radical challenge to the political and cultural establishment, over time they gained access to this establishment, and as they did, their radical energies dissipated. At the same time, they had inspired a new generation of writers who hoped to follow them, but when these writers arrived at the gates of the "High Enlightenment," they found these gates largely closed and the lush precincts beyond already occupied. The result was to drive them "underground," in Darnton's phrase, and to prompt them to write even more radical critiques that would ultimately feed the fierce anger of the French Revolution.[10]

Other historians have shown just how much the institution later called the *salon*—social gatherings of high society in which writers participated—helped to shape the intellectual style of the French Enlightenment: the premium placed on wit and amusement, and also the habit of collaborative work.[11] Some Enlightenment works, including some by Denis Diderot, were effectively composed in the *salons*. The New York intellectuals of the mid-twentieth century are a group ideally suited for this social history of ideas, and despite the voluminous amount of work already devoted to them, much remains to be done from this perspective.

The impression of my father's suitability as a subject of "the social history of ideas" has been reinforced for me by the other contributions to this volume. Jenny Andersson, for instance, in her essay stresses Daniel Bell's role as what she calls a translator, a transnational mediator, and a broker of ideas. In doing so, perhaps inadvertently, she raises questions about his originality as a social theorist, but she is not the first to do so. As is well known, Daniel Bell was not the first writer to speak of "the end of ideology," or the first to speculate about the nature of "post-industrial society," even if both concepts are now firmly associated with him. Putting an emphasis on his role as a mediator or broker, of course, does not mean discounting his intellectual importance. He put his own distinct and significant stamp on both concepts and forever changed the debate around them. That is a major contribution. But it is intellectual work of a different sort than that of birthing entirely original ideas. Several of the other essays directly or indirectly support Andersson's contentions on this subject.

Even as Andersson is tracing Bell's role as a mediator and broker, she also highlights the various institutional settings in which he did the work in question: in particular, the seminars of the Congress for Cultural Freedom in the 1950s, and then the meetings of the Commission on the Year 2000 in the 1960s. She doesn't say much about these settings, but it is worth noting that both were venues for intense oral interchange, debate, discussion, and conversation. The congress had its large public events, its programs, its publications, and of course its secret backer, the Central Intelligence Agency. But it also had the discussions and debates that might start in a seminar but that would continue over meals, in Parisian cafés, at cocktail parties, and late into the night. When my father talked about his experience spending a year working for the congress in the late 1950s, it was this experience of constant conversation that he often came back to.

Thinking about this point, it strikes me that Daniel Bell spent much of his life moving from one intense talk shop to another. In his childhood, he attended the Orthodox Jewish Sunday schools known as *cheders*, where students learned to read the Torah and to debate the meaning of each line. Then, in his teenage years, came the Young People's Socialist League in New York City, with their intense, incessant debates over socialist doctrine fed by the powerful factionalism of the socialist movement in the city. He moved on from there to the famed Alcove 1 at City College, where the anti-Stalinists congregated and where he became fast friends with the Irvings—Kristol and Howe. After that, he passed into the world of the New York intellectuals itself, where the conversations

continued at cocktail and dinner parties and in editorial meetings
at *The New Leader* and *Partisan Review*. The Congress for Cultural
Freedom represented for him an international extension of these
practices, bringing him into conversation with Raymond Aron,
Bertrand de Jouvenel, Constantin Jelenski, and many others. And
so did the Salzburg Seminar, where he taught for several summers
in the 1950s, along with American colleagues, and established
ties with French sociologists such as Henri Mendras and Alain
Touraine. Back in the United States in the 1960s, there was the
Commission on the Year 2000, as well as *The Public Interest*, which
he founded with Irving Kristol in 1965.

But there is one sort of institution that I have *not* mentioned
here, quite deliberately: the university. Because for my father, universities were, in a way, never quite so important—certainly not
as a place to discuss and debate ideas. It is significant that when
he spoke to me and others about City College—which he did very
often—he almost never mentioned his courses or professors, with
the single exception of the great classicist Moses Finley (born Fin-
kelstein). He had very little to say about his brief time as a graduate student at Columbia, even though he worked there with the
distinguished sociologist Robert Merton. And it is no coincidence
that while he had been at Harvard for six years by the time he published *The Cultural Contradictions of Capitalism*, he does not thank a
single Harvard colleague in his acknowledgments to the book, still
less the Harvard sociology department.

There were two exceptions to this pattern. First, there was
the University of Chicago, in the three years he taught there as
an instructor after World War II. And then, especially, there was
Columbia in the 1960s. But Columbia, for him, was very much
an extension of the New York intellectuals. What mattered to
him most at Columbia was not the teaching, nor the life of the
sociology department, but the exchanges with close friends and

colleagues, especially Richard Hofstadter, Lionel Trilling, and Steven Marcus. He always told me that the most rewarding teaching experiences of his life had been coteaching with Trilling—above all because of the exchanges with Trilling. My father always defined himself as an intellectual first, and a sociology professor second, if at all.

As for Harvard, he liked being there. He liked having an endowed chair. But it was being an intellectual that really mattered. The deepest involvement he ever had in the life of a university came when Columbia president David Truman asked him in 1965 to reappraise the college's Core Curriculum. This led to the so-called Daniel Bell Report, which is still prominently referred to at Columbia and led to a book that has received somewhat less attention of late than his others: *The Reforming of General Education* (discussed in this volume by Steven Brint).[12] But that book, too, was the product of an intensive process of consultation, discussion, and debate.

The intellectual remove from universities is yet another point that my father and the New York intellectuals had in common with the French Enlightenment. Unlike the Scottish Enlightenment or the German Enlightenment, the French Enlightenment took place almost entirely apart from universities. French universities were mostly intellectually moribund in the eighteenth century, especially after the authorities cracked down on heterodoxy in the theology faculties in the early 1750s. The intellectual life of the country took place elsewhere.

In all the nonuniversity settings in which my father operated, what mattered most was unstructured and largely unhierarchical conversation. True, the conversations sometimes centered on particular texts. But these were not university seminars, where one person would speak for a defined period of time and then respond to questions. Anyone could jump in, interrupt, talk over someone else. To hold the floor required both verbal skill and verbal force. As I have already remarked, Daniel Bell was a gold medalist in the New York intellectuals' sport of competitive talking. He had verbal skill and verbal force. He was very, very good at holding the floor.

I do not claim in any sense to be an expert either in sociology or in recent American intellectual history. I do think, however, that this exercise in the social history of ideas has some implications for our understanding of my father's career. Let me go through a few aspects of it.

To begin with, there is a problem that has always bothered me, and that is certainly a question for his biographers: why did Daniel Bell never manage to write another major work after *The Cultural Contradictions of Capitalism*? It was published in 1976, when he was fifty-seven. He would live for another thirty-four years and remain mentally acute until the very end.

He certainly intended to write more books. He published a fine but relatively minor collection of essays in 1980, at the urging of his friend Clark Abt: *The Winding Passage*.[13] He published other essays as well, including the brilliant, partly autobiographical "First Love and Early Sorrows." He largely completed, but never finished, a manuscript about Britain in the 1970s, which he called *The Exhausted Isle* and which grew out of his experience living in London and teaching at the London School of Economics in 1976–1977. He planned out a book called *The Return of the Sacred*, based on the Hobhouse Memorial Lecture that he delivered at the LSE. He planned out a book on utopia, related to many of the themes that are discussed in the essays for this volume. He planned out a book on information technology and society. When he was lying in the intensive care unit at Mount Auburn Hospital in December 2010, at the age of ninety, after nearly dying on the operating table, he dictated the outline of a new book to my sister and her husband. But he never finished any of these projects. Why?

There are a number of reasons. He developed diabetes, and with it, painful diabetic neuropathies that drained his energy. He had terrible back trouble. He was prey to depression at different times in his life, especially in his last years, after my mother's terrible accident. But above all, and quite seriously, I blame Harvard. In New York, his world had been one of almost constant conversation, in large and shifting groups, among the intellectuals. At Harvard, he had close colleagues and friends: above all, his old friend Nathan Glazer. But Harvard was still different. Faculty retreated into their offices. There were formal seminars, some stimulating, some dreadfully dull. To be sure, Harvard in those years was in no sense intellectually moribund, but the intensive whirl of constant conversation and debate that he knew from his earlier life was absent. Of course, he published two of his great books while at Harvard: *The Coming of Post-Industrial Society* in 1973 and *The Cultural Contradictions of Capitalism* in 1976. But both of them were based in large part on work that he had done in the 1960s, when still in New York. In fact, both of them were in large part *written* before his move to Cambridge, which took place in 1970.

Would it have been better for him to have stayed at Columbia? Here, unfortunately, I am not sure, for the world of the New York intellectuals itself very largely came to an end in the late 1960s. New York City itself changed, falling into the darkness of high crime and financial crisis, becoming for a time the dystopian cityscape of Saul Bellow's *Mr. Sammler's Planet*. Two key members of my father's circle—Richard Hofstadter and Lionel Trilling—died. By 1987, Russell Jacoby's book *The Last Intellectuals* was treating the New York intellectuals as a species that had gone extinct decades earlier.[14] Columbia changed as well, and diminished, after the student takeover of 1968. In addition, the social democratic politics that had originally bound the New York Jewish intellectuals together was fraying. Irving Kristol, Norman Podhoretz, and many others were turning to the right. So staying in New York might not have made much of a difference in the end. "Between Rome and Jerusalem," to quote this great line of my father's once again, "I choose New York." But it was the New York of the 1940s, 1950s, and early 1960s that he chose. Here, in short, is one aspect of his career that my "social history of ideas" may help to illuminate.

A second aspect involves what Jenny Andersson calls attention to in her essay: my father's role as an intellectual mediator, broker, and translator. This role derived directly from the experience of the intellectual milieus in which he flourished for so long. In the original preface to *Cultural Contradictions*, he wrote the following, very revealing line: "Any book—mine at least—is a dialogue, or sometimes a debate, with one's friends."[15] It is easy enough to dismiss these words as a standard piece of acknowledgment boilerplate, but they actually amount to more than that. To repeat the point, Daniel Bell was anything but a solitary scholar, shut up in a library or study. Nearly all his most important work came out of intensive dialogue and debate with fellow intellectuals.

He was certainly a deeply original thinker. But he also had the great strength of taking ideas that were already part of an ongoing discussion—the end of ideology, postindustrial society—and turning them around, testing them, reconfiguring them, appropriating them, and building them up into something new and rhetorically powerful—and then, often, going out in search of supporting evidence. Although I was still very young at the time and may not be remembering this correctly, I do have the distinct impression that he went out and did much of the research for *The Coming of Post-Industrial Society* after he had already determined the general shape of the argument. I do not mean this as a criticism. He had a strong base of evidence for the book already. But his work was not principally driven by his empirical research. He was not that sort of sociologist. His work was driven by the process of dialogue and debate.

Another aspect of his work that followed from the social-intellectual background I have sketched out was that he was, above all, an essayist. He wrote many imposingly long books, but most of them are collections of essays, including *The End of Ideology* and *Cultural Contradictions*. He used to say to me, quite often, that writers have a natural length. For some, it is the 1,000-word op-ed piece. For others, it is the 1,000-page tome. For him, it was the 10,000-to-20,000-word essay. And that fit very well with the social background I am describing. He could write a 10,000-to-20,000-word essay in a week or two of furious work, after taking part in a particularly vibrant and exciting discussion, and show it to the other participants while everything was still fresh in their memories. And, of course, they could read a 10,000- to-20,000-word essay in a few hours, without having to put everything else aside, so the discussion could continue.

This social background was crucial in shaping what could be called my father's intellectual style. As I've already mentioned, he tended to describe himself not as a sociologist or a professor, but as an intellectual. And he had his own definition of an intellectual: someone who can make "relevant distinctions." It is a definition that traces to a passage from William James that he referenced in *The End of Ideology*. In the original, in one of the lectures on pragmatism, James quotes what he calls a "scholastic adage that whenever you meet a contradiction you must make a distinction."[16] My father's books are grounded in analytical distinctions: between ideology and utopia, between industrial and post-industrial society, between capitalism seen as a system of production and capitalism seen as a system of consumption. My father's biographer Howard Brick argued that these sorts of distinctions, in his view, "formalize the basic dualist structure of Bell's thought, the poles of skepticism and morality, interests and ideals, objective structures and subjective purpose."[17] I also wrote about this theme in my essay for the *Festschrift* privately published for my father by Mark Lilla and Leon Wieseltier. In fact, I called it "Daniel Bell's Relevant Distinctions."

This emphasis on relevant distinctions is very much a rhetorical strategy, born out of the incessant discussions and debates in which Daniel Bell took part for so much of his life. There is no better way to reconfigure a debate, and therefore to seize control of it, than to introduce a fundamental new distinction that everyone else has missed. Even if his interlocutors disputed the new distinction, by disputing it, they were still forced onto his rhetorical territory, and generally into areas of empirical and theoretical knowledge that he knew particularly well. As everyone who knew my father personally can testify, he was brilliant at this.

One final point. Paul Starr, in one of his essays for this volume, discusses the "recency bias" in my father's work: the tendency to project the trends of the moment into the future, for instance by assuming that post-industrial society would be dominated, from the top down, by a new class of scientific experts. Obviously, as several of the contributions to this volume stress, things did not always turn out as my father expected. Recency bias is something that all social scientists can fall prey to—all scholars, in fact. But in my father's case, it was exacerbated by the intellectual milieu in which he grew up, and in which he continued to operate until the fateful move to Cambridge in 1970.

The debates and discussions I have been evoking were public ones that were meant to have an immediate public resonance— and, as time went on, a direct political and policy resonance as well. Already in the 1950s, the publications of the Congress for Cultural Freedom had a major impact on political discussions in Western Europe—there was, for instance, the closeness to *Encounter* magazine of several major Labour Party politicians, particularly Anthony Crosland, Shirley Williams, and Dennis Healey. And then in the 1960s, the New York intellectuals found that they had an audience in Washington, DC. The Commission on the Year 2000, which my father chaired, took the long view of the nation's future. I could also cite the direct impact on policy of *The Public Interest*. All of this would soon be surpassed by the influence of the neoconservatives, and particularly the Kristols, father and son, on American foreign policy, although by that point, my father had parted ways politically with them. But in 1979, President Jimmy Carter invited my father, along with a group of other prominent intellectuals, to the White House for a discussion of the country's woes, and this meeting lay behind what is often referred to as Carter's "malaise speech." Few intellectuals since have had this sort of public audience or political influence, and this has led to a long series of lamentations, going back to Russell Jacoby's *The Last Intellectuals*.

There is, indeed, a lot to lament about this loss. But at the same time, it is worth noting that this influence could often lead to an emphasis on what was uppermost in the public mind. It could direct attention to the social trends that seemed most powerful at the moment, whether the rising prestige of scientific experts or, conversely, the rising importance of what Bell called "psychedelic" culture in the 1960s.[18] There was less incentive to stand back and ponder how these trends might actually come to an end and what might replace them. To be fair, few if any observers in the early 1970s were predicting anything like the digital revolution that has taken place since then, and that is described so well in the contributions to this volume by Margaret O'Mara and Fred Turner. As O'Mara notes, Alvin Toffler, whom my father derided and whose book *Future Shock* he mocked as *Future Schlock*, in some ways saw further than he did.[19] But as O'Mara puts it, Toffler was a "countercultural adventurer," meaning that he was an outsider. He was not caught up in the intense debates and discussions that preoccupied my father, and indeed his book would never have stood up to the sort of criticism to which it would have been exposed in my father's intellectual milieus. But for these very reasons, Toffler was free to speculate more wildly than my father ever did, and some of his speculations—although not all by any means—hit the mark.

But before we make too much of this comparison, Enlightenment studies may prove useful again, this time for introducing a note of caution. The philosophers of the eighteenth century thought a great deal about the future and, in their own way, made a great many forecasts. And nearly all of them were wildly off the mark. Before 1789, a few of them predicted some sort of political upheaval to come, but none predicted anything like what would come to pass in the French Revolution. Interestingly, the one who probably came closest—Gabriel Bonnot de Mably—remains a relative minor figure in the Enlightenment pantheon. His lucky speculations about how the convening of the Estates General might lead to a general revolution were not enough to raise him to the level of a Rousseau or Voltaire.[20] After 1789, the Marquis de Condorcet predicted a future in which the human race would embrace French revolutionary principles and move steadily toward moral and physical perfection. Immanuel Kant speculated about the coming of perpetual peace. Neither of them, and indeed none of the *philosophes*, forecast anything like the Industrial Revolution, the rise of nationalism, mechanized total war, or even the coming of extensive political party systems. All of them suffered, in their own ways, from massive recency bias.

But we judge them today by the richness of their thoughts, not by the accuracy of their forecasts. That is the way Daniel Bell will be judged as well.

NOTES

1. David A. Bell, "Daniel Bell's Relevant Distinctions," in *For Daniel Bell*, ed. Mark Lilla and Leon Wieseltier (privately published, 2005), 9–16.

2. This first reminiscence was originally published as David A. Bell, "Daniel Bell at 100," *Dissent*, May 9, 2019; reproduced here with the kind permission of *Dissent*.

3. Peter Steinfels, *The Neoconservatives: The Men Who Are Changing America's Politics* (New York: Simon and Schuster, 1979).

4. Daniel Bell, "First Love and Early Sorrows," *Partisan Review* 48, no. 4 (1981): 532–51.

5. Bell, "First Love and Early Sorrows," 533.

6. Daniel Bell, "Some Serious Thoughts on Jewish Humor: A Commentary on the Nature of Wisdom," commencement address at Brandeis University, May 26, 1991, reprinted in *New Oxford Review*, September 1991.

7. Daniel Bell, *The Cultural Contradictions of Capitalism* (New York: Basic Books, 1976), 21–22.

8. Hugh Trevor-Roper to Hugh Lloyd-Jones, March 2, 1989, in *One Hundred Letters from Hugh Trevor-Roper*, ed. Richard Davenport-Hines and Adam Sisman (Oxford: Oxford University Press, 2014), 289–90.

9. See especially Robert Darnton, "In Search of the Enlightenment: Recent Attempts to Create a Social History of Ideas," *Journal of Modern History* 43, no. 1 (1971): 113–32. Darnton took the phrase from Peter Gay but modified its meaning considerably.

10. See especially Robert Darnton, *The Literary Underground of the Old Regime* (Cambridge, MA: Harvard University Press, 1982).

11. See, for instance, Dena Goodman, *The Republic of Letters: A Cultural History of the French Enlightenment* (Ithaca, NY: Cornell University Press, 1994).

12. A revised edition was published in 2011, with a new preface: Daniel Bell, *The Reforming of General Education: The Columbia Experience in Its National Setting* (New Brunswick, NJ: Transaction, 2011). See also "The Daniel Bell Report," Columbia College, Columbia University, https://www.college.columbia.edu/core/content/daniel-bell-report, accessed December 17, 2019.

13. Daniel Bell, *The Winding Passage: Essays and Sociological Journeys, 1960–1980* (Cambridge, MA: Abt Books, 1980).

14. Russell Jacoby, *The Last Intellectuals: American Culture in the Age of Academe* (New York: Basic Books, 1987).

15. Bell, *Cultural Contradictions*, xii.

16. William James, "What Pragmatism Means," in *Classics of Western Philosophy*, ed. Steven M. Cahn (Indianapolis: Hackett, 2012), 1268. For Bell's use of "relevant distinctions," see Daniel Bell, *The End of Ideology: On the Exhaustion of Political Ideas in the Fifties, with "The Resumption of History in the New Century"* (Cambridge, MA: Harvard University Press, 2000), 211.

17. Howard Brick, *Daniel Bell and the Decline of Intellectual Radicalism: Social Theory and Political Reconciliation in the 1940s* (Madison: University of Wisconsin Press, 1986), 425.

18. Bell, *Cultural Contradictions*, 118.

19. Alvin Toffler, *Future Shock* (New York: Random House, 1970).

20. See Keith Michael Baker, "A Script for a French Revolution: The Political Consciousness of the Abbé Mably," in *Inventing the French Revolution: Essays on French Political Culture in the Eighteenth Century* (Cambridge: Cambridge University Press, 1990), 86–108.

2

DANIEL BELL'S
THREE-DIMENSIONAL PUZZLE

PAUL STARR

D aniel Bell resisted being classified in any one standard way, identifying himself instead as "a socialist in economics, a liberal in politics, and a conservative in culture."[1] How those different commitments could fit together may seem puzzling, and indeed that was probably part of his intention. His account of himself was a sly invitation to read his work more carefully and ignore how other people characterized it. It expressed his antipathy to comprehensive ideologies, which he regarded as all-too-easy substitutes for hard thought and the drawing of relevant distinctions. And it identified him as both an heir and a contributor to three traditions of thought, none of which on its own, he maintained, satisfactorily represented his views.

Bell's threefold self-description also corresponds to a threefold distinction at the core of his sociology. Contemporary societies, he contended, were not well-integrated wholes. They could best be understood as divided into three realms—the economy, politics, and culture—each governed by a different "axial" principle: efficiency in the economy, equality in the political sphere, self-realization in the culture. He saw his own cross-cutting identifications—socialist in one respect, liberal in another, conservative in a third—as fully compatible. But he argued that the "disjunction of realms" in contemporary society, rather than existing in a complementary equilibrium, led to contradictory and destabilizing forces.

These two sets of claims—one personal, the other theoretical—and the curious relationship between them raise a series of questions about how Bell arrived at and understood his ideas, how they cohere and relate to other intellectual currents, and whether they provide any continuing purchase for social analysis. Despite his protests, he is often categorized as a lapsed radical, a Cold War liberal, a technocrat, or a neoconservative—labels that in some cases don't do justice to the distinctiveness of his ideas and in other cases substantially misrepresent them.

Intellectual creativity often comes from spanning social groups. This between-group, bridging role—"brokerage," as sociologists call it—"provides a vision," Ronald L. Burt writes, "of options otherwise unseen." People who fit snugly within a single group tend to be exposed to relatively homogenous knowledge and experience, whereas individuals with ties to two or more groups are better positioned to borrow and recombine elements from each one into new ideas.[2]

Bell's creativity stemmed in part from the bridging connections and experience that enabled him to recombine elements from different intellectual and political traditions. He had the advantage of developing his ideas through an intense oral community of intellectuals in New York and a transnational intellectual world. The members of his local community were themselves cosmopolitan bridge-builders. The "New York intellectuals," as Irving Howe wrote in the 1968 article that gave them that name, served "as a liaison between American readers and Russian politics, French ideas, European writing."[3] During the postwar decades, Bell himself developed strong connections with both western and eastern

Europeans, spent a year in Paris in 1956–1957, and borrowed key terms ("the end of ideology," "post-industrial society") from his European connections. Later, he developed intellectual ties in Japan—yet more intellectual bridging capital.

In his passage from his immigrant Jewish upbringing to elite mainstream institutions, and from political journalism to the academy, Bell spanned other social boundaries. He grew up in so marginal a relation to American society that he was virtually an immigrant himself. "It was a kind of double consciousness," he later recalled about his childhood. "We'd go to school and we'd sing 'My country 'tis of thee, sweet land of liberty, land where my fathers died,' and people would say, *Russia.* 'Land of the pilgrim's pride'—*Jerusalem.* 'From every mountainside'—*the Alps.*"[4] He entered fully into America only as a young man, and his entry came through the battles on the left. From that experience, he acquired a deep knowledge of Marxism, the labor movement, and the socialist tradition, which he later synthesized with critical reading in the social sciences. As his moral and political views matured, he recombined ideas from diverse sources, notably John Dewey and Max Weber. But it was mostly in confronting theory with experience—typically European social theory with American historical experience—that Bell developed his distinctive contributions. If theories based on European conditions didn't work in the United States, he had to work out alternatives that did.

BELL'S SOCIALIST INHERITANCE

The collapse of American socialism and the failure of Marxism to explain social and political change from the 1930s to the 1950s were formative intellectual experiences for Daniel Bell. But despite being forced to confront the limitations of his early commitments, he never left either socialism or Marxism entirely behind. Beginning in the 1970s, he would have a standard formulation to explain how he could be a socialist in economics as well as a liberal in politics and conservative in culture: "I'm a socialist in economics," he said in *Arguing the World*, a 1998 documentary about the New York intellectuals, "because I believe that every society has an obligation to give people that degree of decency to allow them to feel that they are citizens in this society. In the realm of economics, the first lien on resources should be that of the community in a redistributive way."[5] Yet this idea of the "first lien" as belonging to the community and going to establish a floor of decency understates the continuing imprint of both the socialist experience and Marx on his thinking.

At the macro or system level, Bell continued to believe in the necessity of a collective, public role in economic and social choices that ought to reflect the moral ideals of socialism. Early in his career, Bell thought of these choices in terms of government planning and public ownership; later, he saw them as problems of what he called "the public household." But he consistently argued for the priority of public or communal interests and sought to set out principles for identifying what those were. At the micro level (or "lifeworld," to use the phenomenological term), Bell was concerned about the dehumanization of labor, a focus of his thought in *Work and Its Discontents* and *The End of Ideology* even after he had abandoned socialist politics.

It wasn't only socialist politics that Bell abandoned. As a young socialist, he tended to frame problems in both the system and lifeworld as arising from capitalism and the power of business. Replacing capitalism with socialism would therefore be the solution. In the years after World War II, he turned away from that understanding as he became persuaded that all industrial societies, capitalist or socialist, shared the same problems in collective choice and the humane organization of work. But, on the basis of the New Deal in the United States and social democratic governments in postwar Europe, he thought that liberal democracy gave capitalism a potential for reform, while the tyranny in the communist world left little hope.

This was not as much a shift for him as it was for many others of his generation who were radicals in the 1930s. From his teenage years, Bell had sided with social democrats against the revolutionary-minded left. In a 1977 article, "Memoirs of a Trotskyist," Irving Kristol recalled Bell from their days at the City College of New York as "that rarity of the 30's: an honest-to-goodness social-democratic intellectual" who believed in such "liberal heresies" as a "mixed economy." Bell's "evident skepticism toward all our ideologies," Kristol wrote, would ordinarily have disqualified him from admittance to the alcove in the student lunchroom where the Trotskyists gathered. But Bell "had an immense intellectual curiosity, a kind of amused fondness for sectarian dialectics, knew his radical texts as thoroughly as the most learned among us and enjoyed 'a good theoretical discussion' the way some enjoy a Turkish bath—so we counted him in."[6] In a study of Bell in his formative years, the historian Howard Brick writes that not only did Bell stay on good terms with those to his left in college, he also appropriated ideas from them, and "at several moments in the coming decade [the 1940s] he would turn in that direction politically, radicalizing by shades, before returning to his social democratic anchorage."[7]

Both the continuities and changes in Bell's views of collective choice emerge from a comparison of an article he wrote on planning for *The New Leader* in 1943 and the theory of the public household that he had worked out by 1976. The title of the 1943 article, "Planning by Whom for What?" raised the central question of whose goals would dominate. Bell quoted approvingly from the report of the Natural Resources Planning Board that Franklin Delano Roosevelt had just sent to Congress, which proposed that "the government should underwrite permanent prosperity . . . and maintain reasonably full employment." The lesson, Bell wrote, was clear: "*planning*, an idea viciously derided only a decade ago, is here to stay." But "the nub of the problem now is shaping up as: Who shall do the planning, Government or Business?" The article's subtitle, "Business Menaces FDR Schemes: Vested Interests Plan Own Boards for Economic Control," expressed Bell's fear about what would happen. This was the anxiety at the root of a book to be called *The Monopoly State*, which he began to write over the next two years but abandoned as he came to regard the argument as simplistic.[8]

By 1976, Bell had long given up the idea of business as a unified interest menacing public-minded planning, but he still saw collective choice about the economy from a perspective recognizably similar to his outlook as a young socialist. Three developments, he argued, had transformed the arena of the public budget, which he preferred to call the "public household" because of "its sociological connotations of family problems and common living." First, since the 1930s, "the direction of the economy has become a central government task" in the sense that the government, regardless of its policies, had become accountable for economic performance. Second, government now also underwrote advances in science and technology. Third, it had become responsible since the 1960s for "normative social policy" to redress social and economic inequalities. The political scientist Charles Lindblom, Bell noted, had asked why people don't try to achieve greater equality through the state: "My argument is that such an effort will now be made." Bell had reservations about that effort, but he sought to provide just principles for it, not to reject it.[9]

Here we come back to Bell's view that the community should have "first lien" on resources, expressed in part by the collective obligation to provide every citizen a "social minimum," which he defined as "the amount of family income required to meet basic needs." To that requirement he also added a principle of "illegitimate convertibility": Wealth should not be "convertible into undue privileges in realms where it is not relevant. Thus it is unjust . . . for wealth to command undue advantage in medical facilities, when these are social rights that should be available to all."[10]

In his writing about work and the problem of alienation, Bell also maintained earlier socialist concerns even after his abandonment of socialist politics in the late 1940s. He argued that there had been "two roads from Marx"—one concerned with exploitation and the other with dehumanization in work—and that while socialists and communists had been preoccupied with the first, they had abandoned the second. Marx had recast Hegel's concept of alienation, or the failure to realize one's potential as a self, as being based in work rather than in the ontological facts of human existence and consciousness. In Marx's view, workers become means for others' ends and therefore suffer a double loss—loss of the *product* of their labor (exploitation) because a portion is appropriated by the employer as surplus value, and loss of control over the *labor process itself* (dehumanization)—as a result of a division of labor intensified by technological change. If Hegel had been correct, alienation had to be accepted because it was an inescapable fact of human existence. But if, as Marx argued, alienation was rooted in private property and the social relations of production, it could be overcome by changing that system.

Bell pointed out, however, that in transforming the concept of alienation, Marx ran two risks: the risks "of falsely identifying the source of alienation only in the private property system; and of introducing a note of utopianism in the idea that once the private property system was abolished man would immediately be free."

As the subsequent history of the communist world showed, these two risks proved fatal to Marx's solution. Nonetheless, this was the direction that Marxist thought had followed, down the "narrow road of economic conceptions of property and exploitation, while the other road, which might have led to new, humanistic concepts of works and labor, was left unexplored."[11]

Bell was equally severe in his judgment of the prevailing non-Marxist approaches to work. Early-twentieth-century Taylorism, with its time-motion breakdowns of factory work as well as later studies in industrial social psychology, exemplified what Bell referred to as "the cult of efficiency" in America. Bell rejected the researchers' defense that they were merely studying what existed. "One of the functions of social science," he insisted, "is also to explore alternative (and better, that is, more human) combinations of work and not merely to make more effective those that already exist."

Workers' concerns, Bell argued, involved two separate types of problems: equity in treatment and the work process itself. Equity demanded that workers be free of arbitrary or capricious control by supervisors and that wages be fair. Unions legitimately focused on these issues. But they had failed to challenge the work process itself, which "would require a radical challenge to society as a whole" because it would call into question "the logic of a consumption economy whose prime consideration is lower costs and increasing output." Still, if one was to deal meaningfully with dehumanization in the modern world, concrete changes in the workplace, such as the rotation and enlargement of jobs and decentralization of production, were a place to begin.[12]

As his analysis of work and alienation illustrates, Bell was concerned in nearly all his writing to establish his relation to Marx. In *The Coming of Post-Industrial Society*, he linked his account of changes in the economy and social structure to volume three of

Capital.[13] The *Cultural Contradictions of Capitalism* turned Marx's understanding of capitalism's dynamics on its head. While critical of the substance of Marxism, Bell took Marx as a model. For example, in the midst of criticizing C. Wright Mills for relying on Vilfredo Pareto's "ahistorical" theory of elites, Bell remarked, "My own masters, in this respect, are Dewey and Marx." He revered Dewey, he wrote, for his emphasis on problems and sources of change rather than fixed structures, while he looked to Marx "for the interplay of ideology and power: for the emphasis on history, on crises as transforming moments, on politics as an activity rooted in concrete interests and played out in determinable strategies."[14]

But although Bell admired Marx's historical method, he abhorred the Marxist theory of history and its eschatological vision of an inevitable breakdown of capitalism, revolutionary upheaval, and communist future. That theory was not only wrong, Bell argued; it had historically misled socialists about the practical tasks of politics. And it was on this issue, the relation of ideology to politics, where Bell parted with his socialist upbringing and turned to liberalism.

FROM SOCIALIST TO LIBERAL POLITICS

Bell's first book, *Marxian Socialism in the United States*, originally published in 1952, sought to reckon with the political failure of American socialism.[15] The question "Why is there no socialism in the United States?"—the title of a 1906 book by the German sociologist Werner Sombart—had drawn a long series of answers focused on America's distinctive social and political conditions, including the relatively high standard of living, opportunities for mobility, deep ethnic and racial divisions, and early extension of the franchise to white working men and their integration into the dominant political parties. Shifting from "external" to "internal" causes of failure, however, Bell turned attention to the social-ist movement itself, arguing that "its inability to resolve a basic dilemma of ethics and politics"—namely, how to deal with the "here-and-now, give-and-take political world"—had prevented it from achieving influence.[16]

In a striking analogy, Bell wrote that the Socialist Party had operated, like Martin Luther's church, as though it could live "*in* but not *of* the world," and, as a result "it could only act, and then inadequately, as the moral, but not political, man in immoral society." *Marxian Socialism in the United States* sought to show how moral posturing and ideological obsessions stymied social-ism in practice. Sectarian splintering was one consequence: "the Socialist Party has never, *even for a single year*, been without some issue which threatened to split the party and which forced it to spend much of its time on the problem of reconciliation or rup-ture." At crucial moments such as the two world wars, socialists and their leaders, like Eugene Debs and Norman Thomas, chose moral purity and political irrelevance over responsible politi-cal choice. What Bell said of Debs—"he lacked the hardheaded-ness of the politician, the ability to take the moral absolutes and break them down to the particulars with the fewest necessary compromises"—could have been his verdict on other Socialist leaders as well.[17]

Critics of Bell's argument object that it lacks a "comparative dimension": after all, weren't socialists elsewhere also dogmatic, yet nonetheless more politically successful?[18] But Bell was not denying the relevance of America's distinctive social and political conditions. As he wrote in a 1967 preface to *Marxian Socialism in the United States*, the questions that he had attempted to answer, and that others had previously avoided, was why "the socialist movement, as an organized political body, *fail[ed] to adapt to American conditions.*"[19] Socialists, Bell suggested, could have made different choices. In 1934, for example, the novelist Upton Sinclair, a longtime socialist, won the Democratic nomination for governor of California on the basis of a radical platform and, while losing, he did far better than any Socialist Party candidate ever had. "Sinclair's quick and spectacular rise, like that of the [North Dakota] Non-Partisan League before him, showed that socialists could utilize the primary system to great political advantage"—a point that democratic socialists today have come to appreciate. But the Socialist Party at the time denounced Sinclair for obtaining the Democratic nomination and abandoning orthodoxy.[20]

The problem, Bell argued, lay with the failure of militant socialists to appreciate the distinctiveness of "the American scene." Their attention "was riveted on Europe, because, as Marxist theory foretold, the fate of capitalism there foreshadowed the course of capitalism here." When Bell revisited *Marxian Socialism* in a 1996 afterword, he emphasized this point: the Marxian theory of history had been "mischievously misleading" for American socialists. "Socialism," he wrote, "remains a moral ideal independent of a theory of history," a moral ideal of equality and "condemnation of exploitation and domination," but achieving those aims "necessarily involves politics."[21] And socialists had failed to adapt their politics to American conditions.

❧

Many of the essays that Bell wrote in the 1950s and went into *The End of Ideology* had a similar theme. The Marxist schema was only one example of a theory derived from European conditions that did not fit the United States well. Summing up the six essays that make up the first third of that book, Bell attributed "the inadequacy of many social theories about America" largely to "the uncritical application of ambient ideas from European sociology to the vastly different experiences of American life."[22]

The first essay in the book is a withering critique of the theory of "mass society," which had been developed by a wide variety of European critics—aristocratic, Catholic, existentialist, and left-wing—and picked up in the United States. The general idea was that modernity had broken up traditional communities and faiths and left people rudderless, alienated, and therefore susceptible to manipulation through the mass media by charismatic leaders like Hitler and Mussolini. As mass production in industry turned out standardized goods, so the mass media produced uniform, lowest-common-denominator entertainment. To be part of a mass was to lose one's individuality. But these accounts, Bell wrote, had little to do with "the complex, richly striated social relations of the real world." Americans were joiners; there were some 200,000 voluntary associations in the country. Churches, unions, and civic groups had more members than ever. Civil society was alive and well in the United States despite the tragic stories that the mass-society theorists told about modernity.[23]

Bell was similarly critical of Mills's *The Power Elite* because it was both too dependent on European theory (Pareto's theory of elites) and too little grounded in analysis of American politics. Bell and Mills had been close both personally and intellectually in the 1940s, and *The Power Elite* was in some ways the book that Bell had started to write under the title *The Monopoly State*. But Bell now considered that vision of a cohesive elite controlling American politics out of touch with the realities of a diverse, pluralistic society with multiple centers of power. Like the Marxists and the mass-society theorists, radicals like Mills needed to come to terms with America's liberal complexities.[24]

BELL'S LIBERALISM

Bell's understanding of what had gone wrong with American socialism—its excessive dogmatism and failure to grasp American realities—influenced how he conceived of liberalism. At times, he defined liberalism entirely as an anti-ideological temper. "I'm a liberal in politics," Bell said in an interview for *Arguing the World*, "but liberalism has no fixed dogmas. . . . It's a skepticism. It's a pluralism, it's agnostic."[25] In other contexts, though, he did identify liberalism with a set of principles, which supported representative democracy and qualified his socialism. Individual achievement, for example, should be the basis for allocating social positions; the public and private spheres needed to be kept distinct to avoid politicizing all behavior: "Once a social minimum is created, then what people do with the remainder of their money (subject to the principle of illegitimate convertibility), is their own business, just as what people do in the realm of morals is equally their own business, so long as it is done privately."[26]

Yet these efforts at self-clarification did not get at the heart of Bell's politics. In the last line of *Marxian Socialism*, he quoted a sentence from Weber's lecture "Politics as a Vocation": "He who seeks the salvation of souls, his own as well as others, should not seek it along the avenue of politics." Bell continually returned to Weber's distinction between an ethics of ultimate ends, which demanded an unstinting dedication regardless of costs, and an ethics of responsibility, which required a weighing of consequences and acceptance of limits. To Weber, dangers existed on both sides. But politics required a choice, and Bell made his. Looking back in his 1981 essay "First Love and Early Sorrows," he wrote, "The ethics of responsibility, the politics of civility, the fear of the zealot and the fanatic, and of the moral man willing to sacrifice his morality in the egoistic delusion of total despair—are the maxims that have ruled my intellectual life."[27]

Bell's concern about damage control reflected the experience of a generation that had lived through the rise of fascism and Stalinism, the Holocaust, and World War II, and it had much in common with Judith Shklar's "liberalism of fear," the liberalism that puts the prevention of cruelty above all else.[28] But Bell was particularly concerned with preventing another danger: being sucked into an all-consuming cause that blinds its true believers to the realities of the world and the consequences of their actions. This was a central motivation behind *The End of Ideology*.

Some books, Bell later lamented, are "better known for their titles than their contents," and *The End of Ideology* was one of them.[29] But in choosing the title, he had invited confusion about his intentions. In one of the chapters in the book, an essay on unions, he does the same thing. The essay begins with a line from George Bernard Shaw: "Trade-unionism is the capitalism of the proletariat," which Bell calls "a half-truth, calculated to irritate the people who believe in the other half." The other half was that unions were still a social movement, and indeed Bell saw that movement tradition, rather than "market-unionism," as the half that unions needed to build upon and expand.[30] Nonetheless, Bell appropriated Shaw's disparaging phrase, "the capitalism of the proletariat," for the title of his essay. Likewise, "the end of ideology" was also "a half-truth calculated to irritate the people who believe in the other half," and Bell nonetheless used it for the title of his book, surely knowing whom it would irritate and why their attacks would focus controversy on what he wrote. As marketing, the title was brilliant, but it has left a cloud over the book that it can never escape.

Bell used the phrase "the end of ideology" in both a descriptive and a normative sense. First, it described the political mood of a moment. The subtitle—*On the Exhaustion of Political Ideas in the Fifties*—signaled this descriptive meaning, which was simply that the grand systems of ideas that dominated politics earlier had been drained of vitality and, in particular, no longer captured the imagination of intellectuals. In the introduction, Bell wrote that he was using "ideology" not to denote any "belief system," but to refer to "a special complex of ideas and passions that arose in the nineteenth century," applying the term "largely to left-wing thought." In the epilogue—the only essay in the book directly about the end of ideology—he emphasized that he was referring to "total ideologies," "all-inclusive" systems of "comprehensive reality . . . infused with passion" that sought "to transform the whole of a way of life."[31] This had a definite historical reference in Marxism, but it was a small part of what most people understood then, or understand now, as "ideology."

Bell wrote that the phrase "end of ideology" applied to more than Marxism. Utopian visions of social engineering were not alone in being exhausted: "At the same time, the older 'counterbeliefs' have lost their intellectual force as well. Few 'classic' liberals insist that the State should play no role in the economy." Western intellectuals had arrived at a "rough consensus" in favor of a welfare state and political pluralism. This was the view of Bell's colleagues in the Congress for Cultural Freedom, who included many of the leaders of Britain's Labour Party—though it was by no means an idiosyncratic opinion of Cold War social democrats. The "end of ideology" referenced a narrowing of major-party differences in Western democracies and the collapse of ideological extremes. In the United States, Eisenhower Republicans had accepted the main achievements of the New Deal; in Britain, Conservatives had accepted the reforms of the postwar Labour government, such as the National Health Service. This was the chief basis of the half-truth of "the end of ideology": it described a political reality of the 1950s.[32]

Bell made it clear that he wasn't predicting that ideology would disappear forever, but he also left no doubt that he welcomed "the end of ideology" in the 1950s, and that the phrase had a second, positive, normative meaning for him. Ideology oversimplifies reality, and it was this oversimplification that he opposed. His perspective, he insisted, was "anti-ideological, but not conservative." He did not intend the end of ideology to be an endorsement of the status quo: "A repudiation of ideology, to be meaningful, must mean not only a criticism of the utopian order but *of existing society as well.*" In the book's final pages, he said that people still need the idea of utopia, a "vision of their potential, some manner of fusing passion with intelligence." But now, rather than being a "faith ladder," the ladder to "the City of Heaven" had to be an "empirical" one: "a utopia has to specify *where* one wants to go, *how* to get there, the costs of the enterprise, and some realization of, and justification for the determination of *who* is to pay."[33]

Bell's work as a policy intellectual in the 1960s followed from that understanding of the need for an empirical basis for public remedy. He criticized the "patristic writings" in the Marxist tradition for saying nothing of substance about how a socialist planned economy would work in practice.[34] When he served on a federal commission on automation between 1962 and 1964, he was struck that much writing on the subject lacked grounding in research. In the inaugural issue of *The Public Interest*, Bell and his coeditor, Irving Kristol, wrote that "it is the essential peculiarities of ideologies that they do not simply prescribe ends but also insistently propose prefabricated interpretations of existing realities—interpretations that bitterly resist all sensible revision." The aim of the new journal, they said, was "to help all of us, when we discuss issues of public policy, to know a little better what we are talking about—and preferably in time to make such knowledge effective."[35] This emphasis on the need for empirical knowledge hardly made Bell a technocrat.

During the mid-1960s, Bell cast himself as a practical-minded liberal. In a 1964 speech to the annual dinner of the Sidney Hillman Foundation—Hillman had been the head of the Amalgamated Clothing Workers Union and one of the founders of the Congress of Industrial Organizations (CIO)—Bell suggested that the leaders of the Black protest movement should learn from the CIO. The late 1930s, like the mid-1960s, saw "spreading violence, the seizure of property, sit-downs and sit-ins, complaints from employers about 'outside agitators,' the quick emergence of new, natural leaders from the rank and file." The industrial unions had turned successfully to collective bargaining, and now too, Bell argued, "responsible" Black leaders should organize themselves for "political collective bargaining" (though exactly whom they could have bargained with wasn't entirely clear). With little appreciation for the obstacles to wealth formation among Blacks in the United States, Bell also reprimanded the Black middle class for failing to build "communal" organizations to deal with problems in family life, as the Jewish immigrant community had done. His basic message to Black leaders was that European immigrants had advanced through collective bargaining strategies and communal self-help, so they should do likewise. But he ended by saying that progress also depended on white liberals and "can only start when the Negro has begun to achieve his legitimate political demands."[36]

Bell's speech about Black advance at the Sidney Hillman dinner—still an important annual event on the labor left—illustrates a more general failing among his generation of sociologists in their understanding of racial politics. Like many other white social scientists of the time, Bell saw the Black struggle through the prism of the "immigrant analogy," assuming that Blacks could follow the same path that white immigrant groups had traveled since arriving in the United States.[37] Although he criticized others for failing to take into account America's distinctive history and social conditions, he failed to do so himself on the crucial issue of race.

Bell's insistence in *The End of Ideology* that he was not ruling out utopian ideas—they just needed to be empirically grounded—did not impress his critics on the left. After all, the phrase "end of ideology" suggested that big, radical political ideas were finished everywhere and forever. It suggested a narrowing of criticism of the status quo, even though Bell denied it. Few of Bell's critics disagreed with what he was saying about the political mood of the 1950s. But by the mid-1960s, "the end of ideology" looked outdated as a description of politics, and inadequate as a guide to moral responsibility.

One stinging attack on Bell came in 1967 from Noam Chomsky in a long essay, "The Responsibility of the Intellectuals," published in the *New York Review of Books*. "Intellectuals," Chomsky wrote, "are in a position to expose the lies of governments, to analyze actions according to their causes and motives and often hidden intentions." His main thrust was to lay responsibility for the Vietnam War at the feet of prominent intellectuals who had misled the public about the war, justified it, or provided technical advice in support of it. Bell, however, had never done any of these things, and Chomsky did not say that he had. His indictment of Bell was that *The End of Ideology* provided a general justification for dismissing radical ideas and confining change "within the framework of a Welfare State in which, presumably, experts in the conduct of public affairs will have a prominent role." Like conservatives who would later attack liberals as part of a "new class" that had a self-interest in expanding government bureaucracies, Chomsky saw self-interest at work in Bell's defense of a liberal welfare state: "Having found his position of power, having achieved security and affluence, he has no further need for ideologies that look to radical change."[38]

Although Bell regarded Chomsky's criticism as illogical and unfair— "I have *never* defended American policy in Vietnam," he protested, "on the contrary, as far back as 1965 I began to oppose the war"[39]—it was representative of a wave of attacks from the New Left in the late 1960s. Bell had interpreted Weber's ethics of responsibility as an obligation to weigh moral consequences, which meant, among other things, shedding ideological blinders and assessing empirical effects. But to a new generation who saw the responsibility of intellectuals differently, he had become too close to power and too circumspect when outright opposition was necessary. And in the 1970s, the rise of a movement with which he was initially identified—neoconservatism—seemed to confirm suspicions that he had shifted to the right with other members of his generation.

A CONSERVATIVE ONLY IN CULTURE?

Although Bell had earlier insisted that he was not a conservative, by the 1970s he was saying he was a conservative in one respect—culture. But what was a conservatism specific to the realm of culture?

In *The Cultural Contradictions of Capitalism*, Bell used the term "culture" in a restricted sense. He equated it with "the realm of symbolic forms," and more particularly in the context of his book's argument, with "the arena of *expressive symbolism*: those efforts in painting, poetry, and fiction, or within the religious forms of litany, liturgy, and ritual, which seek to explore and express the meaning of human existence in some imaginative form." Or as he restated it: "Culture, for me, is the effort to pro-vide a coherent set of answers to the existential predicaments that confront all human beings in the passage of their lives." By those universal existential predicaments, he meant "how one meets death, the nature of tragedy and the character of heroism, the definition of loyalty and obligation, the redemption of the soul, the meaning of love and of sacrifice, the understanding of compassion, the tension between an animal and a human nature, the claims of instinct and restraint." Bell identified himself as a conservative in culture, he wrote, because he respected tradition, which "provides the continuity of memory that teaches how one's forebears met the same existential predicaments," and because he believed in "reasoned judgments of good and bad about the qualities of a work of art," and regarded "the principle of authority" to be necessary for "the judging of the value of experience and art and education." He saw religion as having historically embodied "the quest for the unity of culture."[40]

Over the previous century, however, modernism in culture and capitalism itself broke down the respect for tradition and standards of judgment that had prevailed in "bourgeois society." Modernism disrupted the earlier unity established through religion "by insisting on the autonomy of the aesthetic from moral norms; by valuing more highly the new and experimental; and by taking the self . . . as the touchstone of cultural judgment." In its drive for autonomy, modernist culture took over "the relation with the demonic. But instead of taming it, as religion tried to do, the secular culture (art and literature) began to accept it, explore it, and revel in it, coming to see it as a source of creativity." Instead of cultivating the restraint of impulses, modernism celebrated their release. The same shift took place in everyday economic life: "Puritan restraint and the Protestant ethic" dissolved under the influence of a consumption-oriented capitalism: "The greatest single engine in the destruction of the Protestant ethic was the invention of the installment plan, or instant credit."[41] In effect, capitalism had been destabilized from above and below—not, as Marx had taught, through a contradiction between the forces and relations of production, but through the contradictory cultural tendencies that capitalism unleashed.

The result of these tendencies, Bell argued, was to undermine the traditional moral justifications of authority, leaving self-realization, or self-gratification, as the dominant principle of contemporary culture. Nothing so epitomized this tendency for him as the counterculture of the 1960s, with its rejection of authority, traditional standards of judgment, and reason itself in favor of "prerational spontaneity."[42] By the 1970s, the slowdown in economic growth and rise in inflation were accentuating the crisis brought about by the collapse of traditional moral principles. Democratic governments found themselves in a "double bind" as they faced the two imperatives of capital accumulation (to keep the economy growing) and legitimation (which now depended on meeting popular demands for spending on public services). It was in response to this situation—the mid-1970s economic and political crisis coming on top of the collapse of earlier moral justifications—that Bell offered his conception of the public household as a way of grounding the role of government and mediating the conflicting demands it faced.[43] Bell recognized the potential use of the market as a way of diverting responsibility from government, but he neither predicted the crisis would be resolved that way nor favored it.[44]

Cultural Contradictions was important as both a theoretical and a personal statement. As a work of social theory, it challenged both Marxism and the structural functionalism of Talcott Parsons, which shared the premise that societies were interdependent totalities. Marxism saw the material base of a society determining its superstructure, while structural-functionalist theory saw societies as being integrated through general value orientations. Bell's outlook was antiholistic; societies were not necessarily unified wholes. This skepticism about societies as unified totalities was consistent with other tendencies in social theory at the time that rejected grand, comprehensive narratives of historical change. But it was in opposition to what would be a growing vogue in the next several decades, exemplified by the work of Michel Foucault, who saw the same structures of thought as pervading an entire social order. Bell's antiholism did not imply a retreat to small-scale analysis or deny the possibility of understanding long-term patterns of development. After all, his theory of post-industrial society was also a grand narrative, although Bell described the post-industrial shift as limited to the technoeconomic realm rather than determining how culture and politics would change as well.

The most important contribution of Bell's social theory was not his specific claims about the three institutional realms. The axial principles that he said governed the contemporary economy, culture, and politics were debatable: Why, for example, did efficiency rather than capital accumulation dominate the capitalist economy? Why was it necessary to pick only one principle for each realm? Few theorists have followed Bell down that path. His combination of two seemingly opposed elements has been of greater value: long-term structural analysis of technology and the economy on the one hand, and antiholism on the other, which decoupled those structural patterns from culture and politics (or at least loosened the connections between them). The net result is to open up possibilities for multiple institutional misalignments and contradictions and diverse but constrained paths for societal development. This, at least, is how I see his theoretical contribution.

Bell's own preferences did not line up with the principles that he identified as dominating the economy and culture. Just as he had written that one function of social science was "to explore alternative (and better, that is, more human) combinations of work and not merely to make more effective those that already exist," so he thought that it was the responsibility of social scientists to propose more humane alternatives to a society's principles. And this is what he did in identifying himself as a socialist in economics and a conservative in culture.

Published in 1976, when neoconservatism was emerging as an influential force, *Cultural Contradictions* seemed to confirm Bell as one of the movement's intellectual leaders. In a 1979 book *The Neoconservatives*, with the portentous subtitle *The Men Who Are Changing America's Politics*, the journalist Peter Steinfels devoted chapters to three figures: Irving Kristol (who had embraced and championed the label "neoconservative"), the political scientist and later Democratic senator Daniel Patrick Moynihan, and Bell. "Despite Bell's welfare sympathies and political liberalism," Steinfels wrote, "his perception of the economy and polity caught in the tow of a wildly unrestrained culture elevates his self-proclaimed cultural conservatism to a position of dominance."[45] Contrary to Steinfels, however, Bell's views of economics and politics remained fundamentally those of a social democrat, and as neoconservatism evolved over the next decade, Bell explicitly disassociated himself from it.

Originally, the neoconservatives were concerned mainly with domestic affairs and were critical of the radicalized liberalism of the 1960s, but not of the New Deal. Even with respect to the social policies of the Sixties, their stance was repair rather than outright repudiation. By the 1980s, however, neoconservatism stood for a hawkish foreign policy and grew hostile to liberal government in its entirety as part of the Reagan-era right. "From the 1960s to the 2000s, neoconservatism transformed itself so thoroughly as to become unrecognizable," Justin Vaisse writes in a history of the movement.[46] It had already undergone that change long before the 2000s. In a 1984 article, Bell took note of the "rapprochement" between neoconservatives and the right and said neoconservatism had lost intellectual coherence. When he and Kristol founded *The Public Interest*, Bell wrote, they had hoped "to transcend ideology through reasoned public debate," but "for Kristol today all politics is ideology." Bell still held to his liberalism: "We need a new public philosophy, rooted in liberalism, a liberalism which has the 'negative capability' of not reaching closure on all issues."[47]

Kristol, who so self-identified with neoconservatism that he subtitled a book on the subject "The Autobiography of an Idea," ultimately moved so far to the right that there was nothing "neo" left in his neoconservatism.[48] In 1993, claiming that the "liberal ethos" had "ruthlessly corrupted" American life, he wrote, "Now that the other 'Cold War' is over, the real cold war has begun."[49] Bell regarded these views with contempt and returned in his later years to his social democratic roots. When Robert Kuttner, Robert Reich, and I started *The American Prospect* in 1990 as an alternative to *The Public Interest* and other publications that no longer upheld liberal principles, Bell gladly agreed to become one of the magazine's founding sponsors and helped raise money for it.

But if Bell remained a conservative only in culture, while a socialist in economics and a liberal in politics, this still leaves us with our original puzzle: How did his own cross-cutting commitments and beliefs cohere?

Bell differed from many in his generation by staying close to his early beliefs, his "social democratic anchorage," throughout his life. Others who had been socialists or communists in the 1930s, like Kristol, first repudiated those ideas and became liberals in the 1950s and 1960s, and then changed direction again in the 1970s, repudiating liberalism and becoming conservatives. In contrast, Bell recombined his more slowly evolving commitments, assigning them to different dimensions of his thought: socialism to economics, liberalism to politics, conservatism to culture. That differentiated, multidimensional worldview could not settle every issue. Many questions overlap—some, for example, are inherently both political and cultural—and first principles are insufficient to answer them. Bell's own philosophy of the public household overlapped the political and economic spheres. Every political philosophy requires secondary or derivative rules to resolve conflicts of principle and ambiguities of interpretation.

But Bell's synthesis is worthy of being taken seriously because of the intellectual and moral depth with which he developed it. He was a twentieth-century American heir to Marx and other European theorists, testing their ideas against American experience and the changing social world. Similarly, he combined learning and alertness in his efforts to understand the implications of cultural change, even as he overreacted against the sensibility of the 1960s and shifts in sexuality and popular taste. The moral vision that held his worldview together was rooted primarily in the ethic of responsibility and a tragic sense from the twentieth century's horrors and the failure of socialism's great expectations. He was one of those whom he called the "twice born." The "once born," he wrote, drawing on the psychologist William James, were "sky-blue healthy-minded" moralists, to whom "sin and evil" were transient. "To the twice born, the world is 'a double-storied mystery' which shrouds the evil and renders false the good, and in order to find truth, one must lift the veil and look Medusa in the face."[50] Although those words appear in his first book about socialism, written when he was barely thirty, his later work was in the same spirit. He never gave up hope of social democratic improvement, but he looked to tradition and memory for wisdom, and in that respect, his cultural conservatism was consistent with his other views.

Whether Bell's configuration of values has any future is hard to say. Some young people on the left today identify both as liberals in politics and as socialists in economics and mean approximately what Bell meant. They're unlikely, however, to identify as culturally conservative (the exceptions may be people of color, especially those from recent immigrant groups). But the culture wars of recent decades have so influenced our understanding of the meaning of cultural conservatism that it may throw off judgment about the relevance of Bell's position, which preeminently reflected a respect for memory and tradition in answering the existential problems of human life. We stand at a dangerous moment—environmentally, epidemiologically, politically—that has disturbing echoes of the dark times that haunted Bell. The rise of fascism today resembles the 1930s. Although we hope never to live through anything like the twentieth-century tragedies and disappointments that shaped Bell's worldview, we ought to be attentive to the wisdom of someone who learned from those horrors and still maintained the commitments to equality and a free society that he adopted when he was young.

NOTES

1. Daniel Bell, "Foreword: 1978," in *The Cultural Contradictions of Capitalism*, 20th anniversary ed. (New York: Basic Books, 1996 [1976]), xi.

2. Ronald L. Burt., "Structural Holes and Good Ideas," *American Journal of Sociology* 110, no. 2 (2004): 349–399.

3. Irving Howe, "The New York Intellectuals: A Chronicle and a Critique," *Commentary* 46, no. 4 (October 1968): 29–51.

4. Joseph Dorman, *Arguing the World: The New York Intellectuals in Their Own Words* (New York: Free Press, 2000), 25 (italics in original).

5. Dorman, *Arguing the World*, 174.

6. Irving Kristol, "Memoirs of a Trotskyist," *New York Times Magazine*, January 23, 1977.

7. Howard Brick, *Daniel Bell and the Decline of Intellectual Radicalism: Social Theory and Political Reconstruction in the 1940s* (Madison: University of Wisconsin Press, 1986), 61.

8. Daniel Bell, "Planning by Whom for What? Business Menaces FDR Schemes: Vested Interests Plan Own Boards for Economic Control," *The New Leader*, March 20, 1943, 5, 7.

9. Bell, *Cultural Contradictions of Capitalism*, 221, 224–226.

10. Bell, "Foreword: 1978," xiii–xiv; see also Michael Walzer, *Spheres of Justice* (New York: Basic Books, 1983).

11. For the full theoretical exposition, see Daniel Bell, "The 'Rediscovery' of Alienation: Some Notes along the Quest for the Historical Marx," *Journal of Philosophy* 56 (1959): 933–952. Bell condensed this essay and combined it with sections of other papers in "Two Roads from Marx," in *The End of Ideology: On the Exhaustion of Political Ideas in the Fifties* (Cambridge, MA: Harvard University Press, 1988 [1960]), 355–392.

12. Daniel Bell, "Work and Its Discontents: The Cult of Efficiency in America," *The End of Ideology: On the Exhaustion of Political Ideas in the Fifties* (Cambridge, MA: Harvard University Press, 1988 [1960]), 227–272; Bell, "Two Roads from Marx."

13. Daniel Bell, *The Coming of Post-Industrial Society: A Venture in Social Forecasting* (New York: Basic Books, 1973), 54–63.

14. Daniel Bell, "Is There a Ruling Class in America?" in *The End of Ideology: On the Exhaustion of Political Ideas in the Fifties* (Cambridge, MA: Harvard University Press, 1988 [1960]), 48n.

15. The original publication was a nearly-200-page chapter, "The Background and Development of Marxian Socialism in the United States," in *Socialism and American Life*, volume 1, ed. Donald Drew Egbert and Stow Persons (Princeton, NJ: Princeton University Press, 1952), 213–406.

16. Daniel Bell, *Marxian Socialism in the United States* (Ithaca, NY: Cornell University Press, 1996 [1952]), 5.

17. Bell, *Marxian Socialism*, 5, 9–10, 87 (italics in original).

18. John H. M. Laslett, "Comment" [responding to Bell], in *Failure of a Dream? Essays in the History of American Socialism*, ed. John H. M. Laslett and Seymour Martin Lipset (Berkeley: University of California Press, 1974), 30–45. See also Michael Kazin's essay, "Of But Not in the Left: Daniel Bell on Radical Politics," in this volume.

19. Bell, *Marxian Socialism*, xxxix.

20. Bell, *Marxian Socialism*, 162.

21. Bell, *Marxian Socialism*, 162, 199, 203.

22. Bell, *The End of Ideology*, 13.

23. Bell, "America as a Mass Society: A Critique," in *The End of Ideology: On the Exhaustion of Political Ideas in the Fifties* (Cambridge, MA: Harvard University Press, 1988 [1960], 21–38.

24. Bell, "Is There a Ruling Class in America?"; Brick, *Daniel Bell and the Decline of Intellectual Radicalism*, 80–82, 94–100.

25. Dorman, *Arguing the World*, 174.

26. Bell, "Foreword: 1978," xiv–xv.

27. Bell, *Marxian Socialism*, 193; Daniel Bell, "First Love and Early Sorrows," *Partisan Review* 48, no. 4 (1981): 550–551; Max Weber, "Politics as a Vocation," in *From Max Weber: Essays in Sociology*, trans. and ed. H. H. Gerth and C. Wright Mills (New York: Oxford University Press, 1958 [1946]), 77–128.

28. Judith Shklar, "The Liberalism of Fear," in *Liberalism and the Moral Life*, ed. Nancy Rosenblum (Cambridge, MA: Harvard University Press, 1989), 21–38.

29. Bell, "Afterword, 1988," in *The End of Ideology: On the Exhaustion of Political Ideas in the Fifties* (Cambridge, MA: Harvard University Press, 1988 [1960], 409.

30. Bell, "The Capitalism of the Proletariat," in *The End of Ideology: On the Exhaustion of Political Ideas in the Fifties* (Cambridge, MA: Harvard University Press, 1988 [1960]), 211–226.

31. Daniel Bell, *The End of Ideology: On the Exhaustion of Political Ideas in the Fifties* (Cambridge, MA: Harvard University Press, 1988 [1960]), 17, 400.

32. Bell, *The End of Ideology*, 402. For a survey of the debate over "the end of ideology," see Howard Brick, "The End of Ideology Thesis," in *The Oxford Handbook of Political Ideologies*, ed. Michael Freeden and Marc Stears (Oxford: Oxford University Press, 2013).

33. Bell, *The End of Ideology*, 16, 405 (italics in original).

34. Bell, "Two Roads from Marx," 368.

35. Daniel Bell and Irving Kristol, "What Is the Public Interest?" *The Public Interest* 1 (Fall 1965): 3–5.

36. Daniel Bell, "Plea for a 'New Phase in Negro Leadership': The civil rights movement has reached a point of crisis, says an observer. Here are his

suggestions for what should be done beyond protest," *New York Times*, May 31, 1964.

37. See Michael Omi and Howard Winant, *Racial Formation in the United States: From the 1960s to the 1990s* (New York: Routledge & Kegan Paul, 1994), 10 (citing Robert Blauner).

38. Noam Chomsky, "The Responsibility of the Intellectuals," *New York Review of Books*, February 23, 1967, accessed at https://www.nybooks.com /articles/1967/02/23/a-special-supplement-the-responsibility-of-intelle/.

39. Letter from Bell to Lionel Abel, quoted by Abel in an exchange with Chomsky in "Vietnam, the Cold War & Other Matters," *Commentary* (October 1969), 26.

40. Bell, *Cultural Contradictions of Capitalism*, 12, xv.

41. Bell, *Cultural Contradictions of Capitalism*, xv, 19, 21.

42. Bell, *Cultural Contradictions of Capitalism*, 120–145.

43. Bell, *Cultural Contradictions of Capitalism*, 220–282.

44. See Stefan Eich's essay, "The Double Bind: Daniel Bell and Financialization," in this volume; and Greta R. Krippner, *Capitalizing on Crisis: The Political Origins of the Rise of Finance* (Cambridge, MA: Harvard University Press, 2011), 138–150.

45. Peter Steinfels, *The Neoconservatives: The Men Who Are Changing America's Politics* (New York: Simon and Schuster, 1979), 172.

46. Justin Vaisse, *Neoconservatism: The Biography of a Movement* (Cambridge, MA: Harvard University Press, 2010), 4.

47. Daniel Bell, "Our Country—1984," *Partisan Review*, 50th anniversary issue, 54 (4) and 55 (1) 1985, 620–637.

48. Paul Starr, "Nothing Neo," *The New Republic*, December 3, 1995, 35–38.

49. Irving Kristol, *Neoconservatism: The Autobiography of an Idea* (New York: Free Press, 1995).

50. Bell, *Marxian Socialism*, 182–183.

PART II

POLITICS AND IDEOLOGY

3

OF BUT NOT IN THE LEFT
Daniel Bell on Radical Politics

MICHAEL KAZIN

This will not be a dispassionate essay. Daniel Bell was my uncle, and I loved him. Although we didn't spend a great deal of time together, our interactions were always rich and intense. To talk with him about intellectual and political matters was a daunting experience as well as a thrilling one; I sometimes disagreed with him but usually refrained from telling him so for fear that I couldn't mount as erudite and eloquent a defense of my position as he always would make of his. So to evaluate his writings about the left—as a movement and a way of understanding the world—feels like continuing a discussion or kindling an argument. Unfortunately, Dan cannot answer back.

He was fond of retelling a story about growing up fast in the Marxist left and then soon outgrowing it. At the tender age of thirteen, in the pit of the Great Depression, the son of working-class immigrants from the Czarist Empire joined the Young People's Socialist League (YPSL), which was then enjoying a modest spurt of growth that raised its membership to about 4,000.[1] YPSL, like the rest of the left during the early years of the Great Depression, was a hothouse for doctrinal battles and rapid changes of line. For a brief time, Dan evidently considered "becoming a communist" but soon doused forever whatever flickers of Leninism had flared within him.[2]

An older cousin from Russia who had witnessed the revolution of 1917 and become an anarchist urged him to read Alexander Berkman's diary about his experiences in Bolshevik Russia during the Civil War. There, Dan learned about the regime's brutal repression, led by Trotsky, of the 1921 revolt at the Kronstadt fortress in the harbor of the city then known as Petrograd. The shock of that lesson never left him. "My Kronstadt was Kronstadt," he liked to quip—an apt response to those on the left who were slow to recognize the undemocratic, brutal nature of the first communist government and of all its future emulators, in sites ranging from Pyongyang and Beijing to East Berlin and Havana.[3]

By the time he graduated from the City College of New York in 1938, Dan was not just a committed foe of any brand of Leninism, but also an unremitting critic of the romance of revolution itself. Proclaiming himself a Menshevik, he joined the Social Democratic Federation (SDF), which had split away from the Socialist Party in protest against its militant rhetoric and openness to a tactical alliance with the Communists, whose activism in the Congress of Industrial Organizations (CIO) and in artistic circles had lifted them to a dominant status on the American left. Bell also began reporting for *The New Leader*, which shared the SDF's orientation without becoming its house organ.

While still in his teens, Dan had already come to a decision about the only kind of socialism that would ever claim his support: a welfare state that accepted market relations and protected both partisan competition and civil liberties. Such consistency for seven decades was rare in his generation of left-wing intellectuals, for whom second and third rebirths were quite routine.[4]

As a convert to right-wing social democracy, Dan expressed a lifelong desire (one might even call it a compulsion) to critique other left-wingers for what he saw as their multiple errors of thought and action. When I was an ardent New Leftist back in the late 1960s and early 1970s, he used to pepper me with questions, curious yet needling, about the radical world I had joined. Who were the leaders of the Spartacist League? How did SDS activists in Berkeley differ from me and my comrades in Cambridge and New York? Was the Black Panther Party active on college campuses? Did anyone my age comprehend the archaic doctrine of the Socialist Labor Party? Without knowing it, he was sparking my curiosity about the larger history of the American left. Some two decades later, he asked me to write the introduction to a reissue of his pioneering study of Marxian socialism in the United States. [5]

Dan never lost his fascination with Marx's thought either. In fact, he wrote more warmly about the ideas of the hirsute old Rhinelander than he ever did about his latter-day disciples. "I have devoted half my life to the study of Marx, and that may be insufficient," he declared in a 1976 essay that ridiculed Michael Harrington's attempt to retrieve a Marx that he and his fellow socialists could apply to contemporary issues. As David Bell recently wrote, his father "often described" Marx to him "as the most profound social analyst he had ever encountered." It is fitting that Dan bequeathed his "complete set of Marx and Engels in fifty volumes, published in the Soviet Union" to his only son. [6]

Long after he had abandoned the organized left, Dan demonstrated that admiration in a rather surprising venue: a lecture hall at Leningrad State University in the spring of 1988. During a rambling address that, according to Dan, captivated the audience, he made a reference to a work by Trotsky about Marx. A "dumpy woman" in the back of the hall quickly asked Dan, "in a somewhat strident tone," if he had "read anything else on . . . Capital besides Trotsky." He responded by listing all three volumes of the grand opus, as well as "the unfinished and posthumous collection on surplus value edited by Karl Kautsky" *and* a number of more contemporary Russian economists. After more questions, nearly all of them friendly, Dan stepped down from the podium to "a wave of applause." He was emotionally exhausted but clearly delighted. "I had come home," concluded the child of immigrants from Bialystok, "to the other shore."[7]

THE PASSION OF DISPASSION

That same contentious approach characterized nearly everything Dan wrote about the left. He directed piercing, often satirical, thrusts at individuals and tendencies that may have spurned the Bolsheviks but repeated the same error of seeking to redeem a suffering world by shackling its inhabitants to a new set of ideological chains. Dan warned passionately about the dangers of basing one's politics on a great passion for making the world over. He often quoted Weber's line, from his famous 1919 address to radical students in Munich, "He who seeks the salvation of souls, his own as well as others, should not seek it along the avenue of politics." That sensibility both yielded insights about the plight of the left and betrayed a certain myopia about the motivations that drive radical activists.[8]

His first book set the tone that his future writings on the left would follow. First published in 1952, *Marxian Socialism in the United States* was the first scholarly history of its subject. And its chronological breadth, coupled with a bracing critique of the entire phenomenon, have never been equaled. "Socialism was an unbounded dream," began the young sociologist and labor editor of *Fortune*, evoking the millenarian faith that, over the previous century, had moved countless people on both sides of the Atlantic to imagine a future of social equality amid economic abundance and to dedicate their lives to realizing it.[9]

But then he rendered judgment. American Marxists had utterly failed to build a large or stable movement, Dan argued, because they refused to adapt to the nation that they desperately wanted to transform. "The socialist movement, by its very statement of goal and in its rejection of the capitalist order as a whole, could not relate itself to the specific problems of social action in the here-and-now, give-and-take political world. It was trapped by the unhappy problem of living 'in but not of the world,' so it could only act, and then inadequately, as the moral, but not political, man in immoral society." He brushed away such then-popular explanations for the failure of socialism as the existence of a prosperous working class and the "free gift" of the ballot to men without property. It was the blinkered worldview of Marxists that doomed them to marginality, not adverse external conditions of any kind.[10]

Whether democratic socialist or Leninist, every species of left-ism blinded itself to the political obstacles and ideological diversity of the society that it burned to transform. Dan avowed that the Marxian moment, such as it was, had passed midway through the twentieth century. Perhaps musing about the meager results of his own youthful activism, he did allow that "socialism has, as a pale tint, suffused into the texture of American life and subtly changed its shadings." Yet he concluded, portentously, that "by 1950, American socialism as a political and social fact had become simply a notation in the archives of history." Although socialism has experienced a modest revival since the Great Recession, its adherents have yet to reverse Dan's verdict. [11]

But his argument that ideological rigidity was the main reason for its fate is difficult to sustain. From a comparative perspective, the socialist movement in the United States was no more beholden to a self-justifying, total rejection of the capitalist order than were its larger and more influential counterparts in Europe from the late nineteenth century through the 1930s. After all, Karl Kautsky and Rosa Luxembourg—the leading theoreticians in the German Sozialdemokratische Partei Deutschlands (SPD; Social Democratic Party), the flagship party of the Second International—battled successfully against the revisionist heresies of Eduard Bernstein. Along with their comrades, they built an extensive network of party institutions, from hiking clubs to workers' choruses to cremation societies, that allowed socialists to separate themselves far more effectively from the rest of imperial Germany than their American emulators ever managed to do in their own capitalist republic.[12]

Bell's thesis also neglected the many ways that American Marxists claimed legitimacy for themselves within the boundaries of the nation's civic religion. Eugene V. Debs may have "worn his romanticism like a cloak," as Dan remarked. But he also became a beloved figure, even to many Americans who never voted for him, because he was able to frame socialism as the fulfillment of popular, even consensual, beliefs: monopolies were betraying the egalitarian dream, capitalism was a betrayal of the Sermon on the Mount, and only a cooperative commonwealth could truly be a government of, by, and for the people. There was also a dogmatic side to Debs, however. He preached the Kautskyan gospel that capitalism was destined to collapse, regardless of what its defenders or critics did. And he never clarified a strategy for using existing American institutions—other than the ballot box—to speed the coming of that promised commonwealth.[13]

Dan was on firmer ground when describing—and criticizing—the brief years of influence of the U.S. Communist Party (CPUSA) in the late 1930s through World War II, and then its rapid downfall during the Cold War. Writing in the thick of the Red Scare of the early 1950s, he too glibly labeled the "communist movement" a "conspiracy" that "was being driven out of American life, not always with scrupulous regard for civil liberties." But Dan was correct to disparage the blind faith of veteran party members in what Raymond Aron called "acquiescence in the mysterious and imperative law of history" and "resignation to a future deemed even more inevitable than glorious . . ." No previous American political party had ever sworn its fealty to a foreign power, the decisions of whose despotic leader had to be digested and applied, but never questioned.[14]

Still Dan neither mentioned nor tried to explain why the equally Stalinist Communists in Aron's own nation managed to win more than a quarter of the popular vote and lead the largest labor federation in France at the same time that their American comrades were struggling to keep their jobs and fend off accusations that they belonged to a den of spies.

Dan's explanation for why the CPUSA gained remarkable sway in mass movements and among intellectuals during the period of the Popular Front and then World War II was also less than convincing. He described how the Communists gained control of over a dozen CIO unions, encouraged their followers to vote for Franklin Delano Roosevelt (FDR) and other New Deal Democrats in 1936 and 1938, and captured the leadership of several major organizations of students, writers, and artists. He didn't mention the party's decision to oppose strikes and support the roundup of Japanese-Americans once the United States entered the conflict against the Axis powers.

The consequence of all these acts was an influence far greater than the size of the CPUSA's meager membership. These practical steps may have been part of what Irving Howe once called "a brilliant masquerade." Each served the needs of the Soviet Union and would not have been taken if Stalin and his henchmen had opposed them. But they also showed that the party had the ability to navigate the rapids of U.S. politics rather deftly when its line allowed.[15]

Studies of the CPUSA's history written since the 1950s have supplied abundant evidence that most Communists preferred the engagement with larger social forces that the Popular Front and Grand Alliance made possible to the bristling ultraleftism of the Third Period, and then the defensive crouch the Red Scare required. Most rank-and-filers welcomed the decision of the CPUSA chair Earl Browder in 1944 to abandon Leninist structure and discipline and reorganize the party as the Communist Political Association, a "non-partisan association of Americans" that would no longer seek to overthrow the state. A year later, when their fellow Americans mourned the death of FDR, most comrades mourned, quite sincerely, along with them.[16]

Marxian Socialism in the United States is an old-fashioned kind of political history; it closely tracks the evolution and devolution of organizations whose lofty hopes of radical change crashed to the ground, again and again. Yet in assessing the impact of socialists on American life, the strength of the book is also something of a weakness. Dan said little about the *cultural* influence of the left to that point in U.S. history. When he did remark on the matter, it was usually in bitter jest: Dan mocked "the boyish romanticism" of Jack London; "the tepid social-work impulse of do-gooders" in the Debsian Socialist Party; "the slick writers" in Hollywood who were attracted to the CPUSA's "excitement, purpose, and 'answers' to the world's problems"; and the Protestant ministers "unable to believe evil," who appeared "among the sucker lists of communist fronts" and so on.[17]

His talent for polemical zingers neglected the ways that socialists could fail at politics but succeed at helping to change what Antonio Gramsci famously called the "common sense" of society. Americans enamored with Marxism often cooperated with other types of leftists to initiate alterations in the fabric of daily life that are now considered uncontroversial except on the far right: gender equality, equal opportunity for ethnic and racial minorities and homosexuals, the celebration of multiculturalism, and the popularity of novels, films, music, and fine art with a vigorously altruistic and antiauthoritarian flavor. Socialists like Margaret Sanger and Max Eastman, as well as such sympathizers with communism as Paul Robeson, Woody Guthrie, and Jacob Lawrence, played significant roles in promoting and advancing these changes. So did Betty Friedan, who as a liberal feminist in the 1950s and early 1960s, reshaped ideas about women's economic inequality that she had first written about as a journalist for the *UE News*, the organ of the United Electrical, Radio and Machine Workers, which was led by Communists. All these leftists proved the wisdom of the British historian John F. C. Harrison who, half a century ago, observed, "The most enduring aspects of a social movement are not always its institutions but the mental attitudes which inspire it and which are in turn generated by it."[18]

While serious scholarship on the American left began with Dan's work, it suffered from a conspicuous absence common to most histories of the nation written by white male authors at the time, regardless of the politics of their authors. His book implies that the only Marxian socialists who mattered were men of European origin, and the only issues with which they and their fellow Americans concerned themselves were ones of class, war, and electoral partisanship. The names of a few famous women, such as Sanger and Emma Goldman, are sprinkled throughout the book. But Dan never mentions birth control or any other feminist issue that animated them and their followers.

The history of slavery and racial segregation and the left's struggles against them are completely absent from the text—as is any discussion of what Black radicals may have contributed to the larger narrative. "Evidently Bell does not consider Negroes as an integral sociological category," commented Harold Cruse ironically in his influential 1967 critique of integrationist ideas and politics. "Negroes could not possibly have anything to do with the 'exhaustion of political ideas in the Fifties,' which just happens to be the very decade when Negroes became most insistent on being integrated within Western society."[19]

In a midcentury book explicitly concerned with political leadership, the omission of Black and female figures, while regrettable, was understandable. But since the 1960s, no reputable historian would imagine writing a general history of radicalism without analyzing the significance of the movements for women's rights and African American freedom. Dan's silence on how socialists understood and interacted with these larger insurgencies helps mark the book as an example of a style of history-writing that has long since passed on. His neglect of Black history also prevented Dan from discussing whether stark racial divisions and inequalities played any role in weakening the effort of Marxists to recruit working people to their cause.[20]

After *Marxian Socialism*, Dan never again wrote at length about the history of the left. However, on occasion, he did wage verbal combat against radical intellectuals whom he thought had misrepresented his thinking or were leading their followers down a benighted past similar to that of the socialists he had criticized in that book.

The most important and telling of these figures was C. Wright Mills. Dan and the motorcycle-riding sociologist from Texas had been friends and colleagues for several years in the 1940s. In Manhattan, they rented apartments in the same small building in the East Village (which has since been painted a shade of pink) and both contributed to the *New Leader* and the short-lived *Politics*, edited by Dwight MacDonald. At the time, Mills and Bell shared a critique of the power of corporations over the new warfare state, as well as a hope that organized labor, as the historian Howard

Brick put it, "would realize its progressive potential and break out of its alliance with the Democratic Party toward political independence."[21]

However, as Dan grew dubious about the raison d'etre of socialists and Mills became a leading voice for young rebels, the friends turned into adversaries, albeit ones who were colleagues in the same department at Columbia. In *The End of Ideology*, Dan lodged a wide-ranging, characteristically erudite, and relentlessly negative evaluation of *The Power Elite*, which, as he noted, had "won a ready response among radicals." It was a brilliant, scholarly put-down. Dan skewered Mills's imprecise, hortatory definitions of "the elite," revealed his fuzzy understanding of history, and pointed out how little evidence he offered for some of his most prominent assertions. In the end, he wrote, *The Power Elite* was stronger as a " 'romantic protest' against modern life" than an analysis of its subject. Many liberal reviewers shared his judgment, as does, for the most part, Daniel Geary, Mills's most recent and otherwise sympathetic biographer.[22]

Mills did not respond directly to Dan's critique, but soon he mounted a counterattack of a more potent kind. His iconic "Letter to the New Left," published in the fall of 1960, argued with acidic wit that the thesis of *The End of Ideology* was nothing more than an intellectual excuse for acquiescing to the rule of the power elite. Mills called it "a slogan of complacency, circulating among the prematurely middle-aged" [Dan was 41 at the time], which "rests upon a disbelief in the shaping by men of their own futures." What's more, it was "a weary know-it-all justification—by tone of voice rather than by explicit argument—of the cultural and political default of the NATO [North Atlantic Treaty Organization] intellectuals." The letter ended with a now famous call to arms: "Let the old women complain wisely about 'the end of ideology.' We are beginning to move again."[23]

Mills meant his words to cause pain, and they certainly had the desired effect. That December, *Encounter* magazine published Dan's response. entitled "Vulgar Sociology." Rarely since his days in YPSL had his prose been so vituperative, his terms of censure so vivid. Dan scorned the style of "Letter to the New Left," saying: "it is very hard to know when Mills is talking to himself, anticipating questions and answering them by exhortation and when he is addressing the reader." He blasted the author of *The Power Elite* for equating the United States with the Soviet Union: "any analysis of Russian and American society which ignores the political order . . . makes a mockery of such basic terms as liberty and freedom." And he concluded by scolding the embryonic New Left for repeating the same fatal error as its predecessors:

> If there is any lesson which emerges from the experiences of the past forty years, experiences which fashioned the "end of ideology," it is the realization of the recklessness of social movements which sought to change the social "structure" without specifying the "costs" involved other than claiming that History would erase the bill.[24]

In retrospect, Dan's attack was both perceptive and shortsighted. To argue, as Mills had done, for political equivalence between the two superpowers was absurd, and it probably encouraged New Leftists to downplay or entirely dismiss the repressive nature of the Leninist states that challenged U.S. hegemony both then and in the tumultuous decade to come. Yet Dan missed the real reasons why Mills became a hero to budding radical intellectuals, and as a result, never grasped how the New Left was different from, and arguably more consequential than, the old left. After all, despite its romance with the likes of Ho Chi Minh and Che Guevara and the lack of a coherent strategy to achieve its ends, this movement helped bring an end to legal and gender discrimination, questioned the need and morality of killing millions of people abroad in the cause of freedom, and began to warn, in a serious and sustained way, that industrial growth was imperiling the future of life on Earth.

Mills's "Letter" gave young, college-educated Americans (and their counterparts in Britain, where it was originally published) a sense that they were part of an international movement of people like themselves—men and women who were struggling to break out of the chains, ideological and structural, that the Cold War imposed on the world. Thus, Mills praised young dissidents in the Soviet bloc, as well as protestors against the repressive, pro-American regimes in South Korea, Taiwan, and Turkey. And he coyly hailed the sit-in movement "in our own pleasant Southland," where "Negro and white students are—but let us keep that quiet: it really *is* disgraceful."[25]

The idea that the group Mills called "the young intelligentsia" could be the main lever of successful rebellion was an odd delusion for a political sociologist to hold, particularly one who, a dozen years before, had written *New Men of Power*, a book that called labor unions "the only organizations capable of stopping the main drift towards war and slump." But the white New Leftists that he helped inspire would view themselves more as support troops for uprisings by poor and working-class African-Americans and other so-called Third World people than as the primary agents of change.[26]

More important, Dan ignored the wellsprings of political motivation that Mills had tapped. Why were young radicals, most of whom were raised in comfortable circumstances, so discontented? Why did they cheer Mills's positive reference to utopianism—and his advice that "[i]f there is to be a politics of a New Left, what needs to be analysed is the *structure* of institutions, the *foundations* of policies. In this sense, both in its criticisms and in its proposals, our work is necessarily structural—and so, *for us*, just now—utopian"? These are questions that, as a political sociologist *and* an erstwhile activist, Dan should have addressed with something besides derision and pique.[27]

His suspicion of antinomian rebellion was doubtless at the root of this neglect. As the New Left grew in size during the 1960s, its young adherents increasingly merged their politics with the ludic, norm-smashing practices and discourse of the counterculture. "If it feels good, do it" was a sentiment that Dan could never abide. As David Bell wrote recently, "He often said that what mattered most in politics was temperament, and his own temperament was undoubtedly conservative, precisely because of his painful sense, born out of his own childhood experience and his memories of the Depression, of how fragile the structures of ordinary, civilized life could be." In *The Cultural Contradictions of Capitalism*, published in 1976, Dan summarized "the sensibility of the Sixties" as essentially a mass attempt to shock the comfortable classes.. It was unknowingly emulating the fin-de-siècle modernist rebellion, but in a "shriller and harsher form" that promoted "a preoccupation with the sexually perverse; a desire to make noise; an anti-cognitive and anti-intellectual mood."[28]

But those with a passion to change the world, particularly when they are young, seldom obey calls to respect the boundaries or the reigning sensibility of the order that they yearn to dismantle. Right after his famous line about politics being "the strong and slow boring of hard boards," Weber concluded the lecture that was Dan's touchstone with some rather utopian-sounding words of his own:

> [Politics] takes both passion and perspective. Certainly all historical experience confirms the truth—that man would not have attained the possible unless time and again he had reached out for the impossible.... Only he has the calling for politics who is sure that he shall

not crumble when the world from his point of view is too stupid or too base for what he wants to offer. Only he who in the face of all this can say "In spite of all!" has the calling for politics.[29]

A SOCIALIST STILL?

Yet Dan continued to retain a certain sympathy for the traditional left from which he had sprung, although he never recanted the indictment of it that he made in his first book and in several of the essays in *The End of Ideology*. One can view that sympathy in his profound respect for Marx and the zeal with which he castigated Harrington in 1976 for his "serious violation" of the master's "own method, which is to treat ideas historically." One can view it in his 1990 analysis, published in *Dissent*, of the Soviet Union's failure to build a truly socialist order. There, Dan repeated the Menshevik argument, adapted from Marx, that a nation could not vault from a quasi-feudal, peasant order to a collectivist one without going through a lengthy period of capitalist development. One could view it as well in his disgust at what he saw as C. Wright Mills's clumsy, "vulgar" attempt to update and correct Marx's analysis of ruling elites.[30]

For Dan, the greatest flaw in Marx's writings was his reduction of politics to material forces, a point that Gareth Stedman Jones also makes at length in his recent biography. The welfare state constructed by the New Deal order, Dan wrote in 1996, was not the result of "economic pressures or class forces," but rather of a "recognition of the democratic claims of 'the public household' as a legitimate dimension in the definition of citizenship" in American society. Actually, the misery of the Great Depression and the rise of a large and powerful labor movement did undergird the victories of FDR, Harry Truman, and their Democratic Party.

Still, the fact that changes in political consciousness have a dynamic of their own should be obvious to anyone not blinded by the kind of dogmatic certainty that Dan cogently warned against. The theoretical works of sophisticated Marxists from Gramsci to Nicos Poultantzas to Fred Block elaborate the same point.[31]

Unfortunately, there seems to be scant recognition of the autonomy of politics among the mostly young activists who have fueled the current revival of socialism in the United States. They tend to follow Bernie Sanders in blaming the billionaire class for nearly everything that ails the nation and the planet. Bhaskar Sunkara, whose *Jacobin* magazine became a kind of unofficial organ for the most committed backers of Sanders, mentions neither Dan Bell nor his work in his recent book, *The Socialist Manifesto*. Perhaps it is unsurprising that Sunkara and other recently minted Marxists ignore what was once the most prominent, if always controversial, argument for the failure of socialism in the United States.

If they read Dan's work carefully, however, they might be surprised to discover a valuable nugget of sympathy for their cause. "Socialism remains a moral ideal independent of a theory of history," he wrote in 1996, when that cause was quite moribund in the United States and seemed unlikely ever to rise again. "The moral ideal is one of equality and the opportunity for each of us to fulfill our self and our talents." Quoting Weber again, he warned against the search for salvation in politics. But then Dan added that the need to give all "citizens . . . the resources that give them self-esteem necessarily involves politics."[32]

The ethical claim for socialism dates back to the infancy of the persuasion and has survived the collapse of the Soviet Union and the decline of social democratic parties in Europe and elsewhere. It was central to the appeal of the Owenites and other so-called utopians, and also stimulated Marx's early writings about the alienation fostered by marketplace relationships. The German philosopher Axel Honneth, current director of the Frankfurt School, recently wrote a book dedicated to reimagining "the idea of socialism" as a moral commitment to the notion that "it will be possible to organize entire societies on the model of communities of solidarity." Such communities, Honneth added, would be organized around an idea of "freedom in which each person complements the other, completely resolving this freedom with the demands of equality and fraternity." It's not quite the same as the vision in the *Communist Manifesto* of a future order in which "the free development of each is the condition for the free development of all." But the provenance is unmistakable.[33]

Thus, for Dan Bell, the errors, stupidities, and awful crimes committed by those who kept the red flag flying here and there never quite extinguished the need for imagining a world organized to make exploitation obsolete and mutual aid the norm. In 1932, the same year he joined YPSL, a longtime leader of the Socialist Party told a gathering of his comrades why, despite multiple setbacks, he remained committed to the cause. "I am a Socialist," explained Morris Hillquit, "because I cannot be anything else. I cannot accept the ugly world of capitalism, with its brutal struggles and needless suffering, its archaic and irrational economic structure, its cruel social contrasts, its moral callousness and spiritual degradation."[34]

A little less than three decades later, Dan Bell wrote in the introduction to *The End of Ideology*, "One can be a critic of one's country without being an enemy of its promise." Perhaps he could have said something similar about the future of the left.[35]

NOTES

1. "Growth in the Early 1930s," in *The American Labor Year Book, 1931*, ed. Nathan Fine (New York: Rand School Press, 1931), 153. On the details of the history of YPSL and the Socialist Party, see Jack Ross, *The Socialist Party in America: A Complete History* (Lincoln, NE: Potomac, 2015).

2. Nathan Liebowitz, *Daniel Bell and the Agony of Modern Liberalism* (Westport, CT: Greenwood, 1985), 43.

3. Liebowitz, *Daniel Bell and the Agony of Modern Liberalism*, 44–46.

4. See "The Mood of Three Generations," in Bell, *The End of Ideology: On the Exhaustion of Political Ideas in the Fifties* (Cambridge, MA: Harvard University Press, 2000 [1960]), 299–314.

5. I have paraphrased this paragraph from a brief open letter I wrote in the privately published collection *For Daniel Bell*, ed. Mark Lilla and Leon Wieseltier (no publisher, 2005), 64. See also *Marxian Socialism in the United States* (Ithaca, NY: Cornell University Press, 1995), ix–xxxvii. A revised version of that introduction was published as "The Agony and Romance of the American Left," *American Historical Review* 100 (December 1995), 1488–1512.

6. Daniel Bell, "The Once and Future Marx," in *The Winding Passage: Essays and Sociological Journeys, 1966–1980* (Cambridge, MA: Abt Books, 1980), 114; https://www.dissentmagazine.org/online_articles/daniel-bell-at-100.

7. Daniel Bell, "To the Other Shore: A Visit to the Soviet Union," *Dissent* (Fall 1988), 408, 409.

8. From Max Weber, "Politics as a Vocation," quoted in the 1996 Cornell edition, 193. All quotes hereafter are drawn from this edition, the only one in print, referred to hereafter as MSUS. I have paraphrased several sentences from my introduction to this edition.

9. MSUS, 3. Dan included "The Failure of American Socialism," an essay based on this book, in *The End of Ideology* (Cambridge, MA: Harvard University Press, 2000), 275–298.

10. MSUS, 5.

11. MSUS, 193.

12. In the brief preface that he wrote to a 1967 reprint of *Marxian Socialism*, Bell did say about the SPD and its French counterpart that "at crucial moments" in the 1930s, "their ability to act, or adapt, was paralyzed because of ideological rigidity." He did not, however, account for the SPD's success at becoming the largest political party in Germany before World War I. MSUS, xl.

13. MSUS, 89. The best biography of Debs is Nick Salvatore's *Eugene V. Debs: Citizen and Socialist* (Urbana: University of Illinois Press, 1982).

14. Aron quoted in MSUS, 186.

15. Irving Howe, *Socialism and America* (San Diego, CA: Harcourt Brace Jovanovich, 1985), 87–104.

16. Irving Howe, "The Brilliant Masquerade: A Note on 'Browderism,'" in *Socialism and America* (San Diego: Harcourt Brace Jovanovich, 1985), 87–104.

17. MSUS, 45(first two quotes (153.(second two quotes)

18. John F. C. Harrison, *Quest for the New Moral World: Robert Owen and the Owenites in Britain and America* (New York: Charles Scribner's Sons, 1969), 249. This paragraph is drawn from my book *American Dreamers: How the Left Changed a Nation* (New York: Knopf, 2011).

19. Harold Cruse, *The Crisis of the Black Intellectual* (New York: Morrow 1967), 460. In passing, Bell does identify Langston Hughes, Paul Robeson, and Richard Wright as figures in CPUSA front organizations. He also includes an earlier reference to Lucy Parsons, a Chicago-based anarchist who was born a slave but doesn't note (and may not have been aware of) her racial identity. See MSUS, 66.

20. Neither in the preface to the 1967 edition of MSUS nor in his afterword to the 1996 reissue did he mention either the Black or feminist movement.

21. Howard Brick, Daniel Bell and the Decline of Intellectual Radicalism: Social Theory and Political Reconciliation in the 1940s (Madison: University of Wisconsin Press, 1986), 11.

22. Bell, *The End of Ideology*, 74. For contemporary reviews and analysis, see Daniel Geary, *Radical Ambition: C. Wright Mills, the Left, and American Social Thought* (Berkeley: University of California Press, 2009), 161–165.

23. C. Wright Mills, "Letter to the New Left," *New Left Review*, no. 5 (September–October 1960), accessed at https://www.marxists.org/subject /humanism/mills-c-wright/letter-new-left.htm.

24. "Vulgar Sociology: On C. Wright Mills and the 'Letter to the New Left,'" in *The Winding Passage: Essays and Sociological Journeys, 1966–1980* (Cambridge, MA: Abt Books, 1980), 138. 141, 143.

25. Mills, "Letter to the New Left."

26. See the perceptive reconsideration i by the labor historian Nelson Lichtenstein, "The New Men of Power," *Dissent* (Fall 2001), https://www .dissentmagazine.org/article/the-new-men-of-power. Quoted p. 121.

27. Lichtenstein, "The New Men of Power."

28. David A. Bell, "Daniel Bell at 100," *Dissent*, May 9, 2019, https://www .dissentmagazine.org/online_articles/daniel-bell-at-100; Daniel Bell, *The Cultural Contradictions of Capitalism*, 20th anniversary ed. (New York: Basic Books, 1996 [1976]), 121.

29. "Politics as a Vocation" is widely available on line. For a fairly recent English translation, see *The Vocation Lectures*, ed. David Owen and Tracy Strong (Indianapolis: Hackett, 2004).

30. Bell, "The Once and Future Marx," 113; Daniel Bell, "On the Fate of Communism," *Dissent* (Fall 1990), 188.

31. Daniel Bell, "Afterword," MSUS, 202.

32. Bell, "Afterword," MSUS, 203.

33. Axel Honneth, *The Idea of Socialism* (Cambridge: Polity, 2017), 25.

34. Morris Hillquit, *Loose Leaves from a Busy Life* (New York: Macmillan, 1934), 331.

35. Bell, Introduction, *The End of Ideology*, 17.

4

DANIEL BELL AND THE RADICAL RIGHT

JULIAN E. ZELIZER

Right-wing, reactionary politics has been an integral part of conservatism since World War II. To be sure, Republican leaders such as presidents Richard Nixon, Ronald Reagan, and George W. Bush have used tax cuts, national security, and the concept of "law and order" in their attempt to build coalitions of moderates and conservatives while shedding the rougher edges of the movement. But as the presidency of Donald Trump has demonstrated, a ferocious style of cultural populism retains a strong hold on significant portions of the electorate. The resurgence of "America-first" nationalism, xenophobia, anti-Semitism, and racism within Republican circles, including on the Twitter feed of former President Trump, has been sobering for those who thought the nation had moved into a new era with Barack Obama's election to the presidency in 2008. All the old demons on the right floated back to the surface. The spread of conspiracy theories and disinformation, including an effort by the president to overturn the results of the 2020 election, have become "normal" parts of national political life. As Trump dove deeper into the toxic backwater of right-wing extremism, most Republicans stood behind him. Senate Republicans went so far as to filibuster a bipartisan commission to investigate the violent attack, incited by Trump, that took place against Congress and the vice president on January 6, 2021.

In retrospect, none of this should have come as a surprise. The roots of reactionary conservatism are deep, dating back to the heyday of what Steven Fraser and Gary Gerstle term the "New Deal Order," the decades from the early 1930s through the late 1960s.[1] While often neglected, the role of right-wing extremism in that period emerges clearly from a number of recent monographs.[2] As post–New Deal conservatism took form, a radical right was always part of the program.

In 1965, when Under Secretary of State George Ball warned Lyndon B. Johnson about the growing student antiwar movement, the president responded in his characteristic blunt manner: "Don't pay any attention to what those little shits on campus do. The great beast is the reactionary element in the country."[3] That "great beast," Johnson feared, was going to hurt Democrats by saying that they were weak on defense and by playing to racial backlash politics. Historians—preoccupied with the rise and fall of liberalism and the emergence of a conservative movement in the 1970s—would do well to remember the beast that Johnson was worried about.

Some scholars in the period were keeping a close eye on the forces that Johnson feared. The long history of this right-wing extremism can be seen in one of the products of Daniel Bell's work as an editor and analyst of American politics. The emergence and power of reactionary conservatism at the high point of American liberalism constituted the theme of Bell's *The New American Right*, an edited volume published in 1955 and reissued, with additional essays, as *The Radical Right* in 1962. The book brought together several of the country's smartest sociologists and historians as they took a deep dive into the world of right-wing politics. Together, the contributors painted a world of extreme conservative figures who had been an underappreciated presence in national debate.

When Bell's project took form, domestic politics had been rocked by the politics of anticommunism. Wisconsin senator Joseph McCarthy and his fellow anticommunist crusaders had unleashed a fierce campaign targeting officials in the Harry S. Truman administration, intellectuals, and prominent figures from Hollywood, as well as political activists. McCarthy smeared his opponents with accusations of secret communist affiliations that he counted on reporters to repeat. The corrections, if any, to these accusations would not come until careers were destroyed and lives ruined. Senate Republicans, who distanced themselves from their colleague in private, were happy to let McCarthy do their dirty work until the political costs seemed too high.[4] Meanwhile, the Wisconsin senator traveled in extremist conservative circles, what one historian recently called a "Right Wing Popular Front" inhabited by racists, anti-Semites, and xenophobes who had little tolerance for the social changes that were transforming the country in the post–World War II era.[5]

The appeal of McCarthy's raw anti-intellectualism and false innuendos to some of the same working-class Americans who had been at the heart of the New Deal coalition stunned Bell and other liberals. McCarthyism would later be regarded as an anomaly that was destined to fade away, but in the moment, its strength was frightening and demanded new analysis. The idea for a book about the social roots of right-wing extremism emerged from a seminar on political behavior that Bell codirected at Columbia University with the historian Richard Hofstadter and the sociologist Seymour Martin Lipset. At the time, Bell was lecturing at Columbia while working as the labor editor for *Fortune* after he had left behind the socialist politics that had animated his earlier work. The Columbia seminar honed in on a heated academic debate about whether economic interests continued to drive politics. Through the seminar, Bell and his colleagues became familiar with the work of other scholars who had similar ideas to theirs about right-wing extremism. These included the sociologists David Riesman, Nathan Glazer, and Talcott Parsons, as well as the historian Peter Viereck. Except for Bell's introduction, the essays published in the book's first edition were not originally written for it; rather, they appeared around the same time and shared a common framework of analysis.

By the time Bell assembled the collection, McCarthyism was already finished, but it loomed large over the entire project, and all the contributors dealt squarely with it. It was impossible to read any of the pieces without thinking about the implications of the analysis for the political turbulence that the Wisconsin senator had caused. The authors, who lived in the epicenter of the intellectual universe that had been continually slammed by the right, were desperate to understand where the vitriol was coming from. At a purely analytical level, the strength of right-wing extremism came as a surprise. Liberal intellectuals in the early Cold War had eschewed ideological and dogmatic politics. They saw the New Deal as a great break in the reform tradition, as experimental and pragmatic politics replaced the moralistic bent of populism and progressivism. They favored an incremental approach to politics, believing that institutions could be repaired and that over time, history was moving in the right direction.[6]

What made the phenomenon of McCarthyism all the more puzzling was the fact that the economy was roaring in the 1950s. The support for Father Charles Coughlin during the 1930s made some sense in the context of the Depression; Americans were struggling to make ends meet and thus susceptible to xenophobic and anti-Semitic appeals that promised to bring them relief. Economic anxieties, however, could not explain the appeal of the right wing during the 1950s. New Deal programs had provided unprecedented levels of economic support to industrial workers and farmers. The middle class was growing. Unemployment had been low and inflation remained in check. More Americans were going to college, purchasing suburban homes, and driving their own cars. Why was someone like Senator McCarthy able to find support with his retrograde arguments at a moment when many Americans were doing so well?

The New American Right and its expanded successor, *The Radical Right*, are best known for the argument that right-wing extremism was the product not of a reasonable response to the threat of communism, but rather of status anxieties and resentments. In this view, people could move toward extremism when domestic and international forces put their social standing in question. As economic changes transformed power hierarchies and unsettled conventional social relations, some elites and nonelites responded by embracing radical, authoritarian forms of populism that made nostalgic promises about returning to an old order.

In his introduction to the first edition, Bell said that the book was concerned "with the deeper running social currents of a turbulent mid-century America," a turbulence that was "born not of depression, but of prosperity." Contrary to those who believed that a thriving economy solves all problems, "prosperity brings in its wake new social groups, new social strains and new social anxieties." The new framework provided by the book would explain these new strains and anxieties, which conventional analysis was unable to fathom. Instead of emphasizing the role of economic interests in politics, the book would focus on "the new, prosperity-created 'status groups' which, in their drive for recognition and respectability, have sought to impose older conformities on the American body politic." Even people who were objectively prospering might not feel they were getting their due. "One can be a member of the 'upper class' (i.e. have greater privilege and wealth and be able to transmit wealth)," Bell explained, "without being a member of the *ruling group*."[7]

In another essay called "The Dispossessed," published in the 1962 edition, Bell spelled out the status-group argument in greater detail. "What the right as a whole fears," he wrote, "is the erosion of its own social position, the collapse of its power, the increasing incomprehensibility of a world—now overwhelmingly technical and complex—that has changed so drastically within a lifetime." Changes in social structure were "upsetting the established life-chances and outlooks of old, privileged groups, and creating uncertainties about the future which are deeply unsettling to those whose values were shaped by the 'individualist' morality of nineteenth-century America." The old individualism was no longer tenable: "*collectivities*—corporations, labor unions, farm organizations, pressure groups—have become the units of social action, and . . . individual rights in many instances derive from group rights, and in others have become fused with them."[8]

The group most threatened by these changes was the traditional, small-town middle class, especially those who adhered to a "strain of Protestant fundamentalism, of nativism, nationalism, of good-and-evil moralism." The new "upsurge of American nativism" in the 1950s had its parallels in the 1920s, when the same "nativist" and "old middle-class elements" reacted against "the entry *into* society of formerly 'disenfranchised' elements, particularly the children of immigrants and members of minority ethnic groups—an entry made through the urban political machines, the only major route open to them." Bell also saw other groups as among "the dispossessed" in the 1950s—managers and military officers of an older generation who were resentful of new educated elites that were using their mastery of complex technical skills to gain status and power.[9]

Like the other authors in the volume, however, Bell believed that right-wing populists such as McCarthy, while dangerous, would remain marginal, and ultimately the country's political system was strong enough to outlast them. "The saving glory of the United States," he wrote in his 1955 introduction, "is that politics has always been a pragmatic give-and-take rather than a series of wars-to-the-death." Democratic institutions fostered negotiation and compromise, and Bell believed that those institutions would continue to prevent extremism from gaining power. As he would later write in *The End of Ideology*, the threat from the far left and the far right were one and the same. "The tendency to convert concrete issues into ideological problems, to invest them with moral color and high emotional charge, is to invite conflicts which can only damage a society."[10]

The other author in the volume who contributed the most to the status-group theory was Hofstadter, who sharply distinguished traditional conservatives from the right-wing extremists of the 1950s, whom he called "pseudo-conservatives" (borrowing the term from a book published five years earlier, *The Authoritarian Personality*, by Theodor Adorno and colleagues).[11] Reacting to all the concern in the 1950s about "Americanism," Hofstadter wrote that "pseudo-conservatism is in good part a product of the rootlessness and heterogeneity of American life, and above all, of its peculiar scramble for status and its peculiar search for secure identity." Unable simply to take their national identity and loyalty for granted, many Americans were "tormented by a nagging doubt as to whether they are really and truly and fully American." They responded to those doubts by overcompensating and taking Americanism to an extreme. This was part of the reason for the rise of "status politics," a term that Hofstadter introduced in his essay in contradistinction to "class politics." While class politics is based on economic interests, status politics arises from the "clash of various projective rationalizations arising from status aspirations and other personal motives." Class politics dominates periods of economic stress, while status politics is more prevalent in eras of prosperity, such as the 1920s and the 1950s.[12]

In the most recent incarnation of status politics, Hofstadter argued, the right wing had moved away from blatant anti-Semitism and anti-Negroism and toward "anti-Achesonianism, anti-intellectualism, anti-nonconformism. . . ." But really it was one and the same, and it had little to do with genuine conservatism. In his 1948 book *The American Political Tradition*, Hofstadter had sought to show how different leaders since the founding of the United States had worked within a shared consensus and avoided the extremes found in Europe. The New Deal, in Hofstadter's view, represented a pragmatic adaptation of this tradition, but the pseudo-conservative would have none of it, "He hates the very thought of Franklin D. Roosevelt. He is disturbed deeply by American participation in the United Nations, which he can see only as a sinister organization," Hofstadter wrote in his contribution to Bell's volume.

The only conservative in the volume, Viereck, shared much of the same analysis as Hofstadter, arguing that Senator McCarthy's revolt against the New Deal elite had turned the right into an extremist, radical force that betrayed genuine conservative values. The demagogues, he said, appealed to a number of groups that felt left out as a result of large-scale changes. McCarthy had gained power because he was able to bridge the "hick Protestant mentalities in the west" and "South Boston mentalities."[13]

The other contributors to the first edition offered different versions of the argument about status anxieties and resentments stemming from social change. Talcott Parsons wrote that as a result of its internal transformation into an industrial society and its global entanglements, the United States had been undergoing severe "social strains," and McCarthyism was a "symptom" of these strains, "a crisis of national solidarity in the face of what, for us as a nation, were accumulating and unprecedented political demands and responsibilities."[14] David Riesman and Nathan Glazer turned their attention to the role of intellectuals who had been the target of McCarthyite fury. The coauthors wanted to understand how the generation of left-wing and liberal intellectuals who came of age in the New Deal, and who were central to the heroic war against Germany and Japan, had lost support among the "discontented classes" in the age of McCarthyism. The right "now possesses the enthusiasm and momentum previously held by liberals," they concluded. They believed that workers, many of whom came from parents who had emigrated to the United States, felt as if they were dismissed by cosmopolitan, educated liberals who championed pluralism.[15]

Seymour Martin Lipset also argued that status politics had overtaken class politics. The biggest challenge with these kinds of movements, he said, was that government could not do much to alleviate the problems that concerned them. "It is not surprising, therefore, that the political movements which have successfully appealed to status resentments have been irrational in character, and have sought scapegoats which conveniently serve to symbolize the status threat." Lipset looked at the long tradition of reactionary politics that took form in good economic times. The fragmentation of the American elite, he argued, meant that there would be moments when certain groups lost their status to others.

Like Hofstadter and Viereck, Lipset distinguished between two types of conservatives: moderate conservatives, who accepted changes such as the New Deal, with restraints; and the radical right, which "rejects the status quo." The radical right opposed the welfare state, the labor movement, income taxation, and even American involvement in World War II. According to Lipset, the radical right "views our entire foreign policy from the recognition of Russia to Potsdam as appeasement, treason and treachery. It is opposed to membership in the United Nations and to entangling foreign commitments." Because the radical right couldn't depend on a "socio-economic program" to mobilize their supporters, it needed something else, and "McCarthy's principal contribution to the crystallization of the radical right in the 1950s has been to locate the key symbols with which to unite all its potential supporters." The attack on the educated Northeastern elites was a major theme. The weakness of McCarthy's movement, he noted, was that it failed to build a strong organizational foundation because it had only one issue to speak of: hunting down communists. Dwight Eisenhower's election as president in 1952 posed the biggest threat to the radical right because his coalition of moderate Republicans and big business groups promised to contain the radicals in their midst. Lipset doubted that the radical right would grow "beyond the peak of 1953–1954." Prosperity had fostered its rise, but "a recession will probably cripple its political power. It cannot build an organized movement."[16]

The reviews of Bell's book were largely positive. Many praised the contributors for their use of status anxiety to explain right-wing populism. The work was seen as having done a good job filling out the theories that Parsons had put forward and connecting them to the movement that was right in front of their eyes. The reviewers appreciated the way that the volume made sense of a radical right, as it differed from mainstream conservatism. Daniel Aaron, noting that the authors were "mutually indebted and shared common assumptions," said that they had produced a "provocative and convincing diagnosis of the McCarthyite mentality and conditions that foster it." He questioned whether the contributors were correct to assert that these forces would remain marginal because polls "disclose that the most benighted citizenry are the least active politically."[17] In terms of the specific analysis, Rudolf Heberle speculated about whether the authors downplayed the continued role of economic forces in the phenomenon that they were studying. But Heberle believed that the book was "first-rate" overall and provided a "picture of 'McCarthyist' mentality resembling in a striking and frightening way the familiar one of the followers of Adolph Hitler."[18]

❧

Over the next few years, the radical right changed in unexpected ways. While McCarthyism faded, new organizations appeared on the scene that promoted an intense form of anticommunism, and right-wing politicians like Senator Barry Goldwater seemed to gain momentum. The Christian Anti-Communist Crusade, formed in 1953, grew in size and conducted a number of high-profile events. The formation of the John Birch Society in 1958, and its subsequent expansion, seemed to defy the notion that the radical right would fade away in the near future.

In light of recent developments, Bell asked the authors to revise their chapters for a new edition of the book. In his essay on "The Dispossessed" for the 1962 volume, Bell pointed to the disclosure of the existence of the secretive Birch Society, the growing role of evangelist preachers, and "fanatic" groups like the Minutemen, a militia organization. "What is new, and this is why the problem assumes importance far beyond the question of the right for control of a party, is the ideology of this movement—its readiness to jettison constitutional processes and to suspend liberties, to condone Communist methods in the fighting of Communism."

While Eisenhower was in office, Bell argued, the radical right was trapped by a party that needed to contain it. But no longer—with the Republicans out of power, the right wing was unleashed.

The radical right, Bell claimed, now depended on three psychological appeals: "the breakdown of moral fiber in the United States; a conspiracy theory of a 'control apparatus' in the government which is selling out the country; and a detailed forecast regarding the Communist 'takeover' of the United States." He concluded with a dark warning about the dangers of right-wing violence:

> given the severe strains in American life, the radical right does present a threat to American liberties, in a very different and less immediate sense [than an electoral takeover]. Democracy, as the sorry history of Europe has shown, is a fragile system, and if there is a lesson to be learned from the downfall of democratic governments in Italy, Spain, Austria, and Germany . . . it is that the crucial turning point comes . . . when political parties or social movements can successfully establish "private armies" whose resort to violence . . . cannot be controlled by the elected authorities, and whose use of violence is justified or made legitimate by the respectable elements in society.[19]

Bell solicited two new chapters in the book. Alan Westin, a law professor at Columbia University, offered an examination of the Birch Society that emphasized the similarities between the left after World War II and the radical right in the early 1960s. Based on research in John Welch's speeches, Westin highlighted the ideological and strategic similarities. In his chapter, Herbert Hyman, an expert in polling at Columbia University, offered a look at the different climates of tolerance in England and the United States. In his estimation, England's political institutions privileged tolerance and the English were more open to accepting restraints.

The other authors updated their pieces. Hofstadter revised his essay, arguing that class and status had taken up too much space in the first incarnation of the book, and he added the concept of "cultural politics" to capture ethnic divisions and religious fundamentalism. Hofstadter also put forward the concept of "projective politics" to describe pathological interests.

Turning back to his and Glazer's piece at how intellectuals lost their hold on the masses, Riesman argued that intellectuals had regained some of their standing in the domestic sphere, but changes overseas were too complicated for many people to understand. The bombastic militancy of the radical right proved appealing. Still hoping that the radical right could be contained, Viereck argued that traditional Burkean conservatives, as well as adherents of the John Stuart Mill tradition of classical liberalism, needed to fight back against the political extremes. Parsons argued that the Birchers sought to be free from any sort of public control, in contrast with the followers of McCarthy, who wanted to subsume private rights to government. Lipset provided the most original revised piece, contrasting the extremism of Father Coughlin in the 1930s, Senator McCarthy in the 1950s, and the Birchers in the early 1960s. Based on extensive public opinion data, Lipset showed that Coughlin drew his support from Catholics and Lutherans, small-town and lower-income rural communities, and older Americans in the Midwest and New England. McCarthy, by contrast, drew his base from farmers, small businesspeople, and undereducated and industrial workers. Finally, the Birch Society, he said, was supported by ideologically driven conservatives and Republicans who were relatively well educated and wealthy.

The revised version of the book had great appeal because it came out at a time when politicians and other intellectuals were taking note that right-wing extremism had not died with McCarthy and seemed to be gaining organizational strength. When President

John F. Kennedy instructed Myer Feldman, an aide, to study the organizations, donors, and activists of the radical right, he produced a massive compendium cataloguing their power. Feldman found that the radical right spent about $425 million a year and had put out thousands of radio broadcasts. Major foundations and philanthropic donors funded the movement. There had even been scandals within the military, with revelations of right-wing propaganda that was being disseminated among troops. Most important, Feldman argued that the radical right had ties closer than most thought to mainstream conservative movements. "The radical right wing constitutes a formidable force in American life today" and it was more "successful, politically, than is generally realized."[20]

More mainstream Republican Party leaders, like Goldwater, were comfortable in an alliance with these forces. Wyoming senator Gale McGee, a strident opponent of these organizations, argued that the Western region was more receptive to these movements. "There is a reservoir of public opinion susceptible to their ideas. This is made up of pre–World War II isolationism and the remnants of a 19th-century rugged individualism. In fact, it would be fair to say that segments of our population in the West already believed the extreme right-wing line before the current group of extremists invented it."[21]

Over the years, the book, in its different incarnations, drew several kinds of criticism.[22] Two lines of attack were particularly trenchant in challenging how Bell's colleagues understood the nature of American conservatism in the early Cold War. The first emanated from conservatives, who rejected the entire project that Bell had undertaken. They disputed the basic premise of the volume—namely that McCarthyism and the Radical Right were unreasonable responses to the communist threat and should thus be analyzed in social psychological terms. According to the prominent conservative intellectual Russell Kirk, "One simple fact is scarcely mentioned in this book: that we are in the midst of a natural reaction against practical communism; and that such a reaction from a social catastrophe, at any period in history, always has displayed intolerance and imprudence, together with healthy and necessary indignation against the authors of that catastrophe and their friends." The authors, Kirk wrote, were also dismissive of nonradical conservatives: "The sneer of Mr. Riesman and Mr. Glazer at 'the soured high-principled reaction' of Senator Taft, 'the 'colonial' conscience at its worst,' suggests the general tone."[23]

This kind of assessment revealed as much about the mainstream conservative point of view in the 1950s and 1960s as it did about Bell's work. It showed that the voices in the conservative establishment could not always distinguish a form of anticommunism that worked within necessary restraints from an all-out campaign of character assassination, political smears, and scattershot attacks on opponents, along with disinformation, conspiratorial theory, and falsehoods. The resistance among some prominent conservatives to separate these two approaches to anticommunism suggested early on that mainstream Republicans could be seduced into alliances with an extreme right that trafficked in reactionary politics and threatened the democratic culture.

Another important line of criticism gave more weight to partisan strategy than to status anxiety in driving the Radical Right. Nelson Polsby and others believed that Bell and his fellow travelers had overemphasized status conflicts and psychological factors. They believed that McCarthyism and the Radical Right could best be understood as rational political behavior—strategic moves by the GOP to gain power in Washington. The historian Robert

Griffith would make this case in his landmark book *The Politics of Fear*, published in 1970, when he showed how Senate Republicans capitalized on anticommunists like Senator McCarthy.[24]

Yet this kind of criticism downplayed the importance of the social-psychological feelings of those who supported radical conservative extremism. While elected officials in the GOP might have been calculating how this sort of rhetoric could strengthen their partisan standing, the strategy depended on the resonance of these arguments at the grassroots. The Republicans in Washington were relying on voters who could be swept up by these sorts of conspiratorial arguments. Partisan polarization and elite factionalism didn't explain why this rhetoric worked as much as it did, only the reason that many leaders decided to employ these ideas as a political tool.

🖋

Both editions of Bell's book made an important contribution to understanding modern conservatism that has become more pronounced over time. By emphasizing the ways in which status and culture informed the attachment to right-wing politics, Bell's work opened a window into the ways that the GOP could advance regressive economic policies and yet still retain the hold of many working- and middle-class voters. Americans did not always make decisions about their leaders, as Bell showed, based on bread-and-butter issues. Cultural arguments and concerns about the stress on voters as a result of changing demographic trends mattered. Republican leaders since Richard Nixon have played on these concerns about identity and social status, as well as the cultural divisions that Hofstadter anticipated would be important, to build their coalitions and wrestle working-class voters away from a Democratic Party whose economic policies better addressed their daily concerns. Bell and his coauthors captured the reactionary, nativist, and anti-Semitic character of parts of conservatism that other commentators ignored. By moving away from the kinds of strictly economic arguments that had animated the Beardian worldview of American history, Bell's edited books unpacked a key characteristic of conservative politics that would be essential to understand throughout the post-1960s era.

If there was one major issue that most of the authors failed to fully integrate into their work, it was the role of racism in driving reactionary conservatism. Although a few of the authors incorporated short discussions of race relations into their narratives, with particular attention to the South, racism and white supremacy didn't serve as a central thread of their interpretations of what lay behind backlash politics, even though these were published at the height of the civil rights era. Indeed, civil rights activism would reshape scholarship about the right over the next few decades, making it clear how the protection of white power was often at the root of right-wing conservatism in all regions. The anxiety about status often revolved around the threats to the racial standing of white Americans.

Nevertheless, Bell's arguments have found renewed relevance in the era of Trump. Recent social science has found that white anger has driven voters toward antiestablishment politicians. As the Stanford sociologist Cecilia Ridgeway notes, "As a basis for social inequality, status is a bit different from resources and power. It is based on cultural beliefs rather than directly on material arrangements." Peter Hall and Noam Gidron argue that "across the developed democracies the lower people feel their social status is, the more inclined they are to vote for anti-establishment parties or candidates on the radical right or radical left."[25]

At the same time, both versions of Bell's book made fundamental errors about the nature of politics that exposed some of the blindness of mid-twentieth-century American liberalism. A premise of all the essays here was that the Radical Right could not survive. The ideological and institutional structures of American society would render the right a marginal force at best. Even though the nation's politics allowed this kind of extremism to take form, it could never become the norm—or so they said. It would remain on the fringes, even if there were times like 1953 when it could flare up.

Bell and his coauthors imagined a world of conservatism in which the responsible voices on the right were and would remain dominant, even as radical elements lurked within the coalition. But they were wrong. The balance between responsible and extreme conservatism was never as stable as Bell's generation thought. Over time, the Radical Right became the dominant force in the party. In the decades that followed the publication of the second edition of the book, the Republican Party kept veering sharply to the right. After an interlude between 1965 and 1976 when moderates continued to hold their ground, right-wing conservatism took hold within the GOP from the bottom up. A number of historians, such as Rick Perlstein, have documented the way in which the mainstream Republican movement embraced key ideas from this period.[26] Although Goldwater lost the presidential election in 1964, his ideas and followers became the major voices in conservative politics.

The conservative movement of the 1980s and 1990s not only shifted the political debate sharply to the right, but also embraced a style of smashmouth partisanship in which almost anything was permissible. Republicans like Congressman (and future Speaker of the House) Newt Gingrich embodied that extreme, slashing partisanship.[27] In a memo to his fellow Republicans, Gingrich advised them to use words such as "sick" and pathetic" to describe Democrats. Backlash politics became the party norm.

After President Obama's election in 2008, the Radical Right wasn't simply a part of the Republican coalition—it had come to define the party. The Tea Party in Congress and Donald Trump as president brought radical ideas to the forefront of politics, including a birther challenge that questioned the legitimacy of Obama, the nation's first African American president. When Trump openly played to the forces of backlash, using conspiracy theories as a foundation of his rhetorical arsenal, almost no one in the GOP said a thing. When the president broke norms and strained institutions, supporters enthusiastically cheered him on and continued to do so after his term ended.

As the 2010s came to a close, the anxiety that loomed in the Republican electorate revolved around rural, white men with a high school education or less who felt that they were losing their power in a country where immigrants and Blacks had remade communities and feminism and the gay rights movement fundamentally displaced older notions of gender and sexual identity. The cities and suburbs were defining the tenor of life as they feared that their hometowns were being left behind. Just as in the 1950s, there were Republican politicians who capitalized on this sentiment for partisan purposes.

The Radical Right remains a landmark work on the history of a movement that had not received the scholarly attention it merited. A Radical Right that appealed to the psychological anxieties of white Americans who were feeling displaced by social, economic, and political changes has been an essential part of conservatism since the 1950s, and it has only grown in power. The error of Bell and his coauthors was, if anything, to underestimate the importance and durability of the forces they had documented. They thought that mainstream Republican leaders would contain these forces rather than making them part of the coalition. They were unwilling or unable to see that the liberal tradition that their generation helped define was never as strong as they hoped. The contributors underestimated the deep hold that illiberal traditions had in American political culture. Racism, sexism, nativism, and anti-Semitism were all much more part of the nation than they wanted to admit. They were therefore unable to see that what was a marginal and extreme force in their own time could eventually take over American politics.

If Bell had lived to see the presidency of Donald Trump, he wouldn't have been shocked by the ideas that Trump expressed. But he would have been dismayed that they were being uttered by the president of the United States, with the support of Republican leaders. The forces that Bell and his colleagues studied in the 1950s were not just a backward-looking rearguard. In fact, they were just at the start of a long-term ascendency to the highest levels of power.

NOTES

1. Gary Gerstle and Steven Fraser, *The Rise and Fall of the New Deal Order, 1930–1980* (Princeton, NJ: Princeton University Press, 1989). I review the new literature in Julian E. Zelizer, "The Unexpected Endurance of the New Deal Order: Liberalism in the Age of Reagan," in *Beyond the New Deal Order*, ed. Gary Gerstle, Nelson Lichtenstein, and Alice O'Connor (Philadelphia: University of Pennsylvania Press, 2020); and Julian E. Zelizer, "Rethinking the History of American Conservatism," in *Governing America: The Revival of American Political History* (Princeton, NJ: Princeton University Press, 2012), 68–89.

2. See, for example, Nicole Hemmer, *Messengers of the Right: Conservative Media and the Transformation of American Politics* (Philadelphia: University of Pennsylvania, 2018); and David Austin Walsh, "The Right-Wing Popular Front: The Far Right and American Conservatism in the 1950s," *Journal of American History* 107, no. 2 (2020): 411–432.

3. Julian E. Zelizer, *Arsenal of Democracy: The Politics of National Security from World War II to the War on Terrorism* (New York: Basic Books, 2010), 194.

4. Robert Griffith, *The Politics of Fear: Joseph R. McCarthy and the Senate* (Lexington: University of Kentucky Press, 1970).

5. Walsh, "The Right-Wing Popular Front."

6. Richard H. Pells, *The Liberal Mind in a Conservative Age: American Intellectuals in the 1940s and 1950s* (New York: Harper Row, 1985).

7. Daniel Bell, "Interpretations of American Politics (1955)," in *The Radical Right*, ed. Daniel Bell (New York: Doubleday, 1963), 39–62. All citations here and in the rest of this chapter are to this edition of this book unless otherwise stated.

8. Daniel Bell, "The Dispossessed," in *The Radical Right*, 1–38.

9. Bell, "The Dispossessed,"

10. Daniel Bell, *The End of Ideology: On the Exhaustion of Political Ideas in the Fifties* (New York: Free Press, 1972), 121.

11. T. W. Adorno, Else Frenkel-Brunswik, Daniel J. Levinson, and R. Nevitt Sanford, *The Authoritarian Personality* (New York: Norton, 1950).

12. Richard Hofstadter, "The Pseudo-Conservative Revolt (1955)," and Daniel Bell "Preface" in *The Radical Right*, 63–80; x–xiii.

13. Peter Viereck, "The Revolt Against the Elite," in *The Radical Right*, 155–174.

14. Talcott Parsons, "Social Strains in America (1955)," and "Social Strains in America: A Postscript (1962), both in *The Radical Right*, 175–192, and 193–200, respectively.

15. David Riesman and Nathan Glazer, "The Intellectuals and the Discontented Classes (1955)," in *The Radical Right*, 87–114.

16. Seymour Lipset, "The Sources of the 'Radical Right' (1955)," in *The Radical Right*, 259–212.

17. Daniel Aron, "Review: The New American Right," *Political Science Quarterly* 71, no. 1 (March 1956): 128–130.

18. Rudolf Heberle, "Review," *American Sociology Review* 21, no. 4 (August 1956): 516–517.

19. Bell, "The Dispossessed," 1–38.

20. I discuss the Feldman memo in Julian E. Zelizer, "American Conservatism from Roosevelt to Johnson," in *Inventing the Silent Majority in Western Europe and the United States: Conservatism in the 1960s and 1970s*, ed. Anna von der Goltz and Britta Waldschmidt-Nelson (New York: Cambridge University Press, 2017), 28.

21. Zelizer, "American Conservatism from Roosevelt to Johnson."

22. David Plotke, "Introduction," in *The Radical Right*, 3rd ed., ed. Daniel Bell (New Brunswick, NJ: Transaction Publishers, 2002), xvi.

23. Russell Kirk, "Review: The New American Right," *Annals of the American Academy*, May 1956, 185.

24. Griffith, *The Politics of Fear*.

25. These and other recent studies are cited in Thomas B. Edsall, "The Resentment That Never Sleeps," *New York Times*, December 9, 2020.

26. Rick Perlstein, *Before the Storm: Barry Goldwater and the Unmaking of the American Consensus* (New York: Hill and Wang, 2001).

27. Julian E. Zelizer, *Burning Down the House: Newt Gingrich, the Fall of a Speaker, and the Rise of the New Republican Party* (New York: Penguin, 2020).

5

THE END OF IDEOLOGY, THE LONG NINETIES, AND THE HISTORY OF THE PRESENT

JAN-WERNER MÜLLER

I think that all ideology is bound to self-destruct. Ideology is a reification, a frozen mimicry of reality, a hypostatization of terms that gives false life to categories. And that is also its fatal flaw, its Achilles heel, which leaves it vulnerable in the end to other forms of cognition and faith.

—DANIEL BELL

Liberalism is not a dogma. It may only be, in fact, a temperament or an attitude towards other persons and society.

—DANIEL BELL

A cynic might say that the surest way to become famous as an intellectual or, if nothing else, to rack up citations as a scholar is to declare the end of something or other.[1] Everyone who doesn't have much else to say will spend a lot of time and energy on claiming that whatever was supposed to have ended in fact did *not* end after all. Such supposed insights—served with smaller or larger doses of Schadenfreude—are made a lot easier if one does not bother much with the actual arguments advanced by those who had felt justified in declaring an end to something or other.

I am, of course, referring to a pattern that has been most visible in the wake of Francis Fukuyama's declaration of the end of history. The number of books and articles announcing "the return of history" or even "the restart of history" are too numerous to count.[2] Less obviously, they already had begun to appear in the mid-1990s. One of the observers who disputed Fukuyama's thesis was none other than Daniel Bell. At the dawn of the new century, Bell diagnosed a "resumption of history," but decidedly not a "return of ideology." The social theorist also insisted that the "end of history" and the "the end of ideology" should under no circumstances be equated.[3]

Bell himself, of course, was intimately familiar with the perils of what we might call "endism." His 1988 afterword to *The End of Ideology* betrayed more than a little annoyance with critics who, Bell felt, had not bothered to read him properly.[4] He was particularly incensed by observers—mostly on the left—who casually dismissed him as a complacent "Cold War liberal," a "NATO intellectual," some kind of technocrat, or, perhaps worst of all for a man curious about and engaged in so many aspects of the life of the mind, someone intellectually celebrating apathy (as C. Wright Mills put it).[5]

There was an ambiguity in Bell's account of ideology that perhaps made it more likely for him to be misunderstood: he invoked a broader sense of ideology, understood as a strong emotional investment in particular political projects; here, Bell wrote about "the yearning for a 'cause,' or the satisfaction of deep moral feelings." This broad sense allowed him to analogize ideology and religion, and also to speak of a "crossover from religion to ideology" in modernity. But, in addition, there was a narrower, somewhat more conventional (or at least conventional in the context of the Cold War) sense: namely, ideology as dogmatism, as an inflexible attachment to a doctrine, regardless of the particular moral psychological profile that might or might not be typical of such attachment. Depending on which understanding of ideology is deployed, one's sense of an ending at various points in history will clearly differ.[6]

Bell actually agreed with Fukuyama that comprehensive doctrines—ideology in the narrower sense of dogma—appeared to be depleted, if not in the process of disappearing, at the end of the twentieth century.[7] But ideology in the wider sense—passion in politics—had evidently not vanished. Bell saw its most visible manifestation in nationalism. His thesis of a "a resumption of history" seemed to imply that passionate attachment to cultural collectives somehow constituted a kind of historical normality that had just been interrupted by the rise of ideological belief systems in the eighteenth century (or even earlier, in some of Bell's accounts of the chronology of ideological politics). In Bell's eyes, the breakup of empires and the strident pursuit of national self-determination were the most important developments at the end of the twentieth century; the history of ideology as chiliastic belief systems was finished, but "the history of peoples" remained something like the default option for humanity.[8]

This chapter revisits the enormously influential "end of" theses advanced by Fukuyama and Bell. It does so with a view to understanding an era that has clearly receded but which, I think, remains little understood: what might be called "the long nineties," the supposed age of liberal triumphalism. It is not a stretch to say that often, the era that has just passed might be the one most difficult to comprehend. But unless we gain a firmer grasp of what really happened after the end of the Cold War, we are also bound to misjudge the present. It has become all too fashionable among self-declared liberals to disavow "triumphalism," offer some kind of mea culpa, and confess that one ruefully underestimated—take your pick—the power of community, belonging, the nation, the fate of the "left-behind," the "Somewheres" as opposed to the "Anywheres," etc., etc.

I do not mean to ridicule all these concerns (maybe just some of them), or suggest that liberals have no reason for self-criticism. But they should be clear-headed about what they think they need to distance themselves from. And they have to wonder whether, ironically, they might not be currently committing the same mistakes that some already made in the 1990s.

THE END OF WHAT, EXACTLY?

As is well known (or at least as *should be* well known), Fukuyama never suggested that conflicts, including armed conflicts, had somehow come to an end with the Cold War (in fact, who would have found that remotely plausible in the face of the wars in the Balkans and the genocide in Rwanda going on at that time?). Rather, he argued that there was no plausible comprehensive account of politics and the economy other than liberal democracy plus markets—if one took "plausible" to mean something like "genuinely attractive to millions of people"—in the way that, during the twentieth century, millions had found fascism and communism persuasive.[9] And the reason, derived from Hegel via Alexandre Kojève, was relatively straightforward: only liberal democracy with markets (a combination that Fukuyama tended to portray as frictionless) satisfied the fundamental human desire for recognition.

Even in Fukuyama's original version, there was a pessimistic basso continuo in this story, which made the ubiquitous diagnosis of "triumphalism" seem so tone-deaf. After all, Fukuyama, drawing on Nietzsche and channeling Allan Bloom, had also mused that the end of history might be a "sad" time, as a postheroic era populated by "last men" would not allow for the full exercise of certain human virtues.[10] Even worse, the denizens of a *posthistoire* world might eventually become just simply *bored* with liberalism: politics ceased to be a source of real meaning; as the frisson of struggling over rival ideas would disappear from human life, only technocratic tinkering would remain. Politics, one might say, would be replaced by the administration of things. Or, alluding to Fukuyama's concrete example: in the end, all the world would be like the European Union (EU).

For Daniel Bell, this vision would not have been too disconcerting, or perhaps it would have seemed like a luxury to worry about this problem. While Bell had already diagnosed a form of exhaustion of particular political ideas decades before Fukuyama's volume, he did not think that the only challenges to liberal politics emanated from comprehensive doctrines or ideologies understood as "secular religions." When he wrote about a "resumption of history," he observed the "return" of something that, if one takes his own account of ideology seriously, had actually never quite disappeared: strong or even vehement passions in politics. But these passions were no longer connected to anything recognizable as philosophical (and more or less dogmatic) systems, but rather to national self-assertion. The end of the "age of ideologies" (to quote the German historian Karl Dietrich Bracher) did not usher in a postpolitical, let alone an entirely peaceful age. Fukuyama eventually was to agree: he increasingly flagged the "thymotic" dimensions of politics, understood in particular as the desire for collective recognition and dignity; he also admitted in retrospect that he probably underestimated the power of "identity politics" in his original diagnosis of an end of history.[11]

All of this goes to say that, given the tremendous anxieties about nationalism at the time, it is hard to maintain a one-dimensional story that complacent liberals were simply basking in the afterglow of their victory in the Cold War. Communitarians appeared to be making large gains in normative territory across Western philosophy seminars, and while something called "globalization" was increasingly portrayed as the sign of the age, its actual justification was usually framed in terms of national interests: the inhabitants of nation-states were going to be better off integrating into global markets and supranational regulatory regimes; globalization's normative promise was hardly anything that could be called "global justice."

To be sure, not everyone agreed that a normative justification was even necessary. Prominent leaders associated with the Third Way—the idea of a middle road between the supposedly outdated socialism of the twentieth century and neoliberalism—deemed it simply inevitable: it wasn't a question of deciding on the basis of different values; it was effectively a matter of adapting to the inevitable. U.S. president Bill Clinton demanded that his fellow citizens "embrace the inexorable logic of globalization"; British prime minister Tony Blair claimed, "I hear people say we have to stop and debate globalization. You might as well debate whether autumn should follow summer."[12]

If one is looking for ideology in the sense of a policy area where argument was effectively shut down, this seemed to be it: globalization was simply uncontested; whatever remained by way of political conflict was disappearing in a process that Fukuyama had described in his book on the end of history as "the steady narrowing of the already narrow policy differences between political parties in the United States and elsewhere."[13] Those engaged in this narrowing seemed to refuse, as Mills had put it in 1963 in his criticism of Bell's end-of-ideology thesis, "to work out an explicit political philosophy"; they were simply accepting what had to be accepted.

But even here things weren't so simple. After all, both Clinton and Blair thought that they had a philosophy—namely, the Third

Way. Like Bell's original end of ideology, this was presented as a pragmatic convergence on an effectively social democratic program, except that it was not nearly as social democratic as the consensus that the likes of Raymond Aron, Edward Shils, Seymour Martin Lipset, and indeed Bell had favored in the 1950s and 1960s. Before backing up this point, I will situate Third Way thinking in the larger context of the 1990s, which, I submit, were in fact far less triumphalist and far more suffused by political anxieties than is usually thought.

The Search for Certainty: Three Pathways—Three Dead Ends?

Quite apart from the profound concerns about "blood and belonging" (to quote a prominent TV series and book of the era), there was much more intellectual uncertainty than one would have thought in light of the triumphalism narratives.[14] The end of the Cold War was experienced as a kind of identity crisis—during the global conflict, liberals (and conservatives) had known what they stood for because they were sure about what they had to fight against.[15] Less obviously, they also had a sense of liberalism's weak points and felt the need to engage with liberalism's strongest critics.

It is no accident that thinkers often subsumed under the label "Cold War liberalism"—Bell, Aron, Isaiah Berlin—prominently made a point of expressing their respect for Marx (see also Paul Starr's chapter on "Daniel Bell's Three-Dimensional Puzzle" in this volume for the ways in which Marx's thought continued to inspire Bell's theorizing). Not least, they appreciated the fact that they faced intellectually serious opponents. As Berlin once put it, "I have always said to myself that I preferred Jesuits to muddled men of good will. At least one knows what one is fighting for and against, and the weapons are kept sharp."[16] On another occasion, he observed, "Hatred lends sharpness to vision as much as love: there is surely a sense in which one can learn more from enemies than from friends."[17]

Berlin and his fellow Cold War liberals also stressed the importance of self-doubt; they flagged the danger of mirroring what they perceived as communist dogmatism with liberal dogmatism. But, ultimately, their "fighting faith," in Arthur Schlesinger, Jr.'s famous phrase, provided political and intellectual orientation.[18]

That orientation did not entirely disappear with the end of the Cold War, but as a collective orientation, liberalism was increasingly in doubt—even if it could seem that concepts originating in nineteenth-century liberalism, particularly choice and individualism, suffused the culture more broadly.[19] Eventually, liberals thought they had found certainty again. They did so, I argue, in three particular ways. None of them was obviously ideological in Bell's narrow sense, but at least two of them would have qualified as ideological, in the broader meaning of appealing to strong political passions. And one, arguably, satisfied the criterion of an old-fashioned, *Marxisant* understanding of ideology.

First, there was the attempt to reduce liberalism to a barebones, practically uncontestable belief system concerned with protecting body and soul. That attempt was broadly inspired by Judith Shklar's liberalism of fear (to which, as Starr underlines in his essay on the three-dimensional puzzle, Bell had been partial). Shklar had famously argued in an essay published in 1989 that cruelty was the *summum malum* that absolutely had to be avoided.[20] Politics needed to be viewed not from the heights of lofty ideals, but from the perspective of the victims; her liberalism, she emphasized, was that of "permanent minorities." This kind of liberalism seemed most convincingly to have absorbed the lessons of a century in which totalitarian states had generated the greatest threats to individuals and proved to be a source of systematic cruelty—often in the name of ideology, understood in both Bell's wide and narrow senses of the term.

This kind of liberalism served well to justify humanitarian interventions and what, in the course of the 1990s, was fashioned by international lawyers and activists as the international community's new "responsibility to protect." As Michael Ignatieff wrote toward the end of the decade:

> In the twentieth century, the idea of human universality rests less on hope than on fear, less on optimism about the human capacity for good than on dread of human capacity for evil, less on a vision of man as maker of his history than of man the wolf toward his own kind. The way stations on the road to this new internationalism were Armenia, Verdun, the Russian front, Auschwitz, Hiroshima, Vietnam, Cambodia, Lebanon, Rwanda, and Bosnia. A century of total war has made victims of us all, civilians and military, men, women, and children alike.[21]

As critics eventually pointed out, from Corey Robin to Samuel Moyn, such a liberalism had a distinctly depoliticizing impetus: suffering, especially physical suffering under the eyes of the world's cameras, was so obvious (and horrific) that it always seemed clear-cut what had to be done. Or, as the German jurist and novelist Bernhard Schlink put it in a critique of what he saw as the emergence of a new "victim culture," the perception that some situations were just morally unambiguous created large blind spots, which made it very difficult to even see empirical questions about causes and consequences of these situations.[22]

This is not to malign the many idealists who threw themselves into humanitarian work, nor to suggest any kind of moral equivalence between different sides, such as in the war in Bosnia. But it is to say that this kind of liberalism, among other things, promised a kind of certainty: suffering was obvious, and so was the urgency to intervene. It also mobilized passions and pity—but at the same time, it understood itself as clearly *unideological* in Bell's narrow sense, thereby again seemingly heeding a clear-cut lesson from the "age of ideologies."

Second, there was certainty as a result of discovering a new enemy. After September 11, a number of liberals seemed positively to celebrate the possibility of fashioning a new "fighting faith";[23] or, as Daniel T. Rodgers put it more broadly, a "reaggregation of the social imagination," in contrast with the Nietzschean last men, bored individualist consumers wandering around aimlessly in Fukuyama's "universal homogeneous" (God forbid, EU-like) state.[24] It seemed time to refound something like the Congress for Cultural Freedom, but this time dedicated to teaching Muslims the benefits of genuine freedom and pluralism. The battle with what was often called a "third totalitarianism" promised relief from any boredom that might arise in a liberal *posthistoire* universe. As Christopher Hitchens rejoiced at the time:

> I should perhaps confess that on September 11 last, once I had experienced all the usual mammalian gamut of emotions, from rage to nausea, I also discovered that another sensation was contending for mastery. On examination, and to my own surprise and pleasure, it turned out to be exhilaration. Here was the most frightful enemy—theocratic barbarism—in plain view . . . I realized that if the battle went on until the last day of my life, I would never get bored in prosecuting it to the utmost.[25]

For critics, such an attitude seemed to suggest that liberals always desperately need a fighting faith because they have no faith in any of their own principles or practical prescriptions being attractive in the absence of an enemy. Again, this new antitotalitarian liberalism would have disavowed any ideology in Bell's narrow sense—but it obviously was passionately devoted to a cause, and hence very much seemed to fit Bell's wider conception of ideology.

Third, there was indeed the Third Way—maybe the most long-lasting of the ideational legacies of the 1990s. Prophets of the Third Way consciously presented themselves as anti-ideological. The twentieth century had been about opposing dogmatism, or so they suggested; now it was time decisively to move "beyond left and right" in the name of "modernization"; one had to combine resources from any point of the political spectrum, so long as it was reasonable and worked in practice. This relentless will to synthesis was also reflected in a political language abounding in oxymorons; a Third Way theorist like Anthony Giddens kept offering up expressions like "utopian realism" and "radical center" and whatever else seemed to promise the best of all possible worlds, while causing no social costs and requiring no political choice.[26]

Nominally left-wing (or at least center-left) parties insisted that they wanted all the supposed benefits of a market economy while rejecting the notion of a "market society."[27] De facto, such parties imported neoliberal thought patterns—not just the emphasis on consumer choice, but also the less obvious valorization of discipline—into their programs.[28] It was no accident that Blair, Clinton, and German chancellor Gerhard Schröder all placed a particular emphasis on workfare programs, which were justified by a language that was both moralistic and technocratic. The conclusion, whether from a more moral or a more technocratic angle, was always the same: there was no alternative; there was just one singularly reasonable policy. Of course, having no alternative is also a way of having certainty.

The Third Way was not intended to mobilize political passions; it was not a "cause," and it had nothing like nuanced political and economic doctrines. If anything, its doctrine was a self-conscious pragmatism. Less obviously, it also marked a curious shift from universities to think tanks. In Britain, for instance, Demos and the Institute for Public Policy Research were at least as important in generating arguments (or maybe just slogans) as anyone operating in universities (with the possible exception of Giddens), let alone political parties.[29] Authoritative expertise also increasingly came from what Stephanie Mudge has identified as the figure of "the transnationalized, finance-oriented economist," understood as the "bearer and guardian of the truth of markets."[30] This figure was, of course, presented as entirely unideological—in both senses that Bell specified; the language of economics was one of adaptation (to globalization) and discipline (exercised by markets), even in an age that, more broadly, appeared to celebrate choice and contingency.[31]

The obvious critique of thinkers like Giddens consisted in saying that the seeming pragmatism, modernization, or synthesis of the supposedly best ideas from all sides simply masked particular (and highly contestable) value choices. The self-consciously post-ideological pretense of "There is no alternative" was the most ideological stance of all; and, more particularly, the French philosopher Alain's famous quip that nobody on the left would ever say that we're beyond left and right would seem to have been confirmed yet again.[32] De facto, the Third Way proved to pave a path along which social democracy further disintegrated. It generated no lasting concepts or categories that would have allowed politicians, or citizens for that matter, to formulate a solidaristic language in the wake of the financial crisis—which nominally may have seemed like a clear end of the long Nineties (but in many ways actually was not).

THE LONG NINETIES AND THE PRESENT

I have suggested that the long Nineties were not so obviously a time of triumphalism, after all; in many ways, they were actually a time of intense anxiety about liberalism's foundations. Certainty was sought in the immediacy of feelings—negative experiences of cruelty and state-inflicted violence in particular—as well as a new fighting faith against what at the time appeared as a comprehensive "third totalitarianism." Less obviously, the Third Way promised a path beyond twentieth-century ideological oppositions and a uniquely pragmatic politics with, in varying degrees, seemingly uncontestable moral and technocratic justifications.

All of this is another way of saying that Bell's diagnosis of an exhaustion of political ideas in a very narrow sense might well apply to the 1990s—there were no new comprehensive belief systems comparable to what had emerged in the nineteenth century. But it should also be clear that exhaustion is not the same as a calm, let alone uncontested, reign of what Berlin once nonchalantly called "compromise and balance and adjustment and empirical Popperism etc."[33] In fact, the search for certainty led to particular traps and dead ends. It is worth examining them one more time, at a somewhat more abstract level.

First, politics, as one of Bell's most important intellectual heroes, Max Weber, would have insisted all along, is rarely a matter of the normatively unambiguous. Suffering is real, but effective strategies for combating it have to be based on complex accounts of what exactly causes what, and what the likely consequences and costs of different forms of political conduct are likely to be. Such strategies also have to move beyond just seeing everyone as a victim. Above all, they need to complement Shklar's liberalism of fear with what Shklar herself actually advocated as a "liberalism of rights"—one that empowers people as opposed to treating them as passive recipients of assistance.

Second, liberalism must stand for something without the props of more or less imaginary threats and enemies. Obviously, some threats are real, and explicating them is crucial for mobilizing citizens in defense of a liberal democratic order. But there is something perverse about a celebration of enmity along the lines of "Now, at last, we know again what we stand for!" (let alone: "Now we know again that life under liberalism doesn't have to be boring!").

Liberals have not entirely escaped this temptation in confronting what today is often described as "populism"—a phenomenon usually understood as inherently antiliberal. In particular, there has been an attempt to identify the ideologues of populism—and then deploy liberal conceptual weaponry against them. Alas, it is a questionable legacy of the Cold War to assume that every political conflict must ultimately have a deep philosophical dimension. The first imperative for many observers in a very perplexing political present remains: *cherchez le maître-penseur!* Want to understand Vladimir Putin? Look for the intellectual power behind the throne of the new czar, and you find the "Eurasianist" philosopher Alexander Dugin. Getting to the bottom of Trumpism? Even now, the man to watch and listen to is not Donald Trump, but Steve Bannon, and the task is to figure out his secret reading list (which, we are told, includes figures like the Italian traditionalist Julius Evola, a major inspiration for the European New Right).[34]

And yet: are we really dealing with political actors inspired by comprehensive worldviews? Is populism in fact an ideology at all? I would submit that it is a mistake to treat populism as if it were a doctrine, or to assume without further empirical evidence that it evokes particularly strong political passions (to invoke Bell's two senses of ideology again). Populists claim that they, and only they, represent what they usually call "the real people" or "the silent majority."[35] As a result, they deny the legitimacy of their political competitors, who are accused of being corrupt (and "crooked") characters; less obviously, populist leaders suggest that all those citizens who do not share their particular conception of the "real people"—and hence do not support populists politically—do not properly belong to the people at all. Right-wing populists attack "liberal elites" and vulnerable minorities simultaneously to secure and solidify power. Hence, it is a mistake to think about the conflict between liberalism and populism as primarily a matter of more or less good-faith disagreements on policies such as trade and immigration. Populists tend to reduce all political questions to questions of belonging—Trump declares opponents simply "un-American"; mobilization always takes the form of creating (or at least intensifying) culture wars. Trump's rhetorical question in a speech he gave in Warsaw in 2018—"Do we have the confidence in our values to defend them at any cost?"—could be mistaken for a sound bite from the height of the Cold War. But, tellingly, it was immediately followed by a further rhetorical question: "Do we have enough respect for our citizens to protect our borders?"—suggesting a world in which "real Americans" are constantly threatened by caravans of Middle Eastern terrorists and Latin Americans who might pass for citizens, but are actually the enemy within.

There is an elective affinity between right-wing populism and nationalism, as well as nativism. After all, populists invoking "the real people" have to specify who exactly those people are—and, in many cases, the most obvious answer seems to be "the nation." But this does not mean that populism, which always pits the people against elites and offers an exclusive definition of the people, and nationalism, which does not have to have an anti-elite element, are the same thing. Moreover, neither populism nor nationalism has to aim at actually mobilizing citizens. One of the peculiarities of today's populist leaders is that they are *not* all that interested in increasing popular participation in politics—in striking contrast with twentieth-century movements driven by ideologies. Mobilization in the name of ideas is simply not the point.[36] And while many of them talk the anti-neoliberal talk, in practice, they tend to accommodate business elites, and even multinationals—think of Narendra Modi, Viktor Orbán, or Jair Bolsonaro, who are nationalists, but at the same time are careful to make sure that their countries remain open for business.

Liberals should ask themselves whether some of the policies they have been advocating in recent decades should be rethought. "Free trade" and the supposedly inevitable globalization have turned out to be mixed blessings, to say the least. The promise that they were in everyone's interest clearly has not been kept. Here, a dose of the Cold War liberals' crucial insight that there are always trade-offs between different genuine human values is important (even if talk of trade-offs can also be instrumentalized to deny particular citizens equality, as a trenchant critique of Berlin by Ronald Dworkin has long made clear). In fact, though, liberals have been tempted to settle once again for a technocratic mind-set, according to which there is only one correct, rational answer to every policy question, with the implication that those who disagree basically reveal themselves to be irrational. (Given former president Trump's lying and Republicans complicity in his assault on the very notion of shared reality, it is all the easier to assume that liberals must necessarily possess truth and rationality.)

Yet such an attitude, often reminiscent of Third Way rhetoric, has allowed populists to raise the reasonable objection that a democracy where the people do not have a choice is not a democracy at all. If populists succeed at the polls, technocrats see their prejudices about the great unwashed opting for crazy demagogues confirmed. They are likely then to advocate even more vigilant "gatekeeping" (i.e., fewer decision-making opportunities for citizens, such as primaries). While it might seem that two extremes, technocracy and populism, confront each other here, the two have one thing in common. Both are forms of antipluralism: for the technocrat, there is only one rational policy; for the populist, there is only one authentic will of the people (and only he—it is usually a "he"—represents it).

Thinkers like Berlin, Karl Popper, Aron, and, to some extent, Bell—the last three all avowed Weberians—kept returning to the importance of pluralism: they emphasized that there are many attractive but incompatible values in both individual and collective life, so that compromise was not dirty, but in fact indispensable. This notion was at the time plainly (and sometimes unfairly) directed at supposed Marxist utopians who promised to solve the riddle of history. But it still applies today: calling someone who disagrees plainly irrational or, as in the populist playbook, a traitor to the people misses the possibility of having good-faith disagreements about these values. As Berlin once put it, even "compromising with people with whom you don't sympathize or altogether understand is indispensable to any decent society."[37]

Of course, not all disagreements are made in good faith: when populists rage against "globalists," they are battling an imaginary enemy. Few liberals have advocated completely "open borders" (when Popper advocated the "open society," he opposed both doctrinal intolerance and tribalism as a mindset; the argument was epistemological, not about immigration policy). Hence, it is also a mistake to think that populist leaders would be satisfied if only liberals adopted a stance of what is now sometimes called "immigration realism" (or what the Dutch prime minister Mark Rutte, a self-declared liberal, called "good populism").

If it is true that populists always wage culture wars, one might be tempted to think that Berlin—much more so than Bell—might be of renewed significance in yet another respect. After all, Berlin, a lifelong committed Zionist, had great sympathy for nationalism; he always emphasized human beings' fundamental need to belong. He explained many of the ideological developments since the eighteenth century on the basis of a "state of wounded consciousness"—which is to say: a sense of not being recognized, of having one's way of life disrespected, of not being up to the supposed standards of a liberal cosmopolitan culture. In the age of *Hillbilly Elegy*—J. D. Vance's memoir of an Appalachian childhood that liberals lapped up as an explanation of the Trump vote— a stance that sensitively asks about the psychological sources of political discontent (and encourages more work than reading one memoir) might be especially important; in particular, it might orient us away from a futile search for new ideologies that need to be fought by self-declared militant liberals.

But there are two distinct perils here. We do not exactly seem to suffer from a lack of attention to the emotional side of politics. Terms like "anger" and "resentment" are used routinely—in all likelihood, unthinkingly—in contemporary commentary on populism in particular. Such long-distance diagnoses are not just often deeply patronizing, as they treat citizens more like therapy cases than as autonomous sources of political claims. They also make serious debate more unlikely, as they separate emotion from reason. Yet the two cannot simply be kept apart; after all, people are angry for a reason; and looking at discontents primarily through a psychological lens makes it less likely that we ask them directly about those reasons and how they arrived at them.[38]

The other peril is almost the opposite. In an effort to understand—what Berlin often referred to as *Einfühlen*, feeling oneself into the thought and emotions of another—one becomes *too* understanding: the problem of *tout comprendre c'est tout pardonner*. There is no universal panacea of how to avoid this, other than a more or less helpful call to hold firm to one's moral compass, while exercising empathy and imagination to the best of one's abilities. There is also one obvious precaution: it is one thing to engage with people's lived experience; it is another to take descriptions of that experience by self-appointed representatives (be it political leaders or right-wing talk radio hosts) at face value. Surely not every voter of a populist party is a committed antipluralist (or, more specifically, a xenophobe or racist—which is not to deny that there are plenty of racists out there). Even within the electorate of such parties, what one hears about is more likely a loud minority, not the frequently invoked silent majority.

A misguided effort at understanding—what Germans call *Populismusversteher*—can have pernicious long-term consequences. It assumes that populists are somehow most likely to reveal the so-far-ignored "anxieties" of the "ordinary citizen." This notion of populist leaders as telling us the ultimate, so-far-hidden truth about society is based on a profoundly misguided notion of how representation in a democracy actually functions. Representation is not a kind of mechanical reproduction of preexisting interests or even identities, so that the populist can be assumed to have at last discovered these interests and identities—and, if successful in elections, have them reflected in the political system. Rather, democratic representation is a dynamic, in many ways creative process—and how people perceive their interests, and even identities, is at least partly shaped by what politicians, as well the media, neighborhood association, friends and family, and so on, offer them as possible descriptions of themselves.[39] It would be foolish to assume that therefore, anything is possible—or that populists are simply dealing in fiction; of course, what they represent to people resonates for a reason. But it is not simply the ultimate, objective truth about society; here as well, a potential pluralism of representations is not only possible, but a resource for liberals to use to oppose populists.

Finally, "the center" is not per se reasonable, let alone nonideological, and neither oxymorons nor false equivalences can substitute for actually persuasive arguments rooted in always contestable value choices. The obvious second coming of the Third Way in our day, so to speak, is the self-image of French president Emmanuel Macron, who often presents conflict as between reasonable and unreasonable (though on occasion Macron acknowledges genuine conflict, one that he describes as a new cleavage between progressives and nationalists).

Equidistance from seeming extremes is not automatically the same as pragmatism; it is also not in and of itself a desirable form of moderation. One of today's fateful tendencies is precisely the hope that a compulsive symmetrical distancing from left and right (which then also involves a compulsion to equate left and right) can somehow provide orientation.[40] In fact, such distancing amounts to a kind of relativism (one's self-definition is at the mercy of what left and right mean at any moment) or falsely equates what are in fact profoundly different threats to whatever is more or less arbitrarily construed as "the center."[41] *Pas trop de zèle* (not too much zealousness) is not in and of itself a political philosophy.

This leads to one final thought: because of the ambiguity between ideology as passion on the one hand and as dogma on the other, the status of liberalism in Bell's thought—and what its implications for today might be—are also not always clear. Was liberalism really for the most part a matter of temperament? Then woe to those inevitably attracted to passion in politics. Or could one hope that ideology would self-destruct anyway, regardless of the dispositions and psychological stances of political actors, as the other quotation from Bell at the beginning of this essay suggests? Could one educate oneself to resist blind passion (and blind dogma)? Could one find, as Weber had claimed, a proper balance between passionate commitment and a sense of responsibility, in turn grounded in probabilistic reasoning about causes and consequences?

Bell, in one of his last interviews, not only affirmed his allegiance to Weber—the "lynchpin" of this thought, as he put it— but also drew a suggestive contrast between messianism and utopianism.[42] The supposedly complacent Cold War liberal came out in favor of the latter, underlining, just as Weber did, that a proper political mindset meant having ideals (and emotions, for that matter). This is perhaps the crucial lesson Bell has for our age: a seemingly rational pragmatism and incrementalism beyond left and right can themselves become perversely ideological if they turn into doctrines.

NOTES

1. I am grateful to Paul Starr for his comments on an earlier version of this chapter. I partly draw here on arguments first developed in Jan-Werner Müller, "What Cold War Liberalism Can Teach Us Today," *New York Review of Books Daily*, November 26, 2018, https://www.nybooks.com /daily/2018/11/26/what-cold-war-liberalism-can-teach-us-today/; on my book *Furcht und Freiheit: Für einen anderen Liberalismus* (Berlin: Suhrkamp, 2019); and on my essay "Populism and the People," *London Review of Books*, May 23, 2019.

2. For instance, see the volume by Ralf Dahrendorf, a close friend of Bell's, *Der Wiederbeginn der Geschichte* (Munich: C. H. Beck, 2004)

3. Daniel Bell, *The End of Ideology: On the Exhaustion of Political Ideas in the Fifties, with "The Resumption of History in the New Century"* (Cambridge, MA: Harvard University Press, 2000), xii.

4. In particular, he rejected the notion that *The End of Ideology* justified the status quo or amounted to advocating a form of technocracy. Bell, I believe, was right to do so.

5. See the analysis by Howard Brick, who rightly describes the first *End of Ideology* debate as not much of a debate at all, but as a "combination of misunderstandings." Howard Brick, "The End of Ideology Thesis," in *The Oxford Handbook of Political Ideologies*, ed. Michael Freeden and Marc Stears (Oxford: Oxford University, 2013), 102.

6. Bell wrote of a fusion of ideas and passion in the 2000 edition, but in the book as a whole, the two notions of passionate commitment to ideas and doctrinal rigidity ran alongside each other, as opposed to necessarily being fused. See Bell, *The End of Ideology*, xi. Thus, depending on one's

diagnosis, one can see the primary problem with ideology as cognitive or psychological. Note also how Bell's critics, in *tu quoque* moments, charged him with trying to craft a neoconservative ideology as a fusion of ideas (centered on restraints on individual behavior) and emotional bonds. Peter Steinfels, *The Neoconservatives: The Men Who Are Changing America's Politics* (New York: Touchstone, 1979), 180.

7. For a debate on this topic at the time, see Alexsandras Shtromas (ed.), "The End of 'Isms'?" in: *Political Studies*, special issue, vol. 41 (1993), 4–20.

8. The obvious objection is that nationalism can be as much of a chiliastic religion as certain refined doctrinal systems.

9. In this context, see also my *Contesting Democracy: Political Ideas in Twentieth-Century Europe* (New Haven, CT: Yale University Press, 2011).

10. Francis Fukuyama, "The End of History," *National Interest*, no. 16 (Summer 1989), 3–18.

11. Francis Fukuyama, *Identity: The Demand for Dignity and the Politics of Resentment* (New York: Farrar, Straus and Giroux, 2018).

12. Both men are quoted in John B. Judis, *The Nationalist Revival: Trade, Immigration, and the Revolt against Globalization* (New York: Columbia Global Reports, 2018), 17.

13. Francis Fukuyama, *The End of History and the Last Man* (New York: Free Press, 1992), 317.

14. Michael Ignatieff, *Blood and Belonging: Journeys into the New Nationalism* (New York: Farrar, Straus and Giroux, 1994).

15. Witness Irving Kristol proclaiming after the end of the Cold War: "In politics, being deprived of an enemy is a very serious matter. You tend to get relaxed and dispirited. Turn inward." Quoted in Corey Robin, "The Ex-Cons," *Lingua Franca*, no. 1. (2001); available at: http://linguafranca .mirror.theinfo.org/print/0101/cover_cons.html.

16. Isaiah Berlin to Bernard Williams, March 7, 1969, in *Building: Letters 1960–1975*, ed. Henry Hardy and Mark Pottle (London: Chatto & Windus, 2013), 377.

17. Isaiah Berlin to Stepan Volk, July 9, 1962, in Hardy and Pottle, *Building: Letters 1960–1975*, 102.

18. Arthur Schlesinger, Jr., *The Vital Center: The Politics of Freedom* (Boston: Houghton Mifflin, 1949).

19. Daniel T. Rodgers, *Age of Fracture* (Cambridge, MA: Harvard University Press, 2011).

20. Judith Shklar, "The Liberalism of Fear," in *Liberalism and the Moral Life*, ed. Nancy L. Rosenblum (Cambridge, MA: Harvard University Press, 1989), 21–38. Of course, Shklar's contribution to political thought is not exhausted by the liberalism of fear, even if it seems likely that she will be remembered, above all, for this particular theory (or sketch of a theory). See Katrina Forrester, "Hope and Memory in the Thought of Judith Shklar," *Modern Intellectual History* 8 (2011): 591–620.

21. Michael Ignatieff, *The Warrior's Honor: Ethnic War and the Modern Conscience* (New York: Henry Holt, 1997), 18–19.

22. Bernhard Schlink, "Der Preis der Gerechtigkeit," *Merkur* 58 (2004): 983–997.

23. Peter Beinart, "An Argument for a New Liberalism: A Fighting Faith," *The New Republic*, December 13, 2004, and *The Good Fight: Why Liberals—and Only Liberals—Can Win the War on Terror and Make America Great Again* (New York: Harper Collins, 2006). No comment on the subtitle.

24. Rodgers, *Age of Fracture*, 258.

25. Corey Robin, *Fear: The History of an Idea* (New York: Oxford University Press, 2004), 24.

26. Anthony Giddens, *Beyond Left and Right* (Cambridge: Polity, 1994) and *The Third Way: The Renewal of Social Democracy* (Cambridge: Polity, 1998).

27. As Blair and Schröder argued in their manifesto about the Third Way/ Die Neue Mitte: "We need to apply our politics within a new economic framework, modernized for today, where government does all it can to support enterprise but never believes it is a substitute for enterprise. The essential function of markets must be complemented and improved by political action, not hampered by it. We support a market economy, not a market society." They also stated bluntly: "The weaknesses of markets have been overstated and their strengths underestimated," only to then add: "For the new politics to succeed, it must promote a go-ahead mentality and a new entrepreneurial spirit at all levels of society." Tony Blair and Gerhard Schröder, "The Third Way/Die Neue Mitte," annot. Joanne Barkan, *Dissent* (Spring 2000), https://www.dissentmagazine.org/article /the-third-waydie-neue-mitte, last accessed April 1, 2020.

28. For the argument that neoliberalism is *not* the same as "market funda-mentalism" (or in fact any conception of freedom), but rather discipline, see, for instance, Melinda Cooper, *Family Values: Between Neoliberalism and the New Social Conservatism* (New York: Zone Books, 2017); Quinn Slobodian, *The Globalists: The End of Empire and the Birth of Neoliberal-ism* (Cambridge, MA: Harvard University Press, 2018); Nancy MacLean, *Democracy in Chains: The Deep History of the Radical Right's Stealth Plan for America* (New York: Viking, 2017), Niklas Olsen, *The Sovereign Con-sumer: A New Intellectual History of Neoliberalism* (Cham, Switzerland: Palgrave Macmillan, 2019), and James G. Chappel, "A Servant Heart," *Boston Review*, November 15, 2015, http://bostonreview.net/books-ideas /james-chappel-servant-heart-religion-neoliberalism.

29. Stephanie L. Mudge, *Leftism Reinvented: Western Parties from Socialism to Neoliberalism* (Cambridge, MA: Harvard University Press, 2018).

30. Mudge, *Leftism Reinvented*, 35.

31. Rodgers, *Age of Fracture*.

32. Steven Lukes, "Epilogue: The Grand Dichotomy of the Twentieth Cen-tury," in *The Cambridge History of Twentieth-Century Political Thought*, ed. Terence Ball and Richard Bellamy (Cambridge: Cambridge University Press, 2003), 602–626.

33. Isaiah Berlin, *Enlightening: Letters, 1946–1960*, ed. Henry Hardy and Jen-nifer Holmes, with the assistance of Serena Moore (London: Chatto & Windus, 2009), 352.

34. Benjamin R. Teitelbaum, *War for Eternity: Inside Bannon's Far-Right Circle of Global Power Brokers* (New York: Dey St., 2020).

35. I have developed this account more extensively in *What Is Populism?* (Lon-don: Penguin, 2017).

36. India might be a partial exception. The Rashtriya Swayamsevak Sangh (RSS) organization is a genuine mass movement; Modi has made clear enough that the movement openly persecuting Muslims is acceptable.

37. Isaiah Berlin, "Notes on Prejudice," in Isaiah Berlin, *Liberty: Incorporat-ing Four Essays on Liberty*, ed. Henry Hardy (Oxford: Oxford University Press, 2002), 346.

38. For an important argument for the role of anger in politics, see Amia Srinivasan, "The Aptness of Anger," *Journal of Political Philosophy* 26 (2018): 123–144.

39. Michael Saward, *The Representative Claim* (Oxford: Oxford University Press, 2010).

40. Jürgen Habermas has used the term *zwanghafte Symmetrisierung* in this context—the compulsion to suggest symmetry when in fact one is faced with an asymmetrical situation. Jürgen Habermas, "Für eine demokratische Polarisierung," *Blätter für deutsche und internationale Politik* (November 2016), https://www.blaetter.de/ausgabe/2016/november/fuer -eine-demokratische-polarisierung.

41. As an obvious example, see Adam Gopnik, *A Thousand Small Sanities: The Moral Adventure of Liberalism* (New York: Basic Books, 2019).

42. Roberto Foa and Thomas Meaney, "The Last Word," *The Utopian*, February 10, 2011, https://www.the-utopian.org/post/3217295807/the-last-word.

PART III

THE POST-
INDUSTRIAL
TRANSFORMATION

6

"POST-INDUSTRIAL" VERSUS "NEOLIBERAL"

Rival Definitions of Our Age

PAUL STARR

In the introduction to *The Coming of Post-Industrial Society* (1973), Daniel Bell characterizes the forecast he makes in the book as "an 'as if,' a fiction, a logical construction of what *could* be, against which the future social reality can be compared in order to see what intervened to change society in the direction it did take."[1] Nearly half a century later, we can take up that invitation not only to "see what intervened," but also to reexamine Bell's theoretical framework and compare it to alternative ideas about the central forces and tendencies of modern societies.

Post-industrial society—the conception of the contemporary stage of socioeconomic development that Bell did more than anyone else to elaborate—has been one of the most influential definitions of our era. The ambiguity of the concept has probably contributed to its adoption. Like any name with the prefix "post-," it identifies a phenomenon only by what it has come after. In Bell's usage, "post-industrial society" is similar to several other widely used terms such as "information society" or "knowledge society" that do not look back to a previous era. Each of these has somewhat different connotations, but all the associated theories call attention to the role of knowledge and technology as a principal force of change in the economically advanced societies of the late-twentieth and early-twenty-first centuries.[2]

"Post-industrial" now vies, especially on the left, with another conception of our time that emphasizes the role of ideology and politics in a return to market forces and relations. This is the idea that we live in a "neoliberal" age. Although neoliberal thought is usually traced to Friedrich Hayek and his circle in the 1940s, neoliberalism as a political force dates to the late 1970s, and it wasn't until the 1990s that "neoliberal" emerged as a general characterization of politics and society.[3] Some uses of "neoliberalism" are indistinguishable from such older phrases as "laissez-faire," "possessive individualism," or "classical liberalism." Insofar as "neoliberalism" has had a distinctive new meaning—and not been used as a vague term of abuse—it typically refers to ideas and policies that seek to reorient the state, nongovernmental institutions, and the self to market forces. Paradoxically, rather than calling for a general retreat of the state, neoliberalism has often involved the active use of state power to create markets and to rein in or discipline pressures for social protection. The neoliberal policy arsenal includes such measures as privatization, free-trade agreements, deregulation (often actually reregulation in favor of business interests), tax cuts, and reductions in social spending. Like "post-industrial," "neoliberal" is defined by what it has come after. The neoliberal age is an age of capitalist revival, following a period when the market and the power of capital were subject to significant limitations.

These two conceptions of our time reflect the sequence of political change in the twentieth century. Bell formulated his ideas about post-industrialism and social forecasting during the 1960s and published his book on the subject just before the end of the post-war boom (and before the neoliberal political shift). The succession of global crises from World War I through the Great Depression, World War II, and the Cold War had brought about a sustained expansion of the state throughout the West, originally for wartime and economic emergencies, and then for ongoing social and economic purposes. From the late 1940s to the early 1970s, economic growth surged, inequality declined, and the old class conflicts between capital and labor appeared to be receding into the past. To many social scientists of the time, this was the new normal for understanding society and a new baseline for projecting the future.

The mid-1970s, however, initiated a series of shocks: *economic shocks*, with oil crises, spiraling inflation, and a sudden end to steady growth; *political shocks*, with tax revolts and the rise to power of Margaret Thatcher in Great Britain and Ronald Reagan in the United States; and *intellectual shocks*, with the collapse of confidence in Keynesian economics and planning and the return of free-market ideas that many had thought dead and buried, or at least irrelevant to the future of liberal democracies. The collapse of Soviet communism and the Chinese embrace of capitalism and opening to trade then helped legitimate the turn in the West from the state to the market, all of it seemingly part of the same worldwide, free-market awakening. Just as Bell's theory of post-industrialism elaborated and extrapolated the ideas and trends of the postwar era, so accounts of neoliberalism elaborated and extrapolated the political reversal of the late twentieth century.

Like ordinary mortals, social theorists are subject to recency bias: the latest developments weigh more heavily on their minds than earlier ones, especially when they are trying to pick out the seeds of the future. But theories that suffer from a marked recency bias may nonetheless have two sources of redeeming value. First, even if they do not succeed at a general and abstract level, they may still capture the historical moment and identify distinctive patterns of their own time and place. Second, they may yet provide the basis for understanding long-term patterns of social development if later work is able to correct for the original biases and blind spots. Here we need to distinguish between two types of error in a theory: irremediable conceptual problems and flaws of execution. If the problems stem from the execution rather than irremediable problems with the concepts, the theory may be revised and still serve as a useful frame for analysis, and possibly for action as well.

This is what I hope to show we can do with Bell's theory of post-industrialism. There is no way to avoid confronting the glaring problems in his original formulation. In *The Coming of Post-Industrial Society*, he overgeneralized from the immediate past. He expected government and social planning to grow and the role of corporations and markets to diminish. Despite a variety of indications in his own analysis, he missed the coming rise in economic inequality. More generally, he failed to anticipate the brutal aspects of post-industrialism. While correctly forecasting the continued decline of employment in manufacturing, he did not devote any attention to the fate of workers and communities that would lose industrial jobs or to the minorities who would never be able to use those jobs as a ladder into the middle class. There is no sense in his work of the tragic aspects of the post-industrial transformation.

In addition, his conception of the emerging changes in knowledge and technology was also almost entirely top-down, emphasizing the use of theoretical knowledge and technology for institutional decision-making. This perspective carries important insights. But Bell had little appreciation, even in writing on technology in later decades, for the impact of the digital revolution on everyday social relations, the rise of a networked economy, or the new structures of private power arising from the form that the new technology was taking.

Yet while these and other problems detract from Bell's work, much of the basic conceptual framework still survives, provided that it is amended with the benefit of subsequent clarifying developments, including an understanding of the neoliberal reversal. Bell's own viewpoint was antithetical to neoliberalism. He describes post-industrial society as "a 'communal' society in which the social unit is the community rather than the individual, and one has to achieve a 'social decision' as against, simply, the sum total of individual decisions which, when aggregated, end up as nightmares."[4] *The Coming of Post-Industrial Society* may productively be reread today not only as an analytical, but also as a normative work. While Bell was wrong in expecting that certain things would happen in the following decades, he was not necessarily wrong that some of them ought to have happened and could still happen. His book reminds us of a lost agenda of social democratic liberalism at the beginning of the 1970s—lost because of the subsequent turn to the right. Whether that agenda can be recovered, and should be, are questions worth exploring.

BELL'S THEORY OF SOCIOECONOMIC DEVELOPMENT

From its title, *The Coming of Post-Industrial Society* appears to be a comprehensive account of a new era in the advanced societies. But Bell rejects the idea that "societies are organic or so integrated as to be analyzable as a single system" and insists that the term "post-industrial" refers to only one aspect of society—the dimension that comprises the economy, technology, and the occupational system. Rather confusingly, in the original book he calls this dimension "social structure," although in forewords in the 1976 and 1999 editions, he identifies it "primarily" as "the techno-economic realm."[5] It is an indication of how much weight Bell gives to techno-economic change that it could be his primary basis for projecting the structure of post-industrial society.

Yet this techno-economic realm, he argues, is not necessarily synchronized with the political order and cultural sphere, which operate on the basis of different axial principles. Here he pointedly distinguishes his position from Marx's: "A post-industrial society is not a 'substructure' initiating changes in a 'superstructure.' It is one important dimension of a society whose changes pose management problems for the political system that arbitrates the society."[6] Consequently, post-industrial society admits variations, depending on culture and especially on the political choices that governments make when confronted by changes in the other dimensions.

Bell's theoretical schema, however, is similar to Marx's in another respect: he posits a tripartite sequence of stages of development on the basis of changes in material life. Instead of feudalism, capitalism, and socialism, these stages are preindustrial, industrial, and post-industrial society—terms that Bell took from Raymond Aron and Alain Touraine to describe ideal-type, techno-economic "frameworks," each of which, he argues, has its own "design" or logic. Preindustrial society is a "game against nature" because it draws resources from "extractive" work (agriculture, fishing, and so on) and suffers from low productivity. Industrial society is a "game against fabricated nature" that "uses energy to transform the natural environment into a technical environment." And post-industrial society is a "game between persons," in which labor increasingly involves services rather than manufacturing, and "an 'intellectual technology,' based on information, rises alongside of machine technology."[7]

When Bell initially breaks down the shift from industrial to post-industrial society, he identifies five major changes. The first pair relate to the economy and class structure: (1) the shift from a goods-producing to a service economy; and (2) the "pre-eminence of the professional and technical class." The next three relate chiefly to knowledge and technology: (3) "the centrality of theoretical knowledge as the source of innovation and of policy formulation for the society" (which he refers to as the "axial principle" of post-industrialism); (4) "future orientation: the control of technology and technological assessment"; and (5) "the creation of a new 'intellectual technology' " for "decision-making."[8] Later, he writes, "The post-industrial society, it is clear, is a knowledge society in a double sense," and then explicitly identifies the two dimensions, technological and economic, that are implicit elsewhere: "first, the sources of innovation are increasingly derivative from research and development (and more directly, there is a new relation between science and technology because of the centrality of *theoretical* knowledge); second, the weight of the society—measured by a larger proportion of Gross National Product and a larger share of employment—is increasingly in the knowledge field."[9]

Bell's simultaneous emphasis on knowledge as a source of change and on politics as the ultimate arbiter of change creates an internal tension in his thought. He could not be clearer about the structural primacy of knowledge: "the major source of structural change in society . . . is the change in the character of knowledge." Bell also claims that societal decisions will depend more than ever on expertise: "The central point about the last third of the twentieth century, call it the post-industrial society, the knowledgeable society, the technetronic age, or the active society, is that it will require more societal guidance, more expertise." Nonetheless, he emphatically rejects the idea that post-industrial society is leading to a technocracy: "No matter how technical social processes may be, the crucial turning points in a society occur in a political form. It is not the technocrat who ultimately holds power, but the politician."[10]

How can we square these seemingly contrary positions? Bell tries to resolve them by saying that the knowledge-driven structural changes create constraints and an agenda for decision-making, leaving politics to determine the outcome. Although the constraints "tend to shape similar actions and force the use of common techniques," they do not dictate the content of the decisions.[11] Still, Bell does claim that post-industrial society necessarily involves more "societal guidance." In *The Coming of Post-Industrial Society*, he did not foresee any chance that government's guiding capacities would be rolled back in favor of markets. In that sense, his theory was deterministic, and he was mistaken about what was going to happen in the late twentieth century. That error highlights a more fundamental problem with a theoretical approach that puts the economy in one realm and politics in another. Rather than just resolving the finer points left open by techno-economic developments, some political decisions fundamentally shape them—or as I would say, they have constitutive effects on technologies and economic institutions.[12]

A second tension in Bell's schema involves the relationship of post-industrial society to capitalism. The concept of industrial society, he wrote, subsumes capitalism and socialism "under a common rubric." What all industrial societies have in common, whether capitalist or socialist, is that they are "*economizing* societies, that is, they are organized around a principle of functional efficiency whose desideratum is to get 'more for less' and to choose the more 'rational' course of action." But Bell rejected theories of "convergence" suggesting that Western capitalist countries and the Soviet Union were becoming alike; the differences in property relations and political systems still kept them separate and distinct. Societies, in this view, vary according to their stage of techno-economic development on one axis (industrial versus post-industrial) and according to their property relations on another axis (capitalism versus socialism).[13]

Nonetheless, Bell often suggests that post-industrial society supersedes capitalism. For example, he says that while the major conflict of capitalist society has been between capitalist and worker, the major conflict of post-industrial society is between professionals and the populace. In discussing his notion of "axial" institutions or principles—"the major lines around which other institutions are draped"—he writes, "In capitalist society the axial institution has been private property and in the post-industrial society it is the centrality of theoretical knowledge."[14] But this formulation fails to clarify what principles would dominate a post-industrial society that remained capitalist. He might have forecast different futures for post-industrial societies with different property regimes. Instead, without much justification, he argues that private property has diminishing social significance and treats capitalism as a fading legacy of an earlier time—an error that accounts for much of what went wrong with his forecast of post-industrialism.

WHERE BELL'S FORECAST WENT WRONG

In the era after World War II, social theorists of nearly all persuasions overgeneralized from the mid-twentieth-century trends toward an expanded state and reduced economic inequality. Karl Polanyi's *The Great Transformation* (1944) interpreted the imposition of limits on the market as an epochal, one-way shift in which societies repaired the damage of the earlier free-market regime.[15] The economist Simon Kuznets saw the decline in inequality as a consequence of the later stages of industrialization and economic growth, while Marxists such as James O'Connor attributed the rise of the welfare state and other state functions to the logic of capitalism.[16]

But rather than being inexorable aspects of linear developments, the expansion of the state and reduced inequalities of the mid-twentieth century are better understood as effects of a singular historical conjuncture.[17] The industrialized capitalist countries confronted the shocks of war and depression in the context of growing working-class and radical movements at home and the challenge of Soviet communism internationally. Their adoption of higher and more progressive taxes and social spending is impossible to understand without taking into account the larger risks that governing parties and business confronted at home and abroad and the crises' impact in discrediting received ideas and opening politics to alternatives. As Thomas Piketty has shown, the world wars and the Depression also took a direct toll on capital income in Europe, led to a compression of earnings in the United States, and therefore reduced inequality in total market incomes on both sides of the Atlantic, even apart from redistributive government programs.[18]

Some of the national shifts in policy in response to the Great Depression had an almost random character, depending on the party that happened to be in office when the crisis struck. The Depression discredited incumbent governments whether they were conservative, liberal, or socialist, and often produced reactive movements toward alternatives on either the right or the left.[19] But the Depression was followed by World War II, and the victors in that war overturned the losers' regimes and spread their own institutions and policies. In the United States, the Democratic Party benefited from being out of power when the economy went into a tailspin in the late 1920s. But while Franklin Delano Roosevelt's election in 1932 fit the reactive pattern of Depression-era changes in government, the New Deal he led had far-ranging consequences. It disproved doubts about the resilience of liberal democracies and their capacity for redistributive reform, and it took on global significance because of the role that the United States played in the war and the forging of a liberal international order afterward.

Like many others in his generation, Bell viewed twentieth-century trends as resulting not from special historical circumstances, but rather from a logic of societal development. In some respects, he was undoubtedly correct about that logic of development. As economic productivity increases, the occupational distribution shifts first from agriculture to manufacturing, and then from manufacturing to services, notably services requiring higher levels of skill and education. As technological development becomes more complex, innovation demands scientific knowledge and large, specialized organizations, not just the ingenuity of inventor-entrepreneurs like Thomas Edison, "talented tinkerers" with no scientific training. Although World War II and the Cold War provided the impetus for much of the growth in public spending on science, technology, and higher education, those investments likely would have been forthcoming, sooner or later, for developmental reasons. So, at least in part, there is a good case that the mid-twentieth-century global crises were only the *occasion* for some of the techno-economic changes emphasized in Bell's theory, not their ultimate cause.

But the mid-twentieth-century era misled theorists of the time about the irreversibility of the state's role, particularly in achieving greater equality. What Bell thought should happen—a broader role for government and social planning—agreed with the whole trend of the twentieth century up to that point, and hence he projected it at the core of post-industrial society. For example, citing damage to the environment and other negative externalities, he argued that the "increasing divergence of private costs and social costs" required more government intervention in the market. He expected major public commitments to technology assessment and "the planning of technology." Just as the federal government had created a system of economic indicators to help monitor and manage the economy, so Bell favored creating a system of social indicators to help monitor and manage the society. He had served on an advisory committee during the Lyndon Johnson administration for a "social report" that would be the sociological counterpart to the annual economic report by the president's Council of Economic Advisers. In *The Coming of Post-Industrial Society*, Bell was confident this would happen: "the idea of a social report is one whose time is coming."[20]

Bell's forecast for the business corporation was the flip side of his forecast for a system of social accounts and public planning. At the time he was writing in the early 1970s, business was at a low point in its political influence, and government was enacting new forms of regulation for environmental protection, occupational health and safety, and affirmative action.[21] In a chapter called "The Subordination of the Corporation," Bell wrote that because of "the collective effects of private decisions," public involvement in corporate decisions was "inescapable." While industrial society had been dominated by the "economizing" mode, post-industrial society would rely on a "sociologizing" mode of decision-making that would take two considerations into account: "the conscious establishment of social justice by the inclusion of all persons *into* the society," and the balance between public and private goods. The legitimacy of the corporation, instead of resting on a belief in private property, had come increasingly to rest on performance—the ability to produce more and more goods—but that too was now in question: "A feeling has begun to spread in the country that corporate performance has made the society uglier, dirtier, trashier, more polluted, and noxious. The sense of identity between the self-interest of the corporation and the public interest [during the immediate postwar years] has been replaced by a sense of incongruence."[22]

Bell was hardly naive about the power of business: "Corporate power, clearly, is the predominant power in the society, and the problem is how to limit it." But in the "communal society" that he foresaw, social decision-making mechanisms would somehow emerge; Bell never provided an analysis of the politics that would be required to bring about the submergence of corporate influence. The logic of development would simply prevail: "New and large powers will be vested in administrative boards. New and complex tasks will confront the Congress." Bell thought that corporate shareholders could be treated not as owners, but "as legitimate claimants to some fixed share of the profits of a corporation—and to nothing more." The employees, in contrast, he thought had more of a stake in the corporation and deserved more say in its affairs.[23]

This view is now commonly referred to as the "stakeholder" conception of the corporation, as opposed to the "shareholder" conception. But the stakeholder view was not going to prevail in the United States, at least not for the next half-century.[24] Despite the anticorporate mood of the early 1970s, business was about to rebound in political influence, and the next several decades would see the emergence of a new market for corporate control and a "shareholder value revolution," transforming corporations in precisely the opposite way from what Bell envisioned. Instead of being bound to uphold social responsibilities, corporations were under even more pressure to deliver the maximum return to their shareholders. In the wake of the civil rights movement, a corporate rights movement in the law was once again able to lay claim to new rights, as corporations had been able to do in the late nineteenth century after passage of the Fourteenth Amendment.[25]

The shareholder value revolution and corporate rights movement were only two of many developments in the following decades that strengthened capital and undermined the position of labor. Curiously, although *The Coming of Post-Industrial Society* did not anticipate the rise in economic inequality, the book did recognize some key developments that would produce that result, such as the decline of unions and the growth of offshoring. Bell repeated an argument that he had originally made as a labor reporter for *Fortune* in 1956: for a variety of reasons, including the cost of organizing workers in small factories and shops, unions had hit a ceiling on membership.[26] The post-industrial shift from manufacturing to services would pose "a very serious problem for American labor. The area where it is best organized, manufacture, faces a serious erosion of jobs." The service economy was "very largely a female-centered economy," and women were hard for unions to organize because so many of them did not see their jobs as "permanent" and worked only part-time. Unions' share of the private-sector workforce was already falling; the only area for growth was in the public sector, and there, as elsewhere, elected political leaders were crucial: "Union growth in the United States has always been dependent on favorable government support." In addition, the changing position of the United States in the world economy was undermining labor's position: "The reduction in costs of transport, and the differential in wages, has made it increasingly possible for American multi-national corporations to manufacture significant proportions of components abroad and bring them back here for assembly."[27]

Yet despite all these indications of trouble for labor, Bell wrote that the "older problems of an industrial society have been muted if not 'solved.' " Post-industrial society was opening a new chapter: "In the economy, a labor issue remains. But not in the sociology and culture. To that extent, the changes which are summed up in the post-industrial society may represent a historic metamorphosis in Western society."[28] As it turned out, however, there was no metamorphosis; instead, the old problems of economic inequality returned with a vengeance. Labor's share of national income began a long decline, while capital's share increased, and businesses offloaded risks for retirement income and health costs to their workers by shifting to fixed-contribution pensions and high-deductible health plans, or by shedding those obligations altogether by outsourcing jobs.[29]

The problem here was not simply that, like everyone else at the time, Bell assumed the postwar patterns would continue. His own analysis of the shift to a post-industrial economy should have suggested that the industrial workers losing jobs would not be the same people gaining jobs in technical and professional fields, and that many cities and regions would lose their manufacturing base without having developed a knowledge-based economy. That "post-industrial" could mean deindustrialized is simply not an idea to be found in *The Coming of Post-Industrial Society*. Bell also does not take any note of the difficulties for Blacks and other minorities posed by the loss of well-paid jobs in manufacturing. Since Bell argued that techno-economic change generated an agenda for politics, it would have been entirely consistent for him to suggest an agenda for those on the losing side of post-industrial change. But the agenda that he laid out did not include such concerns except indirectly, in an abstract discussion of theories of justice. In that discussion, Bell praises John Rawls's difference principle, which requires any policy benefiting the better off "also to be to the advantage of those less fortunate," a requirement that Bell might have applied in thinking about the downside of the post-industrial shift.[30]

Another striking omission from *The Coming of Post-Industrial Society* is Bell's inattention to changes in the position of women and the structure of the family, as well as other issues related to gender. The shift from manufacturing to services was expanding opportunities for women's employment; more mothers were already in the labor force, and in 1971, Congress passed national child-care legislation, only to have it vetoed by President Richard

Nixon. But Bell did not make much of these developments, nor did he consider gender-related or family issues in the agenda for policy that post-industrial society was creating. Even in his 1999 foreword, when he recognized the oversight—"The extraordinary change in the status of women . . . was unanticipated twenty-five years ago"—he still had little to say on the subject.[31]

Actually, a writer in *Fortune* in 1956 had called attention to a "revolution in the character of the U.S. labor force" as more married women took paying jobs. In 1940, only 15 percent of married women were in the labor force, but that share climbed to 30 percent by 1956; even more strikingly, only 7 percent of mother with children under five had paying jobs in 1940, but that had jumped to 18.2 percent by 1956. These women, the writer pointed out, were facing two kinds of pay discrimination: the denial of equal wages "for doing the identical work men do" and the downgrading of occupations where women predominated. The author of that article was the young journalist Daniel Bell.[32] So it was not as though he had never written about gender inequality; he just didn't integrate it into his theoretical understanding of post-industrial society.

Bell's general claim that the post-industrial shift posed choices for politics raised questions for comparative analysis: How would different countries respond politically? In studies of comparative capitalism, others subsequently addressed those issues. In contrast to Bell's work (though not necessarily in conflict with it), the comparative research identified variations in economic institutions and national policy that enabled some countries and industrial regions to retain high-value manufacturing. These studies called attention to changes within manufacturing, particularly the shift from mass production to "flexible production" and the development of specialty products and capacities for "mass customization."[33] Work on the varieties of capitalism emphasized the institutional features of industries and labor markets that enabled Germany and other "coordinated market economies" to maintain more strength in manufacturing than the "liberal market economies" in the face of technological change.[34] To be sure, even the countries that successfully retained more industry have also seen a long-term shift in employment to services. In that regard, Bell's forecast was correct; contrary to his critics in the 1980s, post-industrialism was no myth.[35] But when economic change is less abrupt, people are better able to make adjustments, and societies can reduce the human costs to workers and their communities.

The different paths in economic policy taken by post-industrial societies in the late twentieth century also affected the type of service jobs and the extent of income inequality that developed. The social democratic model, exemplified by Sweden, called for high public spending, expansion of public-sector service employment, and relatively equal wages and social protections; the Swedes also invested heavily in education to prepare workers for post-industrial jobs.[36] In contrast, the neoliberal approach, exemplified by Thatcherism in Britain and Reaganism in the United States, called for cuts in public spending, privatization of public services, reduced union power, and growth in private-sector service jobs and greater wage inequality. In yet a third approach, Christian Democratic governments in continental Europe initially sought to maintain labor and social insurance protections but, unlike the Nordic countries, sought to hold the line on spending on public services and suffered persistently high unemployment rates. Summing up this pattern in a 1998 article, Torber Iversen and Anne Wren argued that the service economy in post-industrial societies confronted governments with a "trilemma"—that is, a three-way choice among employment growth, income equality, and budgetary restraint, in which it was possible to achieve only two of those objectives. The social democratic model sacrificed budgetary restraint, the neoliberal approach sacrificed income equality, and the Christian Democratic model sacrificed employment growth.[37]

Since the turn of the century, however, the countries that followed the Christian Democratic model, and to some extent even the Nordic countries, have sought to increase employment and labor-market flexibility by reducing social insurance and other protections for certain types of employment, such as work on temporary contracts. They have thereby institutionalized a split between labor-market insiders and outsiders.[38] Although not the same as Thatcherism, these "dualization" policies reflect a shift toward the neoliberal pole in economic policy that has persisted into the twenty-first century.

NEOLIBERALISM AND THE
POST-INDUSTRIAL SHIFT

Under the best of circumstances, the post-industrial transition would have been difficult. The decline of manufacturing implied the destruction of the livelihood of tens of millions of workers. Without more education, most of those workers had no realistic chance of reproducing the same living standards with the low-paying jobs available to them in the private service economy. Governments, however, were not powerless in this situation. As the Swedish example showed, they could expand public services, invest in a high-skilled workforce, and maintain relatively high levels of economic equality. The Germans were able to limit the losses in manufacturing and thereby slow the rate of post-industrial change.

But neoliberal policies aggravated the problems of the post-industrial transition. In an era when hundreds of millions of workers in China, the former Soviet bloc, and the Third World were being added to the world economy, free-trade agreements sped up the losses of manufacturing jobs and undermined the bargaining power of workers in the high-income economies. Just when those workers were being displaced from industry, labor unions were in decline and governments were cutting social protections. Neoliberal policies imposed the costs of the post-industrial transition on those with little power to resist.

The term "neoliberalism" has been used so loosely, and often so tendentiously, that we need to take a moment to consider how broadly it applies. "Neoliberalism," Daniel Rodgers writes in a trenchant critique, "is the linguistic omnivore of our times, a neologism that threatens to swallow up all the other words around it." He spells out what's wrong with the term: "Used casually 'neoliberalism' bundles, abstracts, and totalizes. It masks vagueness under faux precision. It imputes a trajectory to history that is overdetermined and simplistic. It smears; it conjures up witches." But turning to what's right with the word, Rodgers says that it "restores economy to the forefront of critical analysis . . . Above all its asset lies in its capaciousness. 'Neoliberalism,' writes Julia Ott, 'references much of what distinguishes our contemporary moment in history, both in this country and around the world.' "[39]

Neoliberalism does reference "much of what distinguishes our contemporary moment," but that also should alert us to the problems of recency bias and overgeneralization that I mentioned with regard to mid-twentieth-century social theory. The Great Depression seemed to discredit laissez-faire forever, and World War II and the mixed economy of the Cold War era created the illusion of an irreversible acceptance of a redistributive liberal state. In parallel fashion, the global economic crisis of the 1970s discredited incumbent governments and prevailing ideas—except that this time, liberal and social democratic policies lost public confidence and the advocates of free markets seized their opportunity. This

reverse shift has similarly lent itself to overgeneralization, especially because of the late-twentieth-century changes in China and
collapse of Soviet communism. It's not just market triumphalists
who connect the communist collapse with the repudiation of
Keynesianism; so does a Marxist like David Harvey, who (in an
argument with rather hazy causal logic) sees the developments in
both the East and West as common responses by capitalists, or
would-be capitalists, to a crisis of accumulation.[40]

The notion of a global neoliberal age, however, sweeps too
much under the same loose concept of neoliberalism. The Soviet
Union's collapse and China's opening to markets stemmed from
chronic, systemic failures of state-controlled economies, including
an inability to keep pace with the innovations in technology and
organization in the West that were leading to a new post-industrial era. "Neoliberal" does not describe the highly centralized,
authoritarian systems that have emerged in Russia and China. In
contrast, the turn toward neoliberalism under Thatcher and Reagan was precipitated by a crisis in the 1970s of a less fundamental
kind, and it led not to a systemic change, but to a shift in policies, an aggressive effort to use the state to create new markets and
strengthen the power of capital.

In fact, neoliberal governments have faced severe limits in how
far they have been able to go. Neoliberal policies did not reduce
state spending as a share of gross domestic product (GDP); in
1997, when Britain's Conservatives finally left office after eighteen
years, government spending stood at 42 percent of GDP, about
the same as when Thatcher was first elected. The National Health
Service remained, as did Social Security in the United States.[41]
But while neoliberal governments have been unable to undo the
welfare state, they have kept it from expanding and adapting to
meeting the new risks and insecurities of a post-industrial economy. Center-left governments, such as those of Tony Blair and

Gordon Brown in Britain and Bill Clinton and Barack Obama in the United States, sought to address those new sources of insecurity and inequality but were limited in what they could accomplish. They were not progenitors of the neoliberal project, but they were unable, and in critical respects unwilling, to confront and overturn it.

In his 1973 book, Bell envisioned post-industrial society as an extension of postwar European social democracy, including greater planning and stakeholder capitalism—the direction in which American liberalism appeared to be moving at the time. But the neoliberal turn shaped a post-industrialism of a different kind. Consider what Bell imagined would be the effects of techno-economic change on social structure and institutions. He saw scientists as the "chief resource of the post-industrial society," expected the professional and technical class to become preeminent, believed that the nonprofit sector would become increasingly important, and considered the universities—by which he meant the top research universities—to be the "primary institution" of post-industrial society.[42]

These tendencies, however, have run up against contradictory developments, including the financialization of the economy, the commercialization of the nonprofit sector, and an entrepreneurial revival. Some expansion of financial services was to be expected as part of the general growth of the service economy. But the deregulation of financial markets and the shareholder value revolution elevated finance to a more dominant position and a higher status than it had during the mid-twentieth century, when banking was a notoriously boring field for second-rate minds. From the 1980s on, finance increased dramatically as a share of GDP, claimed a larger share of the economy's total profits, provided the basis for staggering top incomes, and—not surprisingly—became the career of choice for many of the top graduates of the top universities.

If scientists and professionals were preeminent, those graduates flocking to Wall Street were not aware of it. Financialization had far-reaching economic significance; the inflow of capital into the United States and resulting expansion of credit helped defuse the economic crisis that had erupted in the mid-1970s.[43]

Commercialization advanced far into the nonprofit sector. Compared to most European countries, the United States has long relied more on private nonprofits than on governmental institutions in such areas as health care and higher education. But in the late twentieth century, the health-care system saw a shift from the dominance of a profession (physicians) to increasing corporate control. For-profit corporations made substantial inroads into health services, and even nonprofit health-care systems created for-profit subsidiaries and came to operate on a market-driven basis. Public health planning agencies were disbanded, and the field of health planning became corporate health planning.[44] In education, for-profit colleges and charter schools expanded, and even though universities remained almost entirely nonprofit, both research and educational programs became more geared to market concerns.

The new high-tech industries, the heart of the post-industrial economy, also deviated from the expectations that Bell held out for the preeminence of the professional and technical classes. The dominant ideals in the tech world have been entrepreneurial rather than professional. By the 1970s, the entrepreneur was supposed to be a figure of the past, superseded by management-run corporations with superior organization and access to capital. But the development of venture capital helped support a new generation of entrepreneurs; innovation, rather than being concentrated in big corporate research centers like Bell Labs, now often came from start-ups, while the share of patents going to *Fortune* 500 companies fell.[45]

The occupations in the information economy have also not developed along the lines of the organized professions with standardized educational and licensing requirements or strong professional associations, even though the work requires considerable expertise. The scope-of-practice rules typically demanded by professions are antithetical to the flexibility prized by high-tech companies.[46] In this respect, the postbureaucratic organizations of the tech sector are postprofessional, often disdaining formal credentials. Workers in high-tech and related fields have also come to accept higher risks in pursuit of what they believe could be higher rewards. A study of labor in new media and fashion observes: "The new economy's cutting edge—and its true social innovation—is the production of a new labor force that is more 'entrepreneurial' than previous generations of workers."[47]

Bell's conception of the emerging role of knowledge focused on higher-level, elite functions. He thought the centrality of "theoretical knowledge" was what critically distinguished post-industrial society. The "major intellectual and sociological problems of the post-industrial society," he argued, were "those of 'organized complexity'—the management of large-scale systems." Information technology, for Bell, was chiefly an instrument of decision-making and control; he focused attention on what he called "intellectual technology"—that is, technology involving "the substitution of algorithms (problem-solving rules) for intuitive judgments."[48] This was an important insight: algorithmic decision-making has indeed become central to the working of post-industrial society. Bell's framing of the information revolution, however, underestimated the potential for other kinds of change. Writing originally in the age of the mainframe computer, he did not anticipate how personal computers and the internet would put computational and communication power in the hands of hundreds of millions of people, or how new social relations, new publics, and new markets would develop in the online world. Even later, in the 1980s and 1990s, he did not fundamentally recast his thinking.[49]

As the dominant forces in digital innovation moved from the state to the market in the late twentieth century, they replicated the general pattern of institutional change in the United States. From the 1940s to the early 1970s, the federal government financed and guided most of the development of computers and electronics, largely via the U.S. Defense Department. It was a defense program, the Advanced Research Projects Agency (ARPA), that funded and supervised the creation of the forerunner to the internet (ARPANET). The state's direct involvement began to decline, however, in the late 1970s and 1980s, coinciding with the neoliberal shift toward deregulation and privatization. The internet itself was opened to commercial development in the early 1990s, and since then, the online economy has grown at a time when federal policymakers were backing away from regulation, antitrust enforcement, and public ownership, the three chief means of keeping corporate power in check.

As a result, the online economy has changed dramatically from the open and decentralized form that it appeared to be taking in the 1990s. Over the past twenty years, the emerging tech giants— Google, Facebook, Amazon, Apple, and Microsoft—have been able to acquire potential rivals, expand into adjacent markets, and achieve overwhelming dominance. Now in control of critical platforms for information, communication, and commerce, they have set the rules for whole ecosystems in the online world and thereby acquired extraordinary economic and political power. In the absence of any regulation of their use of personal data, the leading companies, particularly Google and Facebook, have created a new form of enterprise that Shoshana Zuboff calls "surveillance capitalism." Providing services at little or no charge, the firms use the data that they gather on individuals to create new "prediction products" and capacities for modifying the behavior of consumers and voters.[50]

The post-industrial shift was supposed to provide the basis for the growth of information-related professional fields, but the effects have been mixed and, in one respect, a disaster. With the rise of online media and the tech giants' domination of online advertising, newspapers and other publications have lost their primary source of revenue, plunging journalism into a crisis at a moment when social media have become vectors of disinformation and extremism. The number of professional journalists has declined sharply throughout the post-industrial world.[51]

The internet of the 1990s and early 2000s was neoliberalism's greatest triumph and validation. Released from government control, the internet appeared to be empowering individuals to create new connections and new wealth. Now it has become an illustration of how neoliberal policies and the digital revolution have gone wrong. The libertarian dreamworld has turned into a playground for monopolists and propagandists, and as has happened so often in the past, private corporate power has arisen in the absence of government action and is now generating a backlash.

The backlash against the tech industry is only one of many indications of an emerging political and ideological shift. Free-trade agreements have lost support on both right and left. Right-wing populist nationalism is moving toward a more authoritarian state, while liberals and progressives are pushing for more aggressively redistributive policies to combat inequality. One way or the other, the sun may be setting on neoliberalism.

Here lies a crucial difference between neoliberalism and post-industrialism as definitions of the age. The two terms operate at different levels—one at the level of political and ideological currents, the other at the level of socioeconomic development. The neoliberal turn has left its imprint on the post-industrial transformation, but it has been subject to limits and may be nearing its end. The post-industrial transformation itself is irreversible. There is only the question of what kind of post-industrial future we will have.

BELL'S LEGACY IN SOCIAL THEORY

One morning in the fall of 2009, I was preparing a lecture on theories of social change for an introductory sociology course, when it occurred to me that although I could not discuss my criticisms of Marx or Weber with the theorists themselves, I could do that with Daniel Bell. So I gave him a call and, in a wide-ranging conversation of about 45 minutes, raised what seemed to me several clear problems with *The Coming of Post-Industrial Society*. Wouldn't he grant, for example, that societies weren't doing the "planning of technology" that he had expected?

But Bell would have none of it. He pointed to the efforts to stop global warming and control the future of the climate, which involve planning of technology. Of course, he said (I'm quoting him almost verbatim), it's not planning in the old Soviet-style sense; planning has now moved to the international level in climate negotiations. He went on to place himself in an intellectual tradition going back to the Enlightenment that emphasizes the role of knowledge as an innovative force in society. And I went away thinking, who of us would not like at the age of 90, if we should live that long, to be able to defend our ideas as effectively as he did that morning, about a year before he died.

As those who argued with him know, however, Bell was almost too good at defending his ideas, and not good enough at revising them in the face of complicating developments. I am not concerned especially about mistaken forecasts. The more important question is what a half-century's experience since *The Coming of Post-Industrial Society* tells us about Bell's theoretical framework, its limitations, and its strengths.

Some of the shortcomings in his work were flaws of execution—serious flaws, but not decisive for the fate of the theory. *The Coming of Post-Industrial Society* ignored the human costs of the post-industrial transition; like so many in his generation, Bell had blind spots regarding the implications of post-industrial change for women and racial minorities. The top-down perspective on knowledge and information technology reflected the same limitations in seeing how post-industrial change might affect people from the bottom up. But as serious as these limitations are, they require only a more complete analysis of the post-industrial transformation.

Another shortcoming has to do with Bell's understanding of the relationship of politics to technology and the economy. Bell insists that he is not a technological determinist: technology does not, in his account, determine culture or politics, but it does exert an overwhelming power in economic change. He presents knowledge and technology as the shaping forces of the economy, and therefore of post-industrial society, without considering how politics and ideology shape knowledge and technology themselves. Bell did claim, rightly, that politics is ultimately decisive, but he gave politics only a secondary role after techno-economic change sets the agenda. He ignored the possibility that politics—the neoliberal turn, for example—could create a different agenda. This is a case where what's right with Bell's theory—his recognition of the primacy of politics—could have fixed what's wrong with his execution. His conception of techno-economic change needed more political economy and sociotechnical analysis at the front end.

Still, Bell's framework for understanding socioeconomic development and forecasting change has a great deal to commend it.

Remember that he is talking about ideal-types, which by their nature are simplified models that take into account only a limited number of variables and do not pretend to describe every aspect of a society or an institution, much less to predict all their interactions. Bell's aim in using these ideal types is to provide a coherent, parsimonious account of the working-out of certain core relationships and central tendencies. These fundamentally have to do with how growth in knowledge and technology affects the economy and social structure: the sectoral shifts from agriculture to manufacturing to services, with concomitant implications for the occupational distribution and more complex, specialized organization; the increasing centrality of theoretical knowledge, and therefore of the professional and technical class able to create, interpret, and use it; and the pressure that greater complexity creates for higher levels of social and political coordination. This is basically an evolutionary theory of economy and society.

While seeing economic change as substantially driven by knowledge and technology, however, Bell draws the line at extending the chain of causality into politics and culture. In this respect, the theory is open-ended. He wisely rejects the premise that societies are so well integrated that all the parts fit together; instead, he argues for a "disjunction of realms" and the possibility that different institutional spheres conflict with one another.

Let's set aside Bell's specific argument, which I do not find convincing, that there is a contradiction between contemporary cultural sphere and capitalism. At most, there is a *paradox*—that is, an apparent conflict between logics, which, on deeper reflection, turn out to be wholly consistent—not a contradiction, which would imply a negation and require one or the other to change. Although Bell's term "axial principles" has not caught on, the idea that societies have conflicting "institutional logics" plays an important and valuable part in contemporary social analysis.

The commercialization of the nonprofit sphere in health care and higher education, for example, creates a conflict between the institutional logics of the market and those of science, the academy, and the professions. In this respect, neoliberal tendencies do not simply govern the era—they create its characteristic conflicts.

The Coming of Post-Industrial Society had as its subtitle *A Venture in Social Forecasting*, and it is partly on this basis that it ought to be judged. Recall that Bell was talking about "an 'as if,' a fiction, a logical construction of what *could* be." The appropriate criterion for evaluating that kind of forecast is not whether all the specifics were correct, but whether understanding it in the 1970s was of use in planning for the future—and clearly it was. What Bell got right about the forces of change was enormously important. Even today, his framework, with its emphasis on knowledge as a creative force, is more illuminating than analyses more narrowly focused on information technology.

Here I come back to the point that *The Coming of Post-Industrial Society* was as much a normative work as a venture in forecasting. This is especially clear in his discussions of the need for social planning in what he expected to be a "communal society," where individual interests, if left to themselves, would create havoc. It is clear in his preference for a "sociologizing" mode of decision-making based on "the conscious establishment of social justice by the inclusion of all persons *into* the society" and a balance between public and private goods. It is clear as well in his arguments for subordinating corporations to the public interest and for giving more power to stakeholders than to shareholders.[52] Bell was proposing a different kind of post-industrial society, a more communal one, than the version we have known. But, in that respect, the future that Bell believed *would* happen is still something that *could* happen, and his example of global warming in that conversation with me a decade ago is a reminder of how urgently we need it to happen. Politics may prevent that vision from being realized, as it has so far in the case of climate change, a warning about the tragic possibilities of our time. But in the long run, for humanity's sake, we should all hope that Daniel Bell was right about the communally responsible post-industrial society that lies within our power to create.

NOTES

1. Daniel Bell, *The Coming of Post-Industrial Society: A Venture in Social Forecasting* (New York: Basic Books, 1973), 14 (italics in original). All references to *The Coming of Post-Industrial Society* are to the 1973 edition, except for the forewords to the 1976 and 1999 editions.

2. For the various ways in which Bell and others conceived of "post-industrial society" in the period, see Howard Brick, "Optimism of the Mind: Imagining Postindustrial Society in the 1960s and 1970s," *American Quarterly* 44, no. 3 (1992): 348–380.

3. According to a Google Ngram, which is a limited tally of word counts in books, the term "post-industrial" rose first in the 1970s and led "neoliberal" in use until about 1995, when "neoliberal" moved ahead. For histories of neoliberal thought, see Jan-Werner Müller, *Contesting Democracy: Political Ideas in Twentieth-Century Europe* (New Haven, CT: Yale University Press, 2011), 150–154, 221–222; Angus Burgin, *The Great Persuasion: Reinventing Free Markets since the Depression* (Cambridge, MA: Harvard University Press, 2012), and Daniel Stedman Jones, *Masters of the Universe: Hayek, Friedman, and the Birth of Neoliberal Politics* (Princeton, NJ: Princeton University Press, 2012).

4. Bell, *The Coming of Post-Industrial Society*, 128.

5. Bell, *The Coming of Post-Industrial Society*, 114, x; Daniel Bell, "The Axial Age of Technology, Foreword 1999," in *The Coming of Post-Industrial Society: A Venture in Social Forecasting* (New York: Basic Books, 1999), xxx (hereafter "1999 ed.").

6. Bell, *The Coming of Post-Industrial Society*, x,

7. Bell, *The Coming of Post-Industrial Society*, 116.

8. Bell, *The Coming of Post-Industrial Society*, 14.

9. Bell, *The Coming of Post-Industrial Society*, 212.

10. Bell, *The Coming of Post-Industrial Society*, 44, 263, 360.

11. Bell, *The Coming of Post-Industrial Society*, 75.

12. See Paul Starr, *Entrenchment: Wealth, Power, and the Constitution of Democratic Societies* (New Haven, CT: Yale University Press, 2019), especially chap. 1.

13. Bell, *The Coming of Post-Industrial Society*, 73, 75–76, 112–114; for Bell's clearest statement on this point, see his "Foreword: 1976," (1999 ed.) LXVIII–XC.

14. Bell, *The Coming of Post-Industrial Society*, 129, 115.

15. Karl Polanyi, *The Great Transformation* (Boston: Beacon, 1957 [1944]); Mark Blyth, *Great Transformations: Economic Ideas and Institutional Change in the Twentieth Century* (New York: Cambridge University Press, 2002), 4.

16. Simon Kuznets, "Economic Growth and Income Inequality," *American Economic Review* 45, no. 1 (1955): 1–28; James O'Connor, *The Fiscal Crisis of the State* (New York: St. Martin's, 1973).

17. This paragraph and the next draw on my discussion of what I call "The Great Conjuncture" in *Entrenchment*, 146–157.

18. Thomas Piketty, *Capital in the Twenty-First Century* (Cambridge, MA: Harvard University Press, 2014).

19. See Christopher H. Achen and Larry M. Bartels, *Democracy for Realists: Why Elections Do Not Produce Responsive Government* (Princeton, NJ: Princeton University Press, 2017), chap. 7.

20. Bell, *The Coming of Post-Industrial Society*, 273–274, 26, 329.

21. See David Vogel, *Fluctuating Fortunes: The Political Power of Business in America* (New York: Basic Books, 1989).

22. Bell, *The Coming of Post-Industrial Society*, 286, 283, 272.

23. Bell, *The Coming of Post-Industrial Society*, 270, 286, 295–296.

24. While not integrating this development into his conception of post-industrial society, Bell later took note of it in the 1996 afterword to *The Cultural Contradictions of Capitalism*: "In recent years, the social realm has been shrinking and the 'naked' economic relation has been assuming priority, especially in the rights of the 'shareholder' (even though the shareholder is an individual who moves in and out of a company quickly, seeking the highest financial return) as against the 'stakeholder,' who may be an individual who has worked for a company for twenty years only to

find his or her place wiped out overnight." Daniel Bell, *The Culture Contradictions of Capitalism* (New York: Basic Books, 1996), 285.

25. Adam Winkler, *We the Corporations: How American Businesses Won Their Civil Rights* (New York: Liveright, 2018).

26. Daniel Bell, "No Boom for Unions," *Fortune* (June 1956), 136–137, 174–186.

27. Bell, *The Coming of Post-Industrial Society*, 139, 159, 146, 140, 158–159.

28. Bell, *The Coming of Post-Industrial Society*, 116, 164.

29. Tali Kristal, "Good Times, Bad Times: Postwar Labor's Share of National Income in Capitalist Democracies," *American Sociological Review* (2010), 75: 729–763; David Weil, *The Fissured Workplace* (Cambridge, MA: Harvard University Press, 2014); Jacob S. Hacker, *The Great Risk Shift* (New York: Oxford University Press, 2008).

30. Bell, *The Coming of Post-Industrial Society*, 440–442; John Rawls, *A Theory of Justice* (Cambridge, MA: Harvard University Press, 1971), 75.

31. Bell, *The Coming of Post-Industrial Society*, 146; Bell, "The Axial Age of Technology, Foreword 1999," lxxii.

32. Daniel Bell, "The Great Back-to-Work Movement," *Fortune* (July 1956), 91–93, 168–172.

33. Michael J. Piore and Charles F. Sabel, *The Second Industrial Divide* (New York: Basic Books, 1984).

34. Peter A. Hall and David Soskice, eds., *Varieties of Capitalism: The Institutional Foundations of Comparative Advantage* (New York: Oxford University Press, 2001).

35. Stephen S. Cohen and John Zyman, *Manufacturing Matters: The Myth of a Post-Industrial Economy* (New York: Basic Books, 1987).

36. Jonas Pontusson, "Once Again a Model: Nordic Social Democracy in a Globalized World," in *What's Left of the Left: Democrats and Social Democrats in Challenging Times*, ed. James Cronin, George Ross, and James Shoch (Durham, NC: Duke University Press, 2011), 89–115.

37. Torben Iversen and Anne Wren, "Equality, Employment, and Budgetary Restraint: The Trilemma of the Service Economy," *World Politics* 50 (1998): 507–546; for later follow-up, see Anne Wren, ed., *The Political Economy of the Service Transition* (New York: Oxford University Press, 2013).

38. Bruno Palier and Kathleen Thelen, "Dualization and Institutional Complementarities: Industrial Relations, Labor Market and Welfare State Changes in France and Germany," in *The Age of Dualization*, ed. Patrick Emmenegger et al. (New York: Oxford University Press, 2012), 201–225;

Martin Seeleib-Kaiser, "The End of the Conservative German Welfare State Model," *Social Policy and Administration* 50 (2016): 219–240.

39. Daniel Rodgers, "The Uses and Abuses of 'Neoliberalism,'" *Dissent* (Winter 2018), at https://www.dissentmagazine.org/article/uses-and-abuses-neoliberalism -debate, and Daniel Rodgers, "Reply: Fault Lines," https://www.dissent magazine.org/blog/neoliberalism-forum-daniel-rodgers-reply. (Rodgers's essay and response to critics were part of a forum in which Julia Ott was a participant.)

40. David Harvey, *A Brief History of Neoliberalism* (New York: Oxford University Press, 2005), 14–19.

41. On the limits of the neoliberal reversal, see "Entrenching Progressive Change," chap. 5 of Starr, *Entrenchment*.

42. Bell, *The Coming of Post-Industrial Society*, 221, 15, 269, 245–246.

43. Greta R. Krippner, *Capitalizing on Crisis: The Political Origins of the Rise of Finance* (Cambridge, MA: Harvard University Press, 2011).

44. This development was already evident in the decade after Bell's book. See Paul Starr, *The Social Transformation of American Medicine* (New York: Basic Books, 1982).

45. Fred Block and Matthew R. Keller, "Where Do Innovations Come From? Transformations in the US Economy, 1970–2006," *Socio-Economic Review* 7, no. 3 (2009): 459–483.

46. Paul Starr, "The Post-Industrial Limits to Professionalization," in *Oxford Handbook of Expertise and Democratic Politics*, ed. Gil Eyal and Tom Medvetz (New York: Oxford University Press, forthcoming).

47. Gina Neff, Elizabeth Wissinger, and Sharon Zukin, "Entrepreneurial Labor Among Cultural Producers: 'Cool' Jobs in 'Hot' Industries," *Social Semiotics* 15 (2005): 307–334.

48. Bell, *The Coming of Post-Industrial Society*, 29.

49. Bell's later writings take note of the "merger" of computers and telecommunications, but they still did not explore in any depth the implications for communications and exchange. See "Teletext and Technology" (1977), in *The Winding Passage: Essays and Sociological Journeys, 1960–1980* (Cambridge, MA: Abt Books, 1980), 34–65; "The Social Framework of the Information Society," in *The Microelectronics Revolution*, ed. Tom Forester (Cambridge, MA: MIT Press, 1981), 500–549; and "The Axial Age of Technology, Foreword 1999."

50. Shoshana Zuboff, *The Age of Surveillance Capitalism: The Fight for a Human Future at the New Frontier of Power* (New York: Public Affairs Press, 2019).

51. See my discussions in "An Unexpected Crisis: The News Media in Post-industrial Democracies," *International Journal of Press/Politics* 17 (2012): 234–242; and "The Flooded Zone: How We Became More Vulnerable to Disinformation in the Digital Era," in *The Disinformation Age*, ed. Lance Bennett and Steven Livingston (New York: Cambridge University Press, 2020), 67–91.

52. For perhaps Bell's clearest exposition of his moral and political standpoint, see his "Foreword: 1978," in *The Cultural Contradictions of Capitalism*, 20th Anniversary ed. (New York: Basic Books, 1996 [1976]), xi–xxix.

7

ASSESSING DANIEL BELL
IN THE AGE OF BIG TECH

MARGARET O'MARA

Both Daniel Bell and Alvin Toffler gained their fame for ambitious efforts to define a new era that they claimed the United States was entering in the late twentieth century. From Jewish New York boyhoods and left-wing politics to stints as labor journalists at *Fortune* and writing about the future of technology and society, they followed similar paths—up to a point. Toffler had more success with the general public, beginning with his 1970 bestseller *Future Shock*, an operatic, overwrought, and, yes, sometimes prescient book about the acceleration of social change and transience of relationships, lifestyles, and organizations. Bell was a more cautious forecaster, an academic sociologist rather than an evangelizing futurist, and, unlike Toffler, a cultural conservative rather than a countercultural adventurer. He had little patience for the "popularizer" Toffler, the purveyor of what Bell termed "the vogue of 'future schlock.' " Toffler is cited by name twice in *The Coming of Post-Industrial Society*, both times in rather dismissive footnotes.[1]

But while the more sober of the two, Bell was hardly reluctant to make bold claims. "I am a specialist in generalizations," he often said. Bell gave us the term "the post-industrial society," while Toffler gave us "information overload" and "the third wave." As the two men's respective stars rose, the American cultural establishment sided firmly with Bell. The *New York Times* declared the sociologist "an intellectual's intellectual," while the *Washington Post* considered *Future Shock* "a high school term paper gone berserk."[2]

Those evaluations were reversed, however, in the global technology industry and its de facto capital, Silicon Valley. The peripatetic Toffler had an appeal to the business titans of the Valley that Bell, from his Ivied perch 3,000 miles away, did not. The difference in their reputations says a great deal about the tech leaders' understanding of the world and the role they were playing.

"I have read Toffler's *Future Shock* over and over," Intel and Apple marketing guru Regis McKenna noted in the early 1980s, around the time that his client and protégé Steve Jobs was making the media rounds using talking points that sounded much like Toffler's techno-evangelism. As a college student, future America Online chief Steve Case picked up a copy of the second volume in Toffler's futurist trilogy, 1980's *The Third Wave*, which sketched out the ways in which computer technology would reorganize and reanimate communities on more humane, egalitarian terms. "I read that and knew he was right," reflected the man who would build one of the early leaders in online media.[3]

The Toffler-tech mutual admiration society also included two of the industry's most important political champions of the 1990s, Al Gore and Newt Gingrich. As an unknown assistant professor of history in the early 1970s, Gingrich busted his travel budget to fly across the country to hear Toffler speak, and he remained an ardent fan and confidante of both Alvin and Heidi Toffler from then on.[4]

With such enthusiastic and well-placed boosters, Tofflerism percolated into the broader techno-utopian thinking that propelled the Valley from the personal-computer era forward, even among those who had never read the books themselves. Toffler told a story that reinforced many Silicon Valley technologists' worldview: that the computer made everything new, that history didn't matter, that they were changing the world.

Amid its information-overloaded prose, Toffler's 1970 book predicted a number of things about the digital age that Bell either omitted or rejected in his contemporaneous "venture in social forecasting." Toffler wrote of the disintegration of bureaucracies and mass culture, replaced by an "ad-hocracy" that anticipates today's roiling and often precarious capitalist landscape of gig work and shift scheduling by algorithm. "Far from fastening the grip of bureaucracy on civilization more tightly than before," Toffler wrote, "automation leads to its overthrow."[5]

The accelerating pace of life would alter personal realms as well. Instead of a lifetime of work for one employer or in one profession, there would be "serial careers"; instead of marital monogamy, there would be "serial marriage." Rather than considering this development socially destabilizing, Toffler welcomed it with excitement. "We shall introduce irregularity, suspense, unpredictability—in a word, novelty, into what was once as regular and certain as the seasons."[6]

In sharp contrast, Bell's sober-minded account sketched out a post-industrial world rooted in existing institutions, where men of science were scholars and technocrats rather than cowboy capitalists, where people were assumed to live lives of permanence rather than transience. Written against a 1960s backdrop of missile gaps and moon shots, his work failed to anticipate what neoliberalism enabled from the late 1970s forward: the dismantlement of state institutions to a point that tech companies and platforms would step in to replace (in a privatized, piecemeal fashion) some of the goods and services once provided by or regulated by government. He presumed—quite reasonably, given the time in which he was writing—that an expanding public sector, not the private corporation, would be the site and agent through which such dilemmas will be resolved.

In contrast to Toffler's ebullient and counterculture-friendly predictions of disrupted and liberated sexual and social relationships, Bell makes no mention of the sociocultural transformations of the age in *The Coming of Postindustrial Society*. (His omission may have been due to his prudish disapproval of all of it—something that becomes clear when he finally addresses the counterculture in his later work.) No wonder the antiestablishment baby boomer business titans of Silicon Valley tech gravitated to Toffler instead.[7]

Yet, precisely because of Bell's emphasis on government's role, many of his ideas stand up today as a historical account of Silicon Valley and a useful basis for interrogating today's Big Tech moment. Only a few years ago, the message that history, or politics, still mattered to the future of tech was a hard notion to sell among the ping-pong tables and snack stations of prosperous Silicon Valley companies. Entrenched, too, was the mythos of the scrappy start-up, making it hard to recognize that tech has been, and continues to be, the domain of very large firms.

Donald J. Trump's unexpected and software-propelled victory in the 2016 U.S. presidential election and the growing recognition of the power exercised over billions of citizen-consumers by tech's "Fearsome Five"—Amazon, Apple, Facebook, Google, and Microsoft—have challenged these presumptions. Toffleresque techo-optimism remains, but its adherents are more defensive. Now, perhaps, it is time to give Daniel Bell's ideas a second look in an effort to understand where the tech industry has come from and where it is taking us.

SILICON VALLEY AS POSTINDUSTRIAL SOCIETY, 1940–1970

Despite its carefully cultivated reputation as a breeding ground for future-tense iconoclasts, Silicon Valley's origins lie precisely in the staid mid-twentieth-century social and political structures that Bell described in *The Coming of Post-Industrial Society*. The tech hub that grew in the Santa Clara Valley of California after World War II was a creature of the early Cold War military-industrial complex and of the ideas and institutions expanded and empowered by it: defense and national security agencies, research universities, and the electronics and aerospace industries. It also was a product of something largely unmentioned by Bell, but that he assumed would continue: the broader midcentury American welfare state, especially its Californian variety, in which high levels of taxation and relatively generous spending undergirded robust public education systems (primary, secondary, and higher education), as well as social and physical infrastructure that aided upward professional mobility, particularly for white males of the suburban middle class.

When much of the United States was still very much driven by manufacturing, the Valley already was home to an intense concentration of what Bell identified as "a new class, hitherto unknown in society, of the engineer and the technician," filled with adherents of what he termed a "new definition of rationality . . . which emphasizes functional relations and the quantitative," and an early and notable hub of the "new science-based industries" on which so much of his forecasting focused. The early Valley was, in fact, a hyperexample of these characteristics because, unlike in Boston or New York, tech was the only game in town.[8]

Until the 1940s, the Santa Clara Valley was an agricultural place whose generously sized Mexican *ranchos* became ideal vehicles for large-scale fruit production and processing. San Jose, its largest settlement, was a dusty farm town. The train from San Francisco was too slow and irregular for a feasible daily commute. The only thing that set the Valley apart was the presence of Stanford University, opened in 1891 by Leland Stanford, a grieving railroad mogul, and his wife Jane in memory of their late teenage son. By the end of its first half century, the university had established a solid reputation in disciplines such as electrical engineering, and a few faculty and alumni had established small electronics firms nearby, but Stanford lagged its East Coast peers in rank and visibility.

The Cold War defense spending that washed over California—including an unprecedented federal investment in university-based research and education—changed everything. Stanford's postwar administrators reorganized the university to meet the surging needs of Big Science, pumping up physics and establishing specialized expertise in areas of advanced electronics that were key to the burgeoning defense push. The university once viewed as a rich man's folly became home to a major defense-electronics laboratory, multiple federally funded research projects, and a government-sponsored linear accelerator. Southern California–based Lockheed moved its Missiles and Space division to a former fruit orchard in nearby Sunnyvale in 1954, rooting a mammoth and largely top-secret electronics research operation that remained the Valley's largest employer into the 1980s.[9]

The twin magnets of Stanford and Lockheed pulled multiple East Coast–based electronics and computer firms to establish branch operations nearby. While the aerospace-driven defense economies of Los Angeles and Seattle built big, the Valley created small electronics and communications devices, a specialization that proved particularly lucrative as the American space race moved into high gear in the 1960s. By the middle of that decade, the Valley was home not only to outposts of companies headquartered elsewhere, but to a growing cluster of silicon semiconductor companies whose early growth had been buoyed by contracts from the National Aeronautics and Space Administration (NASA).

Physically and psychically removed from the nation's political and economic capitals, the Valley became a techno-entrepreneurial Galapagos, evolving distinctive breeds of companies and service firms devoted to the business of small electronics and networked communications. These firms also exhibited promising tendencies toward what Bell identified as "the sociologizing mode," adopting nonhierarchical organization charts and generously distributed stock options as signals of their commitment to a set of more communal, altruistic values than the typical midcentury corporation.[10]

Setting the tone were the Valley's original home-grown entrepreneurs, Bill Hewlett and David Packard, who modeled their eponymous company on the meritocratic structure of the engineering lab, trumpeting their method of "management by walking around," and declaring that a company needed to be about more than making money. As Packard once said to his employees, "We have to go deeper to find the real reasons for our being."[11]

Here, too, was evidence of Bell's argument of the waning power and relevance of trade unionism—although local resistance to unions was not only structural, but ideological. Under the rubric of "the greater good" as defined by Hewlett Packard (HP) and other local tech companies, the presence of unions would signal that something had gone wrong, and their founders and executives fiercely resisted any efforts to organize their shops. In the brave new world of tech, labor and management were supposed to be on the same side: worker solidarity salved by stock options, labor discontent solved by quitting and taking another job at the firm across the street.[12]

ECONOMIZING OVER SOCIOLOGIZING, 1970–2000

By the time *The Coming of Post-Industrial Society* landed on store shelves in 1973, however, the Valley's political economy had already started to change. Late-1960s defense cutbacks jolted the local economy. Opposition to the Vietnam War dulled the interest among a new generation of technologists in having anything to do with the military-industrial complex. The Valley's focus shifted toward private markets and a growing cadre of local companies that were taking advantage of emerging global supply chains in a way that old-economy manufacturers were not.

Silicon Valley's microchip makers were early movers in outsourcing manufacturing to East Asia, taking advantage of the fact that their small, lightweight products were easily transported over oceans, and their longstanding resistance to unionization allowed them to downsize and offshore labor with ease. At the same time, a growing cadre of young men who'd come west to work in electronics switched gears to become high-tech venture capitalists and financiers, bringing mentorship and money to the next generation of young entrepreneurs.

Ties to older institutions endured. Rather than investing their own money, most venture capitalists made investments for the monied classes of previous generations: the blue-blood family funds of Whitneys and Rockefellers, the Californian fortunes of Folgers and Bancrofts, the great land companies of the Central Valley and the High Sierra. And the defense industry didn't disappear, by a long shot; government-funded scientific research and development remained a major employer and economic driver of the local economy.

Yet the young entrepreneurial class that began to fill the Valley in the 1970s wanted little to do with the institutions that had started it all. Some were what Silicon Valley historian Fred Turner calls "the New Communalists," searching for a better society and believing that digital tools could be a means to achieve it. Others were unapologetic capitalists, who saw technological entrepreneurialism as a way to make a great deal of money. The people behind the personal computer (PC), video game, and early internet industries were a bit of both.[13]

At the start of the 1970s, silicon semiconductors had become such a dominant cluster in the region that an enterprising local trade reporter gave the place its "Silicon Valley" moniker in January 1971. Later that year, a three-year-old Valley company named Intel announced its breakthrough microprocessor, "the computer on a chip," which crammed more computing power into a smaller space than anything else on the market. Computers already were shrinking from room-sized mainframes to refrigerator-sized minicomputers, but the advent of the microprocessor accelerated the process of miniaturization even further.

By the close of the 1970s, Bay Area garages were filling up with little enterprises specializing in microcomputers, which essentially put a box around a microprocessor, added a keyboard and monitor, and brought computing power to the individual desktop. They came to market, and into the public consciousness, as PCs. Increasingly cheap and powerful transistorized technology also enabled mass-market home video games to come to market at the same time. Up to that point, Silicon Valley had chiefly been a producer of enterprise hardware far beyond the view and technical grasp of the ordinary American consumer; now it was the capital of two growing, alluring, consumer-facing industries with huge appeal to a taste-making youthful market.[14]

Yet this was not simply an ascendant moment for garage entrepreneurship, but for a broader political economy in flux. The new industries of Silicon Valley were able to rise so high partly because, nationally and in California, so much else was in crisis. Global competition had hacked away at the markets and innovative credibility of large American manufacturing sectors like automobiles and steel; in California, blue-collar manufacturing jobs dwindled while the costs of social and physical infrastructure rose. The crunch not only drove Democratic governor Jerry Brown to buckle down on state spending, it also precipitated the passage of

Proposition 13 in the summer of 1978, which capped the growth of property taxes and ushered in an age of perpetual revenue short-falls for California's municipal governments.

As Apple IIs and Atari consoles took the market by storm and Governor Brown declared an "age of limits," the big-government history of Silicon Valley's origins slipped into distant memory. The swiftness with which this collective amnesia took hold is remarkable but not wholly surprising. The magic of the region's entrepreneurial Galapagos—and the thing that had made it so entrepreneurial in the first place—was that the massive public investment that flowed into the Valley came *indirectly* into university labs and private industry via competitive contracting systems that allowed firms to build a commercial book of business at the same time.[15]

This is a trait of the post-industrial society that Bell missed. His vision was top-down, one of large-scale institutions orchestrating large-scale changes, of command and control by technocrats and politicians. It was one in which the importance of government-funded "intellectual technology" to the economy meant that public policy would have more, not less, influence on the workings of the corporation.[16]

Silicon Valley later became famous for the networked nature of its relationships across and within firms. The decentralized and federalized nature of federal science and defense spending enabled these networks in the first place. And this meant that technologists who were educated, trained, subsidized, and otherwise enabled by government programs believed that they had done it all on their own.

Leaders readily acknowledged technological and organizational debts that their firms owed to the entrepreneurs and companies that came before them, but they and their compatriots considered the work of the state to be wholly irrelevant, if not antithetical, to the story. Growing large and wealthy in an age of governmental austerity, the new entrepreneurial class of technologists had plenty of reasons to believe that public infrastructure rarely delivered on its promises, and they increasingly regarded government as a taxing and regulating obstacle to their success. "The government had nothing to do with Apple's success," one thirty-five-year veteran of the company told me in the fall of 2014. "If you write a book about the government's role in Silicon Valley"—as I had just indicated I planned to do—"it will end up on the remainder table."[17]

This particular flavor of free-market thinking had a sociologizing power of its own. There was no love lost between Silicon Valley executives of the PC and early internet eras and traditional big business; they agreed that, as Bell wrote, "corporate performance had made the society uglier, dirtier, trashier, more polluted, and noxious." But rather than seeing increased policy intervention as a necessary and inevitable guardrail for corporate excess, as Bell had concluded, tech leaders and their allies argued that the solution lay in swapping old-style business for newer, cleaner, and innovative enterprises like their own.[18]

What gave this argument heft and momentum was not only the charm of the mop-haired tech moguls themselves—although Jobs's lyrical exhortations about the computer being like "a bicycle for the mind" didn't hurt—but the fact that politicians of both parties amplified it as well. To President Ronald Reagan, no one better demonstrated the virtues of American free enterprise than the high-tech entrepreneurs who started out tinkering in suburban garages and ended up leading hugely successful computer companies. "These entrepreneurs and their small enterprises are responsible for almost all the economic growth in the United States," Reagan declared in 1988. "They are the prime movers of the technological revolution." Bill Clinton and Al Gore picked up

the baton a few years later, burnishing their business bona fides
with 1992 campaign endorsements from Silicon Valley moguls and
consulting tech leaders on matters from internet infrastructure to
education and tax and regulatory policy throughout their eight
years in the White House.[19]

As the companies of Silicon Valley were on the verge of amass-
ing what venture capitalist John Doerr quipped was "the largest
single legal creation of wealth we've witnessed on the planet,"
America's political leaders made a case that tech was the means
to a kinder, gentler, more bountiful capitalism. "Information
means empowerment—and employment," read the 1993 report on
a National Information Infrastructure, developed in close consultation with tech leaders. The spread of internet access would overcome "the constraints of geography and economic status, and give
all Americans a fair opportunity to go as far as their talents and
ambitions will take them."[20]

In his introduction to the 1976 edition of *The Coming of Post-
Industrial Society*, Bell worried that the dominance of science
might leave a society unmoored. "It is not at all clear that science, as a 'republic of virtue,' has the power to provide a new
ethos for society," he wrote. "More likely it is science itself that
may become subverted. What this means is that the society is left
with no transcendent ethos to provide some appropriate sense of
purpose, no anchorages that can provide stable meanings for people." Yet Silicon Valley's "new definition of rationality" already
was divorced from its linkages to broader social institutions and
national political projects by the start of the 1980s. Instead of losing their moorings, tech leaders and allies repurposed scientific
thinking into a new guiding virtue of techno-optimistic entrepreneurship, and they brought the rest of post-industrial America
along with them.[21]

WHO WILL RULE? 2000–2020

In the past two decades, Silicon Valley—place, industry, ideology—has grown larger and more market-dominant than ever before. The combined market valuation of American tech's five largest companies (three based in northern California, two in Seattle) is larger than the gross domestic product (GDP) of the United Kingdom. The coastal high-tech hubs groan under the weight of the industry's rapid expansion, while rural and heartland regions feebly clamor for the economic scraps that fall from the table in the form of fulfillment centers, server farms, and call centers. The landscape of tech is one marker of an age of hyperwealth and hyperinequality that is geographic as well as socioeconomic—all conditions that Bell failed to anticipate. As tech critics rail about the suffocating power of "surveillance capitalists," Bell's confident declaration in the coda to *The Coming of Post-Industrial Society* that "the control of society is no longer economic but political" seems woefully off base.[22]

But was it? Events might not have played out as Bell expected, but the reasons why tech was able to become Big Tech in the early twenty-first century have a great deal to do with politics and institutions that were his chief object of study. And while Silicon Valley is certainly powerful, Big Tech's critics not only are selective in their history but also overlook the continued role of the state in shaping the industry's twenty-first-century trajectory.

Take the extraordinary sums that governments around the United States and the world have spent over the past several decades on the chase to build tech hubs of their own. Somewhat surprisingly, Bell made little acknowledgment of the intense geographic concentration of technology in his 1973 volume. He does mention it in the introduction to the 1999 edition, but only as a means to make a broader point about how geography matters less in a world driven by information technology.[23]

Contra Bell (and many other late-1990s prognosticators), geography has only mattered *more* in the internet era. As tech grew, its concentration intensified. Undeterred by high housing prices and unprepossessing surroundings, people flocked to the Santa Clara Valley's freeway-bounded territory of bedroom suburbs and corporate campuses. A need to recruit and retain young and highly skilled employees led tech firms to spill over from suburb to city, putting the pressure on already overstressed housing markets and transportation networks in San Francisco and Seattle.

Undeterred by the downsides of this growth, hundreds of other cities and regions dreamed of building "Silicon Somethings" of their own, devoting considerable public resources to lure tech companies into their regions. This was a global quest. In India, the provincial government of Karnataka created special "export zones" in an around the city of Bangalore (Bengaluru) starting in the 1970s. Singaporean prime minister Lee Kwan Yew spearheaded a succession of big-ticket public infrastructure projects to build research parks and other facilities to encourage the growth of high-tech industry.[24]

In the United States, local and state officials' hunger for high-tech growth intensified as the PC industry gained steam in the 1980s and spiked even higher in the dot-com era. In the late 2010s, the competition to land an Amazon "HQ2" demonstrated the extraordinary—and often fiscally irresponsible—lengths to which local and regional governments would go to land white-collar, high-tech jobs. (Despite many cities' hopes that Amazon would use this search to inject new tech-economy vitality into economically struggling regions, the company chose two established knowledge-economy hubs—Washington, D.C. and New York City—instead.) The tax-cut chase is not limited to Amazon.

Silicon Valley tech firms now have a global geography, and many of the physical spaces they occupy are subsidized in some way by public funds.[25]

Despite this significant public push—which, of course, has diverted municipal assets and potential tax revenues away from infrastructural investments serving a broader population—no would-be Silicon Valley has yet achieved the scale and wealth of the original. A particularly intense strain of agglomeration economics drives high-tech growth, as the most successful regions not only have significant clusters of competing companies, but also develop highly specialized service firms (law, marketing, investment). The strong predilection for dynamic and diverse urban environments among the high-skilled tech talent pool has intensified this phenomenon; tech firms, large and small, go where the workers want to be, from Seattle's South Lake Union to San Francisco's SoMa and beyond. In 1999, Bell emphasized the global, networked nature of information technology, which twenty years later has only become more pronounced. Yet even as Silicon Valley has become a global network with nodes in many countries and continents, two cities on the West Coast of the United States remain tech's command-and-control centers. The geography of the knowledge economy seems as entrenched as that of mining or steel.[26]

Demographically, the tech industry is also highly skewed. The predominance of a class of workers drawn from the nearly entirely white male ranks of midcentury academic science and engineering has had lasting economic and cultural significance Bell's class-based analyses of the technical workforce failed to notice that pattern, much less to interrogate the origins and effects of the hypermasculinity of tech culture.

The Valley's ability to produce multiple generations of market-disrupting tech companies depended on a tightly networked ecosystem that hired and invested in what one venture capitalst termed "grade-A men" and relied heavily on existing personal and academic connections. The successful entrepreneurs of one generation became the venture capitalists who picked the winners of the next, and they rarely wandered out of their relatively small institutional and professional circles to find them. Compounding this bias was a deep-seated presumption, held even among free-thinking Californians who considered themselves to be pretty enlightened on matters of feminism and women's liberation, that women were simply not well suited for nor interested in technical fields. All of these were nuances missed in Bell's belated effort ("a note on women" in his 1999 foreword) to remediate the absence of gender analysis in *The Coming of Post-Industrial Society*. They remain highly relevant to understanding how and why contemporary technology companies function the way they do.[27]

The dearth of technical women employees in Silicon Valley companies did not stem from any specific government policy other than the general family-unfriendliness of an American system that provides little to no support for working parents. The state did play a direct role, however, in shaping another demographic characteristic of tech: its disproportionately high number of foreign-born workers and company founders.

The 1965 Hart-Celler Immigration Act goes unmentioned by Bell in *The Coming of Post-Industrial Society*, which indeed makes no mention of immigration at all. Fair enough: even those who authored and enacted the measure had little inkling of the political and economic transformation that the legislation would precipitate. It turns out, however, that immigration solved "the major problem for the post-industrial society" that Bell identified in 1973: maintaining "adequate numbers of trained persons of professional and technical caliber."[28]

In the case of Silicon Valley, the post-1965 immigration system brought thousands of technically trained migrants from South and East Asia to the region, where they became the engineering backbone for the growing tech sector from the 1970s forward. They and their children also founded new companies at a disproportionate rate, including some of tech's very largest such as Google, cofounded by a Soviet refugee, Sergey Brin. Federal immigration law and specialized visa programs continued to shape tech's post-industrial landscape into the twenty-first century, becoming one of the few public policy issues with which tech moguls weighed in upon with regularity.

The state also has remained a critical customer and investor in the business of tech. Defense and national security work never left Silicon Valley, but it intensified significantly in the post-9/11 national security buildup. The extent to which cybersurveillance was increasingly important to the U.S. national security establishment was made clear in the stunning 2013 leak of materials committed by National Security Agency (NSA) contractor Edward Snowden, which showed how the government had used Silicon Valley's largest consumer-facing social media and communications platforms to spy on users and monitor private communications.

While tech companies presented themselves as unwilling partners in these surveillance operations, the Pentagon's subsequent push to enhance military technical capacity has tightened ties—financial and operational—between Silicon Valley and the national security state. The anger and surprise with which tech-company employees have responded to this defense work over the past year point again to how the indirect nature of contracting allowed Silicon Valley's government ties to remain so thoroughly hidden.

FUTURE SHOCK

Writing at the cusp of the 1970s, Daniel Bell and his popularizing nemesis, Alvin Toffler, both recognized that technology and technocracy had their limits, as well as great hazards. "We frequently apply new technology stupidly and selfishly," Toffler wrote toward the end of *Future Shock*. "In our haste to milk technology for immediate economic advantage, we have turned our economy into a physical and social tinderbox." His prescription was not to turn away from technology, however, but to craft *better* technology.[29]

This has been the impulse of Silicon Valley tech titans as well—and continues to be, even amid today's "techlash." Politicians, too, hew to this techno-optimism even as they fiercely criticize the companies built around it. They call for Big Tech to build better safeguards against the promulgation of online violence, for better policing of the products they sell on their platforms, and for smarter algorithms to catch fakes, hacks, and other bad actors. Silicon Valley and Washington, D.C., may not agree on much these days, but both sides seem to think there is still an app for that.

Daniel Bell was no Luddite, but he was a social realist. "What does not vanish," he wrote at the end of *The Coming of Post-Industrial Society*, "is the duplex nature of man himself—the murderous aggression, from primal impulse, to tear apart and destroy; and the search for order, in art and life, as the bending of will to harmonious shape."[30] Silicon Valley has always wanted to transcend history. Bell rightly recognized that it couldn't be shaken off.

Utopianism has long burned brightly in the sunny precincts of Silicon Valley, boosted by the notion that a *better* technology is the means to achieve a greater social good (or, as many of them still say without irony, "to change the world"). It turns out that some tech leaders have been just as blind to the consequences of technological progress as the old-economy polluters and profiteers upon which the 1960s and 1970s generation heaped such scorn. And, as it turns out, politics and culture *do* matter. They will also matter to where post-industrial society goes next.

NOTES

1. Alvin Toffler, *Future Shock* (New York: Random House, 1970); Bell, "Foreword: 1976," in *The Coming of Post-Industrial Society: A Venture in Social Forecasting* (New York, Basic Books: 1976), lxxxvii; Bell, *Coming of Post-Industrial Society*, 54n, 318n.

2. Bell quoted in David A. Bell, "Daniel Bell at 100," *Dissent*, May 9, 2019, archived at https://perma.cc/W7GW-GYQD; "New and Recommended," *New York Times*, July 7, 1973, 29; Sanford J. Ungar, "Review of *Future Shock*," *Washington Post*, August 7, 1970, B8. Alvin Toffler's wife, Heidi, is now widely considered to have been his uncredited coauthor on much of his life's work, including *Future Shock*. "I don't know where her brain ends and mine begins," Alvin Toffler reflected in 2006 (Keith Schneider, "Heidi Toffler, Unsung Force Behind Futurist Books, Dies at 89," *New York Times*, February 12, 2019, B14).

3. Regis McKenna, *The Regis Touch: Million-Dollar Advice from America's Top Marketing Consultant* (Reading, MA: Addison-Wesley, 1985), 4; Richard Feloni, "Billionaire Investor Steve Case Says a Book He Read in 1980 Set Him on the Path to Founding AOL, and It Still Influences Him Today," *Business Insider*, October 12, 2018, archived at https://perma.cc/4X7T-8KNZ.

4. John Heilemann, "The Making of the President 2000," *Wired*, December 1995, https://www.wired.com/1995/12/gorenewt/; Jacob Heilbrunn, "President Gore's Foreign Policy," *World Policy Journal* 17, no. 2 (2000): 48–55. Also see Margaret O'Mara, *The Code: Silicon Valley and the Making of America* (New York: Penguin, 2019), 323–325.

5. Toffler, *Future Shock*, 141.

6. Toffler, *Future Shock*, 110, 252, 258. "Ad-hocracy" is the focus of his chapter 7.

7. As Fred Turner notes in "The Cultural Contradictions of Capitalism, Then and Now," his contribution to this volume, Bell's *The Cultural Contradictions of Capitalism* (New York: Basic Books, 1978) dilates extensively on the counterculture and its shortcomings, revealing a sharp distaste, and perhaps even fear, of the sexual liberation and familial redefinition that it had helped foster.

8. Bell, *Coming of Post-Industrial Society*, 189, 196.

9. On the early Cold War and the Santa Clara Valley see O'Mara, *The Code*, as well as Rebecca Lowen, *Creating the Cold War University: The Transformation*

of Stanford (Berkeley: University of California Press, 1997); Martin Kenney, ed., *Making Silicon Valley: The Anatomy of an Entrepreneurial Region* (Stanford, CA: Stanford University Press, 2000); Margaret O'Mara, *Cities of Knowledge: Cold War Science and the Search for the Next Silicon Valley* (Princeton, NJ: Princeton University Press, 2005); and Christophe Lécuyer, *Making Silicon Valley: Innovation and the Growth of High Tech, 1930–1970* (Cambridge, MA: MIT Press, 2007).

10. Bell, *Coming of Post-Industrial Society*, 282–284.

11. Packard quoted in Jim Collins, foreword to David Packard, *The HP Way: How Bill Hewlett and I Built Our Company* (New York: HarperBusiness, 2005 edition), x.

12. O'Mara, *The Code*, 33; Bell, *Coming of Post-Industrial Society*, 137–140. I expand further on tech's resistance to unionization in "The High-Tech Revolution and the Disruption of American Capitalism," in *Capitalism Contested: The New Deal and Its Legacies*, ed. Romain Huret, Nelson Lichtenstein, and Jean-Christian Vinel (Philadelphia: University of Pennsylvania Press, 2020), 199–223.

13. Fred Turner, *From Counterculture to Cyberculture* (Chicago: University of Chicago, 2006), 4–5 et seq.

14. For a richly layered discussion of the origin and evolution of these two industries, see Leslie Berlin, *Troublemakers: Silicon Valley's Coming of Age* (New York: Simon & Schuster, 2017).

15. On Brown's oft-repeated warning of an "age of limits," see for example James Ring Andrews, "Jerry Brown Plays the Numbers," *Wall Street Journal*, March 31, 1977, 16.

16. Bell, "The Social Framework of the Information Society," in *The Computer Age: A Twenty-Year View*, ed. Michael L. Dertouzos and Joel Moses (1979), 167.

17. Anonymous, interview with the author, 2014, Palo Alto, Calif.

18. Bell, *Coming of Post-Industrial Society*, 272.

19. Ronald Reagan, remarks and a question-and-answer session with the students and faculty at Moscow State University, Moscow, May 1988.

20. John Doerr, "The Coach," interview by John Brockman, 1996, Edge.org, archived at https://perma.cc/9KWX-GLWK; National Telecommunications and Information Administration, U.S. Department of Commerce, "20/20 Vision: The Development of a National Information Infrastructure," NTIA-Spub-94-28, March 1994.

21. Bell, *Coming of Post-Industrial Society*, xcix.

22. Shoshanna Zuboff, *The Age of Surveillance Capitalism: The Fight for a Human Future at the New Frontier of Power* (New York: PublicAffairs, 2019); Bell, "Coda," *Coming of Post-Industrial Society*, 373.

23. Bell, "Introduction," *Coming of Post-Industrial Society*, xlvi.

24. Margaret O'Mara, "Silicon Dreams: States, Markets, and the Transnational High-Tech Suburb," in *Making Cities Global: The Transnational Turn in Urban History*, ed. A. K. Sandoval-Strausz and Nancy Kwak (Philadelphia: University of Pennsylvania Press, 2017), 17–46.

25. Amazon.com, "Request for Proposals," 2017, https://images-na.ssl-images-amazon.com/images/G/01/Anything/test/images/usa/RFP_3._V516043504_.pdf; Margaret O'Mara, "Winning the Amazon Sweepstakes Will Give One City a Big Boost—If It Happens the Right Way," *Washington Post*, September 20, 2017.

26. Bell, *Coming of Post-Industrial Society*, xlv–liii. On post-industrial agglomeration economies, see, for example, Edward L. Glaeser, ed., *Agglomeration Economics* (Chicago: University of Chicago, 2010).

27. Bell, *Coming of Post-Industrial Society*, lxxxi–lxxxii. On "grade-A men," see Tom Nicholas, *VC: An American History* (Cambridge, MA: Harvard University Press, 2019).

28. Bell, *Coming of Post-Industrial Society*, 232.

29. Toffler, *Future Shock*, 380.

30. Bell, *Coming of Post-Industrial Society*, 408.

8

THE POST-INDUSTRIAL UNIVERSITY AS WE KNOW IT

Daniel Bell's Vision, Today's Realities

STEVEN BRINT

The main line of Daniel Bell's argument about universities is clear: in post-industrial society, universities are a central institution, more central even than corporations, and their gravitational pull will increase as the post-industrial sector of the economy grows. High-tech industry and quality-of-life services create the economic foundations of post-industrial society. The post-industrial sector's class structure is arranged in a pyramidal form consisting of a dominant group of scientists and scientific administrators at the top, a middle stratum of professors and engineers, and a bottom layer of teaching assistants, junior faculty, and technicians. Its ethos is meritocratic and scientific, leavened by a commitment to providing opportunities for talented individuals from families with limited resources.

Yet the book in which Bell lays out this argument, *The Coming of Post-Industrial Society*, cannot be read as a straightforward exposition of an argument about the direction of social change. The text includes many second thoughts in the form of side commentaries, layers of qualification, quotations intended both to support and to interrogate the argument, and instructive stories that illustrate the moral conundrums and open questions facing post-industrial society.

Take one example. On the surface, science appears to be the directing force in postindustrial society, and yet Bell vacillates as to whether science or scientists can be such a force. Government, not the scientific community itself, controls the direction of policy, and it has little appetite for a "coordinated attack on big problems."[1] Moreover, government-funded science is mainly for defense, not for the peaceful uses envisaged in Bell's "Scientific City" of the future. Bell himself raises questions as to whether these realities can be overcome.[2]

Bell later uses the story of J. Robert Oppenheimer to add another layer of ambiguity to the relationship between science and political power. Oppenheimer, the leader of the Manhattan Project during World War II, was alternately chosen by, cowed by, tempted by, and ultimately destroyed by the politically powerful. Bell's Oppenheimer is a symbol of the man of creativity who flies too close to the sun of political calculation. Yet he concludes his reflections by quoting Andrei Sakharov's faith in the method of science as "a defense against any kind of political subjugation."[3] So perhaps science is not destined to be dominated by its political masters: "The charismatic aspect of science gives it its 'sacred' quality as a way of life for its members. . . . It is the tension between those charismatic elements and the realities of large-scale organization that will frame the political realities of science in postindustrial society."[4]

Such are the perplexities and pleasures of Bell's style. What can seem on a first reading to be a relatively straightforward social scientific analysis and confident prediction is better read as a complex literary text, full of uncertainty and doubt and replete with problems that can be resolved in multiple ways. Depending on how the future unfolds, the university could turn out to be axial—or not.

These ambiguities make a reassessment of Bell's thinking about higher education all the more interesting. Despite all his qualifications, he did lay out a grand vision of the future of universities. But how central have universities become to innovation and economic growth? Have the forces driving higher education diverged from the understanding that Bell had of them? Has the content of a college education followed the model that Bell advocated? Confronting Bell's vision with a half-century's experience may help us better understand how universities are continuing to evolve now.

THE CENTRALITY OF THE UNIVERSITY?

Bell's work on knowledge as an engine of development was of a piece with the thinking of other midcentury social analysts. Joseph Schumpeter's emphasis on the role of technological innovation in economic development was a major influence.[5] In the 1950s, Robert Solow formalized Schumpeter's insight by showing that technical advance explained the large residual in growth rates that remained after taking into account the classical factors of production (land, labor, and capital).[6] Economists such as Zvi Griliches[7] and Vernon Ruttan[8] demonstrated that technological innovations in agriculture had greatly improved farm productivity; the sociologist Everett Rogers traced the process of diffusion that allowed technological innovations to spread through relevant sectors of the economy.[9]

By the mid-1960s, a long line of liberal academics had written about the economic power of knowledge. Fritz Machlup provided the first estimate of the size of the contributions to gross domestic product (GDP) by what he called "the information economy."[10] Clark Kerr heralded the rise of the "multiversity" as a central institution providing research and expert advice to help solve society's problems.[11] Peter Drucker coined the term "knowledge worker" to identify individuals who contribute to organizations based on expertise first developed in universities and subsequently honed in professional and managerial occupations.[12] John Kenneth Galbraith's analysis of "the new industrial state" highlighted the significance of a "techno-structure" of engineers, scientists, and professionally trained managers running large organizations and a "scientific and cultural estate" consisting principally of academics, writers, and artists.[13] Not much later, Gerald M. Platt and Talcott Parsons published what amounted to a paean to cognitive rationality as the cultural daemon of advanced societies and of the university as the institution most responsible for producing it.[14]

As early as 1959, Bell was working on related themes. Unsatisfied with his first unfinished portraits, he published a two-part essay on post-industrial society in 1967[15] and his book on the subject six years later. Bell's assertion of the centrality of basic science and theoretical knowledge as the fount of post-industrial society became one of his more noteworthy contributions (as was his interrogation of these claims). In *The Coming of Post-Industrial Society*, he writes that "just as the business firm was the key institution of the past hundred years because of its role in organizing production for the mass creation of products, the university—or some other form of a knowledge institute—will become the central institution of the next hundred years because of its central role as the new source of innovation and knowledge."[16]

The university as a source of theoretical knowledge was crucial to Bell's argument. Nineteenth-century inventors "were indifferent to science and the fundamental laws underlying their investigations,"[17] he argued, whereas innovation in the twentieth century came to depend on theoretical knowledge. Thomas A. Edison is for Bell the epitome of the talented tinkerer of a bygone era, when it was possible for someone to make revolutionary breakthroughs in technology without training in the relevant science. But further development of electrodynamics "could only come from engineers with formal training in mathematical physics."[18] Chemistry for Bell is another example of the primacy of theoretical knowledge: "One must have a theoretical knowledge of the macromolecules one is manipulating in order to recombine and transform compounds."[19] But while Bell provided some other examples, he failed to present any systematic evidence for the claim that university-based theoretical knowledge is the key to post-industrial innovation.

The evidence from the history of science does not support Bell's claim. The current consensus is that scientific progress occurs through a number of channels, including the development and application of theory (or basic research), pure empiricism, and what Donald Stokes refers to as "use-inspired basic research";[20] that is, basic research with an applied goal in mind. Codification is important in the progress of science, but codification is only a means to organize what is known so that others can readily access it. Tinkering remains an important feature of scientific progress, as the history of the personal computer (PC) makes clear.[21] In a study of the fifty most important inventions between 1955 and 2005, I show that some inventions that made the list—such as bulletproof Kevlar—were invented using brute-force experimentation with a wide variety of possible compounds. Many others—magnetic resonance, in vitro fertilization, the human immunodeficiency virus (HIV) protease inhibitor, the polymerase chain reaction, the birth control pill—grew out of a combination of theoretical knowledge and what amounts to inspired tinkering.[22] Those who have looked into the origins of important scientific discoveries have also found a range of forces at work, some tied to theory, others tied to empirical observations, with quite a bit of back and forth movement between the two.[23]

If theoretical knowledge is only one source of innovation, Bell's assumption about the priority of academic research loses force. No one today would argue that corporations such as Apple, Google, and Microsoft depend on universities for innovation. Indeed, corporations are involved in virtually every important invention that succeeds in the marketplace. In contrast, universities figure prominently in about 40 percent of the fifty important inventions that I studied[24]—an exceptional record, given their small share of total research and development (R&D) funds, but not as much as what one might expect from the axial institution of post-industrial society.

New conceptual understandings originate today in a wide variety of institutional settings, not just in universities. For example, total quality management, the triple bottom line (the idea that corporations should evaluate themselves in relation to labor conditions and environmental impact as well as profit), and the balanced scorecard (the idea that managers should rate themselves on financial, customer service, internal process, and organizational learning outcomes rather than only on financial outcomes) all come from the world of business consultants. Formulas predicting film and song success originate in the entertainment industry. Principles of human-centered design were developed first by IBM engineers. Scenario planning originated in the armed forces and oil companies. The role of university researchers in these developments has been to test for validity, to refine or reject their findings, and to feed revised understandings back to the originating institutions, whether for adoption or dismissal.[25]

Bell not only exaggerates the role of academic science, he also idealizes it:

> The community of science is a unique institution in human civilization. It has no ideology in that it has no postulated set of formal beliefs, but it has an ethos which implicitly prescribes rules of conduct. It is not a political movement that one joins by subscription,

for membership is by election, yet one must make a commitment in order to belong. It is not a church where the element of faith rests on belief and is rooted in mystery, yet faith, passion, and mystery are present, but they are directed by the search for certified knowledge whose function it is to test and discard old beliefs.[26]

The limits of this understanding of science are now well known. The so-called science of eugenics legitimized racism. The atomic bomb was a product of the best scientific minds. And the science of artificial intelligence may damage civilization in ways that we are currently unable to anticipate. Science is our best means to discover new truths about the natural world and social relations, but scientists rarely consider the potential of their work for dangerous, unintended consequences. Moreover, science is like other fields in which ambitious people strive to make a name for themselves. When their careers are at stake, scientists may become invested in paradigms that obscure as much as they reveal, and in extreme cases, they may even engage in fraud.

Although he failed to explore the underside of science, Bell did reject the technocratic vision that his conception of post-industrial society might have encouraged. He argued at length against the view that scientists could set the direction for policy, or even the direction of scientific organizations. "The lack of a unified science policy, or a major academy or ministerial system, has meant that the 'technocratic potential' inherent in the growing influence of science and the nature of technical decision making is minimized in the American system."[27] Science is fragmented, dependent on the mission orientation of the federal government's research agencies and the system of individual project grants adopted following World War II.

More broadly, the Saint-Simonian dream of a society run on the principles of rationality is, in Bell's view, unrealizable.

Scientists, engineers, and planners must be taken into account in the political process; they wend their way into administrative leadership, and the ethos of science dominates the value system of these increasingly important figures. But "it is not the technocrat who ultimately holds power, (it is) the politician."[28] Most issues cannot be settled simply based on technical criteria because value choices shape the technical criteria themselves. "Rationality, as an end, finds itself confronted by the cantankerousness of politics, the politics of interest and the politics of passion."[29]

In Bell's vision of post-industrial society, science occupied a position of high prestige and trust—more prestige and trust than it now enjoys. Fewer than half of Americans say that they have a great deal of confidence in the scientific community, a figure that has remained relatively stable over three decades. It is not even clear that the ethos of science holds sway among all segments of the highly educated. Many people with degrees in the humanities, the qualitative social sciences, and the professions linked to these disciplines are skeptical of science. They criticize its unintended consequences and its alliance with powerful patrons, and they are frequently attuned to inquiries that are more sensitive to the lived experiences of disadvantaged and marginalized populations. Within the stratum of professionals and managers, confidence in science is lower among women and minorities.[30]

Bell saw discontent with rationality in the 1960s and 1970s as originating in antibourgeois, romantic impulses, but the antiscientific temper of our current time has different roots and harder edges. On the political right, it derives from religious faith and nostalgia for a past that conservatives prefer to the contemporary world that they see as being engineered by liberal elites. On the political left, criticism of science derives from a commitment to social justice as the singular priority for building a better future. These conflicts play out in the forces shaping universities today.

THE FORCES SHAPING HIGHER EDUCATION

Bell identified the push for equality, more than the need for scientific and professional personnel, as the primary reason for the expansion of higher education.[31] He deplored that a "bright but poor boy" had only about half as much chance of completing college as his "well-to-do counterpart," and he argued that if the necessary expansion of higher education were to occur, increasing numbers of students would "have to be drawn from working-class families."[32] Indeed, for Bell, a just meritocracy required the widest possible opportunities to rise from the position of one's birth.

Bell foresaw that the promotion of equal opportunity could easily become a demand for equal representation. But he failed to anticipate the extent to which the demand for equal representation would become institutionalized in universities and undermine the rationale for meritocracy. University administrators today try to have it both ways. They aspire for excellence and equal representation of minorities among both faculty and students, as well as the administrative staff.[33] They keep elaborate records to monitor their progress toward equal representation, and they devise additional remedies when progress fails to keep pace with their goals.

Bell thought this emphasis on representation was misguided. Quoting W. G. Runciman, he wrote that all people should be accorded respect, but not all deserve equal praise, and the meritocracy, "in the best meaning of that word," is made up of those worthy of praise—the people who are the best in their fields, as judged by their peers.[34] Bell claimed that "a society that does not have its best men at the head of its leading institutions is a sociological and moral absurdity."[35] The omission of women from that statement is only the most obvious difficulty with it. Failures of leadership by people who are thought to be "the best" inevitably raise questions about who the best actually are. Were the best people running the Afghanistan war during its two decades of futility? Were they running ExxonMobil during their many decades of denying climate change? Were they running Lehmann Brothers prior to the Great Recession?

For Bell, the requirement that merit take precedence over representation is particularly strong in the university setting because universities are based on the capacity of those in authority to make valid judgments: "knowledge is a form of authority and education is the process of refining the nature of authoritative judgments."[36] He adds, "There is every reason why a university has to be a meritocracy, if the resources of the society—for research, for scholarship, for learning—are to be spent for 'mutual advantage,' and if a degree of culture is to prevail."[37]

Since *The Coming of Post-Industrial Society*, however, the momentum in universities has been with the egalitarians. The old, allegedly meritocratic regime favoring white men looks in retrospect like a system of opportunity hoarding. Once-marginalized groups, notably women and Asian Americans, now outperform white males on virtually all measures of academic achievement and performance.[38] They have clearly strengthened universities, contributing to the vast increase in research in recent decades. Although leadership in science and engineering remains largely in the hands of white and Asian men, women have made inroads in the other professions—the life sciences, the social sciences, and to an even greater degree in the interpretive disciplines.[39] Among the faculty, full-throated defenders of meritocracy have become rare.[40]

But meritocracy remains, even if its advocates are quiet. Access to faculty and administrative positions has been expanded, but the opportunity to climb the faculty ranks still depends on scientific and scholarly output. Those engaged at the highest levels in their disciplines have often found the drive for diversity irrelevant or an impediment to their interests, while those committed to equal representation have just as often viewed leading disciplinary professionals as elitists. Even in the most liberal bastions of academe, the faculty remains uneasy about the more intrusive policies put into place to advance diversity, equity, and inclusion goals.[41] The scholars who are most in favor of such policies tend to be ones whose work focuses explicitly on the injustices perpetrated against marginalized groups.

Bell assumed a tight connection between university-trained labor and the dynamic industries in our society. Was he right? Certainly a primary source of university strength comes from its monopolization of legitimate credentials for access to well-remunerated and powerful positions in the economy. Here, advanced degrees are particularly important. People with advanced degrees are concentrated in a handful of industries, as Bell indicated. To identify which industries belong to the post-industrial sector, I use a simple criterion: 10 percent or more of their employees need to have postgraduate degrees. Computers, software, and other high-tech industries such as pharmaceuticals and telecommunications, health, legal services, media, museums and galleries, government, finance, insurance, and higher education itself meet this criterion. As contributors to GDP, these "knowledge sector" industries have been gaining ground over time—by my count contributing just one-quarter to GDP in 1959, up to two-fifths in 1997, and nearly 50 percent today.[42]

At the same time, manufacturing of durable and nondurable goods, warehousing and storage, transportation, and sales in wholesale and retail trade are large contributors to GDP, and none of these industries belong in the post-industrial sector. Neither do post-industrial industries account for all the fastest-growing industries. By my calculation using Bureau of Labor Statistics data, they account for about half of them.[43]

Although Bell discusses populist resistance to professional power, he did not envision that such sentiments could be as powerful as the forces driving the rise of science and the universities. The partisan divisions that are now so apparent are rooted, in large part, in the near-even balance between the post-industrial sector and the traditional agricultural, industrial, and commercial sectors. Post-industrial progressivism rules in the big cities and their suburbs, especially on the Northeastern and Western Seaboards; traditionalism rules the exurbs, the small towns, and the heartland.[44] The possibility of an economic victory by the forces of post-industrialism and a political victory by the forces of traditionalism is one that Bell did not contemplate, but we cannot avoid confronting.

What forces, then, are dominating the development of the universities? In the advanced societies, as they now exist, universities are best understood as institutional hubs and innovation partners. They link institutions and elites and contribute to technological progress, but they are no more central than other institutional hubs or other innovation partners such as high-tech firms and federal research agencies. I adopt the term "hub" from the work of Richard Arum, Elizabeth Armstrong, and Mitchell Stevens, who see the university's power as stemming largely from its capacity to connect elites from different institutional spheres: "privileged families" that send their children to selective undergraduate programs; professional schools that train future occupational leaders; prominent figures in government, the arts, and business, who welcome honorary degrees and speaking engagements; and wealthy patrons who donate money and put their names on buildings and entire schools.[45]

The complementary idea of a national innovation system implies that universities, states, and corporations all have roles to play in the creation, dissemination, and ultimately the production of new science-based technologies.[46] States very often provide the funding for foundational research, sometimes supported by corporations with an interest in potential applications. University labs are most important for basic research, but they also work on applications. Corporations are essential for the production and marketing of new technologies, of course, and they also conduct the majority of "downstream" research leading to marketable products. In some industries, corporations are the primary producers of use-inspired basic research; in others, universities are more important. In the United States, the computer software and pharmaceutical industries illustrate two polar cases. New software comes mainly from in-house research in software companies, while new drugs are discovered as often in university life science and medical labs as in the labs of pharmaceutical firms. Nevertheless, high-technology firms, regardless of industry, locate themselves near leading academic centers, sometimes to draw directly on the expertise of their faculty, and even more commonly, to recruit their graduate students. Corporate scientists also benefit from sabbatical periods spent working in the labs of leading academic scientists and engineers.

Undoubtedly, the contributions of universities to economic development have increased since Bell wrote, but so too have the contributions of corporations and governments. R&D statistics suggest a moderate increase in the university's share, going from 10 percent of total U.S. R&D in 1973, the year *The Coming of Post-Industrial Society* was published, to 13–14 percent in recent years.[47] Of course, these statistics only scratch the surface of the complex interactions between R&D-producing sectors and entirely leave out the steady flow of university-trained scientific personnel who are largely responsible for the corporate and government contributions to R&D.

Compared to the state-centered national innovation systems in most of the world, the U.S. system has a wider variety of revenue sources. Philanthropic support, student tuition, and corporate fund supplement national and state research funds and subsidies. In 2015 alone, the federal government alone poured $65 billion into student financial aid, made hundreds of billions available in subsidized loans, and disbursed more than $30 billion to universities for research and development. Donors provided billions of dollars more.[48] The major research universities have consequently grown stronger in the years since Bell wrote about them. But their strength does not derive primarily from the generation and codification of theoretical knowledge, as Bell argued. Instead, their success is due to high levels of investment combined with the interplay of three dynamic growth logics.

Growth logics are guiding ideas joined to institutionalized practices. The first of these, the logic of intellectual progress, is the commitment to knowledge discovery and transmission in the disciplines and at their interstices. The second, the logic of expanding into new markets, results in a proliferation of degree programs and an increased focus on the use of university research to advance economic development. The third, the logic of social inclusion, reflects the effort to use colleges and universities as instruments of social change by expanding opportunities to members of once-marginalized groups. All three have contributed to the distinctive orientation of the leading research universities in the United States over the last forty years.

But if we look beyond the top four dozen or so thriving institutions, we can see that the challenges facing colleges and universities are daunting. The quality of undergraduate teaching and learning is urgently in need of improvement. Since the early 1960s, undergraduate study time has declined by half across every type of institution and major, and academic requirements have followed a similar downward course.[49] A great many lower-division classes are taught by underpaid adjunct faculty, who do not generally perform as well in the classroom as tenured or tenure-track faculty and do not maintain as high academic standards.[50] Few faculty members have tried to implement the findings of the now-extensive research literature on effective teaching practices.[51] The low quality of teaching reflects an implicit pact among students, who do not want demanding coursework; faculty, who would rather spend their time on research and socioprofessional activities; and administrators, who are more interested in maintaining and expanding enrollments than ensuring the quality of teaching and learning.[52]

Affordability is the other great challenge. College and university net costs after financial aid are not as out of control as they are often depicted to be in the media, but they have nevertheless risen faster than inflation.[53] This rise has been accompanied by a well-publicized growth in student indebtedness. Most students do not take on unmanageable debt,[54] but loan repayment *is* a major problem because it begins for new graduates at a time when their salaries are not only low, but also highly variable from year to year.[55] Nor have Pell grants for low-income students kept up with college costs.[56] Low-income students have consequently found themselves unable to afford top-quality public institutions, even if they are qualified for admission, creating a more homogeneous elite stratum in states with leading, flagship universities.[57]

The campus climate for speech may seem a trivial problem in comparison, but it is an issue that greatly concerns the public and consequently contributes to the university's problems of legitimation.[58] The benefits of diversity and inclusion policies have been genuine, but they have come at a price. In politically correct campus environments, students and faculty members are expected to say the "right" words and have the "right" attitudes. In some cases, explicit support for an aggressive "call-out" culture against anyone who is seen as failing to conform to campus norms does inhibit alternative views.[59] All of this creates a tense cultural climate, in which advocates feel that the university has not gone far enough to redress historical wrongs and skeptics find themselves walking on eggshells for fear of giving offense.[60]

THE REFORMING OF GENERAL EDUCATION

Bell's ideas about the social and economic role of universities are captured in *The Coming of Post-Industrial Society*, but his outlook on what should be taught to students can be found only in *The Reforming of General Education*, a now little-read, book-length report written by Bell in 1966 for Columbia University's provost at the time, David B. Truman.[61]

In the 1950s and early 1960s, the Columbia general education program was widely admired as a model for colleges. It consisted of (1) two terms of humanities (sometimes referred to as "lit-hum"), focusing on "great books" from the ancient world to the Enlightenment; (2) two terms of history and social analysis (called, rather misleadingly, "contemporary civilization"), focusing on classical texts in social and political thought; and (3) a two-term science sequence encompassing both the history of science and the methods and principles of scientific disciplines. By the mid-1960s, this structure was fraying for a variety of reasons. Some professors, particularly in the sciences, resisted teaching outside their specialty areas. Science students were also rebelling against a constraining structure that did not allow them to spend as much time as they desired in their areas of concentration. The adoption of departmental requirements for majors in 1956 increased the pressure on the general education courses.

Bell's solution was not to give in to centrifugal forces, but rather to weave general education more deeply into the four-year

curriculum. Instead of a yearlong course in humanities, he proposed three semesters, with the third semester taking up great
works of modernism, such as those of James Joyce, George Eliot,
Sigmund Freud, and Friedrich Nietzsche. Rather than abolish the
yearlong course in contemporary civilization, he proposed two
years of coursework: a first term in Greek and Roman history; second and third terms of work on Western history, with an option to
focus on political, economic, or social history; and a fourth term for
work in a specific social science discipline. This fourth term could
include comparative studies, particularly of non-Western cultures.
Instead of a yearlong science requirement, he proposed a two-year
sequence in either physics and math or biology and math.[62]

Perhaps needless to say, neither Columbia nor any other college
ever adopted this complicated structure. As a curriculum planner,
Bell proved too little concerned about either faculty or student
interests. The model that he envisioned stood no chance of sat-
isfying faculty members who wanted a more compact structure,
particularly those in science, who wanted students to spend more
time in their areas of concentration. And it certainly made no
effort to appeal to students who felt similarly.

But what Bell had to say about the values of general education
continues to resonate. He set out four working principles. The first
was to help students see the big issues looming ahead so that they
would be prepared to address them. The second was to make students aware of the intellectual and civic traditions that they have
inherited, as well as the limitations of those traditions. The third
was to combat premature specialization so that students could
better grasp the underlying human condition, the persistent issues
of morals and politics, and the webs of relationships in which
humans are enmeshed. The fourth was to integrate knowledge
through the use of multiple disciplinary lenses to provide more
insight into both canonical works and contemporary problems.[63]

Throughout, Bell's interest was in expanding the analytical, perceptual, and imaginative powers of undergraduates in the service of mature judgment. For this reason, he opposed orthodoxy of any type, including any fixed list of great works that purported to illustrate moral or aesthetic principles. He emphasized the limitations of even the greatest of conceptual schemes. Quoting William James, he wrote: "Concepts are 'maps of relations,' but by their nature they are 'forever inadequate to the fullness of the reality to be shown,' a reality that consists 'of existential particulars' of which 'we become aware only in the perceptual flux.' "[64] The context of history was essential "for all the schemata of men are bound to the vicissitudes of events and the crossroads they present."[65] One lives, he stated, "often in (the) painful alienation of doubt, not certainty." And yet this, too, is a state of grace, for "doubting pleases . . . no less than knowing."[66] "The ends of education are many," he argued: "to instill an awareness of the diversity of human societies and desires; to be responsive to great philosophers and imaginative writers who have given thought to the predicaments that have tried and tested men; to acquaint a student with the limits of ambition and the reaches of humility; to realize that no general principle or moral absolute, however strongly it may be rooted in a philosophical tradition, can give an infallible answer to any particular dilemma."[67]

In spite of his evident interest in non-Western cultures, Bell did not doubt that the grounding for this approach should be based on works in the Western intellectual tradition. Shortly after *Reforming* was published, the forces of equal representation exploded that conventional assumption. The grounding of general education in the Western intellectual tradition came under fierce attack, beginning in the late 1960s at Amherst and culminating in the Stanford protests of the 1980s.[68] Western civilization stood accused of racism, sexism, and imperialism, overshadowing for campus radicals whatever intellectual merits its greatest thinkers may have had. Since that time, those who advocate the grounding of general education in the Western intellectual tradition have come to occupy a marginalized status in most colleges and universities. Not a single elite college in the country currently requires a course in Western civilization. In contrast, during the twenty-five-year period from 1975 to 2000, courses on diversity and non-Western cultures were among the fastest growing of the new requirements. (The other principal trend was toward greater representation of basic skills courses, such as introductory math and English composition.)[69]

Bell believed that the reliance on distribution requirements as a foundation for general education was "an admission of intellectual defeat" because it served up a "mishmash of courses that are only superficially connected."[70] The majority of colleges and universities have nevertheless gone down this path, finding it a successful method of bringing a degree of peace to academic departments worried about capturing their share of student enrollments, and thereby securing their future prospects.[71]

There are new stirrings in this seemingly moribund territory. Over the last two decades, the American Association of Colleges & Universities (AAC&U) has attempted to shift general education away from a focus on content to a focus on skills. AAC&U initially identified five "core competencies"—analytical and critical thinking, oral communication, quantitative reasoning, and written expression—and has sought to embed these in the general education curriculum, whatever content form it may take.[72] Some promising content models have also been proposed, including the University of North Carolina's "making connections" curriculum, which focuses on how the disciplines study questions and how students might integrate these methods and results in ways that cross traditional disciplinary lines.[73] Harvard now requires just six semester-long general education courses, with at least one from each of four broad areas: aesthetics and cultures; ethics and civics; histories, societies, and individuals; and science and technology in society. These are high-status courses, often taught by celebrated professors, and proposals must be approved by a faculty committee.[74]

None of the dominant models, nor any of the new approaches, provides the depth of thinking about the aims of general education that readers will find in Bell's report. It is debatable whether the lessons of *The Reforming General Education* are transferrable to nonelite institutions. But for those who are interested in the education of elites, the philosophical passages in the text bear more than a single reading.

❧

Bell's greatness certainly does not come from the accuracy of his predictions—that is a mixed bag at best. It stems, rather, from his capacity to help us think more deeply. He provides analytical models that are often illuminating and always worth considering. He criticizes the plausible but naive views of his predecessors, whether these derive from the Marxist insistence of economic determinism or the Saint-Simonian dream of rationalized rule. His asides are rich in erudition, provoking us to expand our own intellectual horizons. He asks the right questions, the provocative questions, even when his answers have proved inadequate to historical developments that he could not foresee.[75]

Individual paragraphs and sections gleam like precisely cut gemstones. Consider, to provide just one example, his justification for great literature as a feature of general education:

> The humanities have a different intent [than the sciences or social sciences]: to heighten sensibility (that fusion of intellect and feeling) and to impart a sense of coherence about human experience—(in

the themes of) heroism, pride, love, loneliness, tragedy, confrontation with death. . . . A great novel has no "nature," as if it were a natural object and therefore subject to some fixed discussion of its qualities and propensities . . . [I]t can be read in different ways . . . and each of these ways is . . . a valid facet of human emotions. . . . Hence the concentric sense of uncovering new meaning as one confronts, over a period of time, a genuinely imaginative work. . . . The humanities . . . combine "fixed reason with wayward spirit." And this unique combination of order and freedom, rule and spontaneity, limitation and potential is a necessary realm of experience for renewing the animal spirits and the guiding intelligence of man.[76]

In the incisiveness of his investigations, the clarity of his analytical frameworks, the scope of his erudition, and even the persistent questioning of his own conclusions, we can see Bell for what, at his best, he truly was: not a great sociologist or a great prognosticator, but a great educator of human sensibility and judgment. He teaches us about how to make necessary distinctions and how to create standards for sorting out the meretricious from the good—two of the tasks he set for a university education. The readers who turn to his work will be rewarded with an intellectually thrilling journey—and the experience of confronting a vivid future that, for better or worse, did not emerge as Bell expected.

NOTES

1. Daniel Bell, *The Coming of Post-Industrial Society: An Essay in Social Forecasting* (New York: Basic Books, 1973), 249.
2. Bell, *The Coming of Post-Industrial Society*, 261–262.
3. Bell, *The Coming of Post-Industrial Society*, 408.
4. Bell, *The Coming of Post-Industrial Society*, 408.
5. Joseph Schumpeter, *Capitalism, Socialism, and Democracy* (New York: Harper & Row, 1947).

6. Robert M. Solow, "A Contribution to the Theory of Economic Growth," *Quarterly Journal of Economics* 70, no. 1 (1956): 65–94; Robert M. Solow, "Technical Change and the Aggregate Production Function," *Review of Economics and Statistics* 39, no. 3 (1957): 312–330.

7. Zvi Griliches, "Hybrid Corn: An Exploration in the Economics of Technological Change," *Econometrica* 25, no. 4 (1957): 501–522.

8. Vernon W. Ruttan, "The Contribution of Technological Progress to Farm Output, 1950–75," *Review of Economics and Statistics* 38, no. 1 (1956): 61–69.

9. Everett Rogers, *The Diffusion of Innovations* (New York: Free Press, 1962).

10. Fritz Machlup, *The Production and Distribution of Knowledge in the U.S.* (Princeton, NJ: Princeton University Press, 1962).

11. Clark Kerr, *The Uses of the University* (Cambridge, MA: Harvard University Press, 1963).

12. Peter F. Drucker, *The Effective Executive* (New York: Harper & Row, 1967).

13. John Kenneth Galbraith, *The New Industrial State* (Boston: Houghton Mifflin, 1967).

14. Gerald M. Platt and Talcott Parsons, *The American University* (Cambridge, MA: Harvard University Press, 1973).

15. Daniel Bell, "Notes on Post-Industrial Society (I)," *The Public Interest*, no. 6 (Winter 1967): 24–35; Daniel Bell, "Notes on Post-Industrial Society (II)," *The Public Interest*, no. 7 (Spring 1967): 102–118.

16. Daniel Bell, *The Coming of Post-Industrial Society*, 344.

17. Bell, *The Coming of Post-Industrial Society*, 20.

18. Bell, *The Coming of Post-Industrial Society*, 20.

19. Bell, *The Coming of Post-Industrial Society*, 21.

20. Donald E. Stokes, *Pasteur's Quadrant: Basic Science and Technological Innovation* (Washington, DC: Brookings Institution Press, 1997).

21. Walter Isaacson, *The Innovators: How a Group of Hackers, Geniuses, and Geeks Created the Digital Revolution* (New York: Simon and Schuster, 2015).

22. Steven Brint, *Two Cheers for Higher Education: Why American Universities Are Stronger Than Ever—and How to Meet the Challenges They Face* (Princeton, NJ: Princeton University Press, 2018), 92–95.

23. Arturo Casedevall and Ferric C. Fang, "Revolutionary Science." *mBio* 7, no. 2 (2016), 1–6; Nathan Rosenberg, *Studies on Science and the Innovation Process* (Singapore: World Scientific Publications, 2010).

24. Brint, *Two Cheers for Higher Education*, 92–95.

25. Brint, *Two Cheers for Higher Education*, 55–59.

26. Bell, *The Coming of Post-Industrial Society*, 380.

27. Bell, *The Coming of Post-Industrial Society*, 249.

28. Bell, *The Coming Post-Industrial Society*, 360.

29. Bell, *The Coming of Post-Industrial Society*, 366.

30. The statement about declines among professionals and managers is based on unpublished analyses that I have conducted with Michaela Curran on General Social Survey data, 1974–2018.

31. Bell, *The Coming of Post-Industrial Society*, 318.

32. Bell, *The Coming of Post-Industrial Society*, 240.

33. Steven Brint, "Creating the Future: The 'New Directions' in Research Universities," *Minerva* 43, no. 1 (2005): 23–50.

34. Bell, *The Coming of Post-Industrial Society*, 454.

35. Bell, *The Coming of Post-Industrial Society*, 454.

36. Bell, *The Coming of Post-Industrial Society*, 423.

37. Bell, *The Coming of Post-Industrial Society*, 454.

38. Thomas A. DiPrete and Claudia Buchmann, *The Rise of Women: The Growing Gender Gap in Education and What It Means for American Schools* (New York: Russell Sage Foundation Press, 2013); Arthur Sakamoto, Kimberly A. Goyette, and ChangHwan Kim, "Socioeconomic Attainments of Asian Americans," *Annual Review of Sociology* 35 (2009): 255–276.

39. See, e.g., Steven Brint, Komi T. German, Kayleigh Anderson-Natale, Zeinab F. Shuker, and Suki Wang, "Where Ivy Matters: The Educational Backgrounds of U.S. Cultural Elites," *Sociology of Education* 93, no. 2 (2020): 153–172.

40. For an interesting exception, see Anthony Kronman, *The Assault on American Excellence* (New York: Basic Books, 2019).

41. Komi T. German, *Diversity, Equity, and Inclusion Policies on a Liberal University Campus: The Faculty's Response* (unpublished PhD dissertation, Department of Psychology, University of California, Riverside, 2020).

42. Brint, *Two Cheers for Higher Education*, 70–74. Some estimates of the share of national economic output produced by the knowledge sector industries are significantly lower than mine. Antonipillai and Lee, for example, find a 38 percent share of GDP in 2014. Their estimate is based on the eighty-one American industries that generate the most patents and trademarks. Justin Antonipillai and Michelle Lee, *Intellectual Property and the U.S. Economy: 2016 Update* (Washington, DC: Economics and Statistics Administration and U.S. Patent Office, 2016), 22.

43. Brint, *Two Cheers for Higher Education*, 74–75.

44. See, e.g., Eduardo Porter, "How the GOP Became the Party of the Left Behind," *New York Times*, January 28, 2020, B1, B6.

45. Richard Arum, Elizabeth A. Armstrong, and Mitchell L. Stevens, "Sieve, Incubator, Temple, Hub: Empirical and Theoretical Advances in the Sociology of Higher Education," *Annual Review of Sociology* 34 (2008): 127–151.

46. Richard R. Nelson, ed., *National Innovation Systems: A Comparative Analysis* (New York: Oxford University Press, 1993).

47. National Center for Science and Engineering Statistics, *Academic R&D in the United States* (Washington, DC: National Science Foundation, 2020), figure 5B-1, https://ncses.nsf.gov/pubs/nsb20202/academic-r-d-in-the-united-states#:~:text=R%26D%20conducted%20by%20higher%20education, NP%202018%3A%20Table%202).

48. Brint, *Two Cheers for Higher Education*, 205–207, 243–247.

49. Philip S. Babcock and Mindy Marks, "The Falling Time Cost of College: Evidence from Half a Century of Time Use Data," *Review of Economics and Statistics* 93 (2010), DOI:10.1162/REST_a_00093.

50. Paul D. Umbach, "How Effective Are They? Exploring the Impact of Contingent Faculty on Undergraduate Students," *Review of Higher Education* 30, no. 2 (2007): 91–123.

51. For a useful guide to teaching practices supported by this research, see Carl Wieman and Sarah Gilbert, "The Teaching Practices Inventory: A New Tool for Characterizing College and University Teaching in Mathematics and Science," *CBE Life Sciences Education* 13, no. 3 (2014): 552–569.

52. Richard Arum and Josipa Roksa, *Academically Adrift: Limited Learning on College Campuses* (Chicago: University of Chicago Press, 2011), 3–13.

53. College Board, *Trends in College Pricing* (New York: College Board, 2019).

54. Beth Akers and Matthew M. Chingos, *Game of Loans: The Rhetoric and Reality of Student Debt* (Princeton, NJ: Princeton University Press, 2016).

55. Susan Dynarski, *An Economist's Perspective on Student Loans in the United States*. The Brookings Institution ES Working Papers Series (Washington DC: Brookings Institution, 2016).

56. Suzanne Mettler, *Degrees of Inequality: How the Politics of Inequality Sabotaged the American Dream* (New York: Basic Books, 2014).

57. Kati Haycock, Mary Lynch, and Jennifer Eagle, *Opportunity Adrift: Our Flagship Universities Are Straying from Their Public Mission* (Washington, DC: The Education Trust, 2010).

58. Karen Tumulty and Jenna Johnson, "Why Trump May Be Winning the War on Political Correctness," *Washington Post*, January 4, 2016, https://www.washingtonpost.com/politics/why-trump-may-be-winning-the-war-on-political-correctness/2016/01/04/098cf832-afda-11e5-b711-1998289ffcea_story.html.

59. For extended discussions of this topic, see Greg Lukianoff and Jonathan Haidt, *The Coddling of the American Mind: How Good Intentions and Bad Ideas Are Setting up a Generation for Failure* (New York: Penguin, 2018); and Keith E. Whittington, *Speak Freely: Why Universities Must Defend Free Speech* (Princeton, NJ: Princeton University Press, 2018).

60. See, e.g., William Deresciewicz, "On Political Correctness: Power, Class, and the New Campus Religion," *American Scholar*, March 6, 2017.

61. Daniel Bell, *The Reforming of General Education: The Columbia University Experience in Its National Context* (New York: Columbia University Press, 1966).

62. Bell, *The Reforming of General Education*, 290–292.

63. Bell, *The Reforming of General Education*, 50–52.

64. Bell, *The Reforming of General Education*, 287.

65. Bell, *The Reforming of General Education*, 289.

66. Bell, *The Reforming of General Education*, 312.

67. Bell, *The Reforming of General Education*, 312.

68. Gilbert Allardyce, "The Rise and Fall of the Western Civilization Course," *American Historical Review* 87, no. 3 (1982): 695–725.

69. Steven Brint, Kristopher Proctor, Scott Patrick Murphy, Lori Turk-Bicakci, and Robert A. Hanneman, "General Education Models: The Changing Meanings of Liberal Education in American Colleges and Universities, 1975–2000," *Journal of Higher Education* 80, no. 6 (2009): 605–642.

70. Bell, *The Reforming of General Education*, 285.

71. Three other relatively popular models for general education are evident, according to my group's study of college catalogs. One of these focused on traditional liberal arts subjects, with a heavy dose of philosophy and literature. This model was most popular at religiously affiliated private colleges, particularly Catholic colleges. Another centered on cultures, both Western and non-Western, and ethics. This model was most popular at politically progressive liberal arts colleges. The final model was distinctive, in that it required courses in economics and government (and sometimes also in technology), under the influence of political conservatives

in some southern and midwestern states, who have made these courses obligatory in their states' public universities. See Brint et al., "General Education Models."

72. American Association of Colleges & Universities (AAC&U), *Liberal Education and America's Promise* (Washington, DC: AAC&U, 2005).

73. University of North Carolina, *General Education Curriculum and Degree Requirements* (Chapel Hill: University of North Carolina, 2019).

74. Harvard College, *General Education Program* (Cambridge MA: Harvard College, 2019), https://gened.fas.harvard.edu/regquirements/.

75. On the future of science policy, for example, he asks: "Will the allocative process simply be one of immediate responses to urgent definitions, either of defense or even of social needs, because of the 'discovery' of pollution, poverty, urban chaos or other social ills, or will there be an effort to spell out a coordinated set of policies based on some considerations of national goals defined in long-range terms? Will the current system of 'administrative pluralism' in which individual agencies hold power be maintained or will there be some coordinated system to unify science? If science has expanded mainly for defense posture will there be an equivalent effort in support of domestic social needs?" Bell, *The Coming of Post-Industrial Society*, 261–262.

76. Bell, *The Reforming of General Education*, 175–176.

9

DANIEL BELL, SOCIAL FORECASTER

JENNY ANDERSSON

Maybe more than any other intellectual of his generation, Daniel Bell was concerned with how to understand and define advanced industrial society, characterized in his terms by the "end of ideology" and the dawn of what he famously chose to label a new "post-industrial" stage of development. Both of these terms lent themselves to oversimplification. The end-of-ideology idea, which was not Bell's own but originated from a much wider debate on the political context of the postwar era, dominated by Raymond Aron and Edward Shils, became a trope for the age of affluence until the unrest of the late 1960s disqualified it both as an accurate description of politics and as a normative ideal. At this point, the end-of-ideology trope came to stand for a technocratic, Cold War conception of the age, which Bell himself resented.

Post-industrialism was a purloined and fraught idea too. Just like the idea of an end of ideology, ideas of a new kind of industrialism marked by knowledge, information, and creativity circulated in a wide context of sociological, often post-Marxist writers on both sides of the Cold War divide. Bell drew influences from Aron's *Dix-huit leçons sur la société industrielle* (1962, in English as *Eighteen Lessons on Industrial Society*); from his rival, the French

Marxist sociologist Alain Touraine (whose *La société post industrielle* was first published in French in 1969 and translated into English as *The Post-Industrial Society: Tomorrow's Social History* in 1971); and from the Czechoslovak sociologist and planner Radovan Richta, whose influence he discussed in the new foreword to the 1999 edition of *The Coming of Post-Industrial Society*.[1] Richta was the key architect of the debate on open futures of the Soviet system in the run-up to the 1968 Prague Spring.[2] *Civilization at the Crossroads* (published in English in 1968), written by Richta's team of planners in the Czech Academy of Science, introduced the idea of a post-industrial revolution driven by human creativity and technological potential, as well as the notion of forecasting.[3] Later, the notion of post-industrialism became associated with Schumpeterian visions of creative destruction and a range of both utopian and dystopian visions of a new knowledge-based, network form of capitalism. It is important that in their time, the notions of the end of ideology and the post-industrial society were both open-ended concepts, descriptions of possibilities and tensions more than of end points and sociological fixtures.

One of the challenges in understanding Bell is to separate out his own usage of terms, which often included a purposeful emphasis on contradiction and tension, from the meanings that they later acquired. At the same time, Bell was happy to use large terms, which may have been a result of his journalistic background, and oftentimes the contradictions in his arguments were complex and easily lost in translation as the trope caught on.

Another challenge to intellectual historians is to put Bell's work in its international context and consider his intellectual strategy of borrowing concepts and merging influences from many directions as an act of transnational translation and adaptation. Bell was a singularly well read and informed scholar, whose European connections probably outstripped most in his generation. He is interesting, therefore, in the postwar American generation of social thought, the modernization theorists who were profoundly concerned with American society and often projected their conclusions from the United States onto the global realm.[4] Bell somehow did the opposite; he took inspiration from his wide networks of French, Polish, and Czech sociologists (and probably Japanese and Korean ones too) and adapted their ideas to his own concern, thinking about the future of what Malcolm Waters describes as the "idealized American polity."[5] This constant shift of gaze from the outer to the inner workings of American society is a key to his work, but it also makes its contradictions come out stronger than may be the case if one considers Bell uniquely in a history of American social science, as has mostly been the case. Seen from within the American context, Bell becomes an agnostic of the era of affluence and the many contradictions of the American 1960s.[6] Seen in a transnational light, he rather appears as a thinker on the future of industrial societies, both liberal and socialist, and, on the related issue of how to make the future of those societies a tractable analytical problem for social scientists.

This essay will focus on Bell's ideas of social forecasting, a venture that he popularized in his 1973 book *The Coming of Post-Industrial Society*. As already stated, his ideas on forecasting originated in a tangled web of ideas and debates between liberal and Marxist scholars about the future of industrial society, beginning in the mid-1950s. Bell's own first observations on post-industrial society appeared as a note to the Salzburg seminar in 1959 (possibly drafted upon his return from his first journey to visit Polish sociologists in 1956).[7] His first contact with future research came during his time as an envoy of the Ford Foundation and the Congress for Cultural Freedom in Paris in the late 1950s.[8] The notion of an end to ideology informed discussions at the 1955 meeting on the social sciences of the Congress in Milan, and it was as an observer of European social science in Paris that Bell encountered Touraine and other Europeans debating the future of advanced societies. Touraine was one of the young French scholars that the Ford Foundation saw as victims of Marxism.[9] Paris, in the 1950s and 1960s, was a hub for translations of Marxist debates. East European thinking about the possible future of socialism was of particular interest to Bell, the Marxist skeptic, who was as interested in revisionist tendencies in Marxist scholarship as in the actual evolution of the communist system.

For a long time, future research has appeared to intellectual historians as a Cold War obsession, and Bell's biographers have also tended to see his interest in forecasting as a quirk and an add-on to a larger enterprise of social theory.[10] But Bell's concern with forecasting illustrates how his work bridged theoretical reflection about social orders and more concrete and practical analysis of the technologies and tools that might be used to shape these orders. Bell also played a key role in institutionalizing future research, in yet another act of translation. He helped bring technical scientific and planning debates into the canon of social science.

Through Bell's mediation, the Ford Foundation funded and set in place several important institutions for future research, including the French philosopher and political theorist Bertrand de Jouvenel's Futuribles think tank in Paris, to which Bell remained as a consultant, and the International Institute for Applied Systems Analysis in Vienna. In the late 1960s, as future research gained acceptance in the Soviet Union, Bell argued that it could serve as a basis of dialogue between the blocs about global and common concerns. These were crucial acts of translation in Cold War social science.[11]

When taken as a theory in its own right, Bell's thinking about social forecasting is particularly revelatory of the contradictions in his thinking: he rejected the term "technocrat" but firmly believed that social scientists had a particular problem-solving responsibility and that post-industrial society required new forms of technical expertise that could and should be applied to value-based issues. The social democrat Bell appraised forecasting as a liberal equivalent of long-term planning for social welfarist purposes, but Bell's later thinking on forecasting, inspired by the ongoing turn to neoconservatism, saw it as a possible correction to a return of irrationality in American politics. While Bell often rejected all kinds of systems thinking and determinism, he was also deeply fascinated by systems logics and their possible application to planning and policy. Maybe the greatest contradiction of all concerns his view of prediction itself. Bell repeatedly argued against prediction, both in its Marxist-Leninist version and in Alvin Toffler's techno-liberal "future schlock" (in Bell's phraseology). Yet he kept coming back to prediction as a kind of test case or experiment in the epistemology of the social sciences, as a practical application of his social theory, and also as a fun intellectual exercise of horizon gazing.[12] These contradictions make it hard to understand Bell as a social theorist, but they say a lot about him as a historical actor, translator, and mediator of social science.

The argument to come will explore three aspects of Bell's interest in future research. First, I will propose that Bell used the idea of future research to conduct a reflection on the future of industrial society, and that his interest in future research and forecasting was also directly related to the end-of-ideology proposal of a secularization of social time. Second, I will examine the notion of forecasting as a particular decision tool or social calculus for post-industrial society, and third, I will suggest that Bell's views on this intellectual technology interacted with his changing view of social change from the publication of *The End of Ideology* in 1960 until the 1973 book *The Coming of Post-Industrial Society*.

THE FUTURES OF INDUSTRIAL SOCIETY

It's useful to distinguish between Bell's interest in the future as a common problem of advanced industrial societies, liberal and Marxist, and his interest in forecasting as an intellectual technology. What initially drew Bell to future research was the problem of the future of liberal society. Like others in postwar American social science, he was also centrally concerned with how communist society would develop, and one of the advantages of systems theory was that it allowed him to think about these two problems—the futures of the capitalist and the communist worlds—together. As Nils Gilman and David Engerman have shown, the modernization theorists who formulated the end-of-ideology thesis regarded Soviet society as a form of modernity to which American modernity could be compared. Communism was not just a scarecrow for them, but also the impetus for an existential reflection on the West.

The resulting tensions were evident in the similarities in epistemological structure between Marxism and modernization theory. While modernization theorists such as Walt Rostow or Edward Shils rejected Marxist Leninist social laws, they still sought to identify and depict laws of stage-driven development for the West. Future research was a product of modernization theory. As such, it was torn between the assumptions of predictability in social affairs and the nagging anxiety that social developments might follow unexpected patterns. This ambivalence marked the postwar generation of American social science, and Bell was one of its key interpreters, from *The End of Ideology* to *The Cultural Contradictions of Capitalism*. It also explains his interest in future research.

Bell's first foray into the problem of the future, in the late 1950s, took the form of a critique of attempts in international relations theory to predict Soviet behavior.[13] He drew the conclusion that prediction in social affairs was impossible, and what could be usefully done instead was informed speculation that drew attention to future choices and the consequences of choosing one alternative over others. The first reflections on this dynamic vision of the future, in which a decision in the present leads to an unfolding myriad of consequences over time that can to some extent be foreseen, appear in *The End of Ideology* in response to C. Wright Mills's notion of a power elite (which had been published in 1956). Bell, a former good friend of Mills who was distinctly peeved by the argument of the 1956 book, argued that it was impossible to pinpoint a power elite at a time when the locus of decision-making was shifting quickly among political leaders, growing bureaucracies, and increasingly autonomous individuals.[14] Who held the power of decision? And who could reasonably foretell where the consequences of a decision led, and ended? These were new problems of power in modern society—and arguably this insight was what formed the core of Bell's analysis of post-industrialism as a new pattern of social struggle over the points of decision, which was one of the key messages in *The Coming of Post-Industrial Society*.

Bell borrowed the idea that in postwar society, a new range of decision-makers turned the act of decision into a complex question of time and consequence from two key influences: Herman Kahn's work at RAND on scenarios, which was an outcrop of wartime operations research and experimentation with stochastic reasoning and mathematics of large numbers; and de Jouvenel's notion of political (as opposed to economic) conjecture. While an economic conjecture followed law-bound movements (or at least that was the big debate in postwar economics), de Jouvenel argued that political conjecture was open-ended, dependent on political decisions, and followed sometimes unpredictable and spontaneous changes in the relations between the large mass of individuals in postwar societies and their leaders. Like Kahn, de Jouvenel was a deeply conservative political thinker who was also a monarchist, a neoliberal, and a redeemed fascist. He stood out, in the circles of the Congress for Cultural Freedom, as an odd figure, but his ideas of conjecture caught the Ford Foundation's and Bell's attention.

To de Jouvenel, conjecture was a necessary antidote to growing public power over decisions and expenditures in the postwar era. Unprecedented individual freedoms in a society of employment and consumption were, to de Jouvenel, a potential source of chaos resulting from the lack of coordination as individuals gained the power of decision over their lives and movements.[15] Some sense of direction to this chaotic social structure had to be achieved, and to de Jouvenel, who was a vehement anti-Gaullist, it could not be through planning. Planning was "power over time," an illegitimate extension of decision to new temporal horizons. In contrast, "conjecture" was a kind of *antiplanning*, a way of increasing freedom over time by entrusting speculation over long-term developments to a particular body of expertise in political scientists.[16]

It is true that de Jouvenel knew and corresponded with Friedrich Hayek, but in the context of the 1950s Congress, the antiplanning message of conjecture was perhaps lost in favor of an appreciation of conjecture as a reflection on open futures and as offering an alternative to the Marxist long-term plans of Soviet society. He was one of the skeptics of the end-of-ideology thesis, while to most intellectuals of the Congress, postwar affluence was an overwhelmingly positive, driving force of modernization. In Bell's analysis, the end-of-ideology state was in itself open-ended, but it included a core tension between, on the one hand, the appraisal of the new individual freedoms in advanced industrial society, and, on the other, the idea that these freedoms in themselves held the potential for new patterns of social conflict that might emerge over time as the struggle for status and resources changed.[17] This notion of the transformation of social conflict—not its end—runs as a line of continuity from *The End of Ideology* to *The Coming of Post-Industrial Society*. In 1965, Bell declared to a seminar of the Congress for Cultural Freedom that the end of ideology had been a mistaken hypothesis that underestimated the social tensions that were sketched in *Post-Industrial Society* and more explicitly discussed in *Cultural Contradictions*.[18]

The 1955 seminar of the Congress for Cultural Freedom in Milan was a defining moment in postwar social science. The seminar was dominated by a debate on the future of a liberal society marked by new forms of acceleration, technical progress, and mass education and consumption. By the mid-1950s, as Giles Scott Smith has shown, the Congress was shifting away from its early emphasis on art and culture in the defense against totalitarianism and toward social scientific work on growth, planning, and the organization of industrial society.[19] Bell presented notes to the seminar that became the first chapter of the 1960 book, originally intended as a response to Shils's notion of modernization as the "entry of the masses into society" and Aron's ideas of a Marxist seduction of Western intellectuals in the absence of more exciting theories.[20] These notes provide one of the clues to Bell's thinking about the future of industrial liberal society and how it could be steered and guided. The chapter was a critique of the dominant ideas of mass society in social science and accepted Shils's view that the masses were the new dynamic element driving progress and integration.

Here was an important shift in social theory: analysis of mass society had dominated interwar social thought, in which the large concern was to understand the mass movements and cult of leaders that had given rise to fascism. Strands of this analysis of mass society resurfaced after 1945, not least in Frankfurt school theory, but also in the cultural and social conservatism of scholars such as Karl Jaspers and Hannah Arendt, not to mention the neoliberalism of

Hayek (and de Jouvenel). Bell singled out Jaspers and Arendt in his argument as propagating an outmoded conservative and determinist mass society idea. Mass society, Bell suggested, had to be seen as an indeterminate social form, an indefinite social organization that was not necessarily either incompetent or prone to authoritarian rule, as were the observations of scholars who had witnessed the rise of national socialism.[21] The mass did not have a predetermined element; rather, it could be seen as a new array of human potentiality as the monopolistic social interests of one dominant social group gave way to unprecedented forms of freedom. This, to Bell, was a promising new situation, but it was not without a set of tensions that arose from the very process of integration.

The key point in Bell's argument here was that the dynamics of mass society in an age of affluence were poorly understood by social scientists. Both *The End of Ideology* and *Post-Industrial Society* were reflections on the political dynamics of a secular society defined by unprecedented forms of interaction in mass participation, communication, and education.[22] As open-ended drivers, these factors required a reflection on the future social order that they might produce. "Mass society is the product of change, and is itself change. It is the bringing of the masses into a society, from which they were once excluded. The theory of mass society affords us no view of the relations of the parts of society to each other that would enable us to locate the sources of change."[23] A task of future research was thus to contemplate the new constellations between the parts and identify key forms of change in status groups, technology, capitalism, and the structures of power "in the complexion of life under mass society." With these changes might well come new anxieties of status, a changed "character structure and moral tempers," and tensions as a result of "unfulfilled expectations."[24]

These arguments fit perfectly into the wider debate about the end of ideology. As Scott Smith insists, the end-of-ideology thesis was far more sophisticated than the common idea that progress had killed ideological strife. The end-of-ideology debate reflected notions that a formerly monopolistic social structure had given way to a plurality of interests in industrial or post-industrial society; that a welfare statist component balanced market arrangements with the greater welfare of the masses but also to the benefit of the economic order; and that technological progress, science, and knowledge were replacing class struggle as the new social force.[25] Central to the end-of-ideology thesis was a notion of the future as a secular problem of the organization and management of social time. Bell's *End of Ideology* also introduced the idea that new individual freedoms and a multitude of choices and decisions created problems of steering and management once ideologically set goals no longer charted a future.

If social time was secular, who would decide its course? The conclusion that Bell drew from this observation is what would later earn him the New Left charge of technocracy. The final chapter of *The End of Ideology* discussed the role that social scientists and Cold War intellectuals like Bell himself played in the process of change. To steer and manage social time, says Bell, is a purposeful task that is even to be seen as a kind of utopia to disenchanted intellectuals in search of a purpose (those whose opium, as Aron put it, might otherwise be Marxism).

The notion of utopia is significant here. Bell uses it in Karl Mannheim's sense in opposition to ideology, in other words as a secular notion of progress, and as a rationality-based and social scientific critique of ideology. Utopia is an incitement to a social science–based reasoning about the proper objectives of social development, their internal consistency, logical fallacies, and hidden determinisms. And utopia, in the final pages of *The End of*

Ideology, is also a dream of a technicized polity in which social conflict can be managed through what Bell sometimes referred to as "the substitution of algorithms for intuitive judgment," by which he meant the new computerized tools of cost–benefit analysis and forecasting.[26] These "intellectual technologies" or "decision tools" would play a central role in the argument of *Post-Industrial Society*, in which they appear as a form of mediation between new social groups and the political order, and thereby, as a way of anticipating emergent forms of social struggle. As he wrote the final chapter of *The End of Ideology* in 1960, Bell was decidedly optimistic about the prospects of such decision tools, suggesting that they might reinject a sense of utopian spirit and "fuse passion with intelligence" in the social politics of the 1960s.[27]

FROM THE END-OF-IDEOLOGY THESIS TO THE POST-INDUSTRIAL SOCIETY

Bell himself had a clear explanation of the relationship of his 1960 and 1973 books: "the theme of the End of Ideology was the exhaustion of old political passions; the theories that developed into *The Coming of Post-Industrial Society* sought to explore technocratic thought in relation to politics."[28] The question of how to reconcile rising social expectations within a new kind of mass society with social order—or "form," as Bell put it—remained at the heart of the argument. In fact, *Post-Industrial Society* contained three complex arguments. The first of these was the message of an ongoing shift from a preindustrial, to an industrial, to a post-industrial society—a triptych that recalled assumptions of stage-driven logics of modernization that had been the backdrop of 1950s American social science and informed works such as Walt Rostow's *The Stages of Growth*.

The second argument of the book also stood in a clear, modernist light. This was the idea that both capitalist and communist systems were essentially industrial societies that were now experiencing forms of convergence toward a post-industrial state driven by intangible goods such as information. This was not a well-received message in the Soviet Union, where the book was nonetheless included in the select library of translated volumes that held specific Communist Party interest.[29] This interest, in turn, was due to the third argument of the book, which concerned the need for forecasting in a post-industrial society marked by a high degree of economic, social, and technical complexity that posed challenges to planning as traditionally conceived (i.e., linear planning). Forecasting was sanctioned by Moscow in 1967 and understood as "total planning"—a quantitative system of long-term performance indicators to be applied to the totality of the communist state. The goal was to demonstrate the full penetration of technology in Soviet society, including in planning and decision making.

The following year, Radovan Richta's critical philosophy of planning with multiple and open-ended future objectives was squashed and banned as a bourgeois activity. What remained was a strictly quantitative approach based on a multitude of indicators.[30] In 1967, forecasting and cost–benefit analysis were also decreed as tools for the federal government in the United States.[31] Bell himself had, as a member of President Lyndon Johnson's Commission on Automation, overseen its chapter on cost–benefit analysis, which was one of the new intellectual technologies that he saw as steering technologies for post-industrial society. During his time on the Automation Commission, Bell had also closely studied technological forecasting as it was conducted in the American defense and aeronautical industries. In these industries, forecasting was used as a tool to predict the evolution of technology in a defense system because it allowed the charting of consequences of investment decisions over time and the depiction of possible technological leaps, or even systems changes.[32] Bell's notion of social forecasting as presented in the 1973 book was a reflection on the transposability of technological forecasting to the social system as an aid to a difficult measuring of investment in social spending. Bell's preface to the 1973 edition mentioned the Richta group and its critical discussion of the process of setting objectives for planning, and the book then went on to propose that a systems-oriented and quantitative kind of social forecasting could be used to conduct an informed speculation on social change and identify the "best" goals.[33]

More specifically, Bell proposed that forecasting was a necessary decision tool for an age of growing public choice (James Buchanan's book *The Calculus of Consent*, which laid the basis of public choice theory, had been published in 1962). In this new era, a growing number of decisions would no longer be made in the individual or market realm, but rather in a realm guided by principles of collective decision-making. This shift posed, Bell argued, a principled problem for a liberal polity characterized by freedom of choice, market mechanisms, and a high degree of individual arbitration. Post-industrial society, he wrote, was a society characterized by the fact that "the large majority of social groups had active 'claims' on the state," and of a new sense of public responsibility for education and welfare that transformed the relationship between the political order and the citizenry by raising expectations of the public. It was crucial, therefore, to develop forms of foresight that could help anticipate and evaluate the consequences of public decisions over time, their effects on the distribution of power between social groups, and the desired or possibly undesirable consequences of a social program for the future.[34]

It is worth pointing out here that there was a significant time lag between Bell's first drafts of *The Coming of Post-Industrial Society* and its publication in 1973. The turbulent ten-year period in American intellectual history when he was working on the book profoundly changed his outlook on American society. In 1964, Bell assumed the chairmanship of the Commission for the Year 2000 in the American Academy of Arts and Sciences, and *Post-Industrial Society* drew on drafts and notes that he prepared for the commission. His first address to the commission said that American society was in the process of becoming, for the first time, a "communal society"—by which he meant a society in which a majority of decisions was made on the basis of a sense of public responsibility.[35] A growing share of the national expenditure went to public welfare purposes and social programs. A growing number of people worked in the federal administration and were in various ways involved in the state apparatus. Presidential power was growing, and the decisions that the government was making promised to transform the future of American society. Also, the emphasis here was on change as open-ended—a set of "open futures"—but, Bell pointed out, while the futures that confronted American society were still open, the decisions made in reaction to them in the present would shape the thirty-year period to come. They therefore necessitated a forward-looking analysis of just how they would transform the United States.[36]

In 1964, these were highly positive notions that reflected a problem-solving spirit. As Otis Graham has shown, the early 1960s saw a "New Deal" moment in debates on public administration and a renewed interest in ideas of planning.[37] Clearly, Bell's first interest in future research was that it could be used to develop a new planning function for a liberal society with welfare ambitions to fulfill those rising expectations that Bell saw in *The End of Ideology* as key to the pacification of social life. He thought that such planning had to be different in kind from the long-term planning of the Marxist system, in which all future objectives were predetermined and individual and market freedoms thus curtailed.

In this context, and borrowing in a slightly breathtaking way from both the arch conservative de Jouvenel and the social pragmatist and democratic theorist John Dewey, Bell defended future research as a form of planning that increased freedom of choice over time, by speculating on the consequences of public decisions and on whether these consequences increased individual and public freedoms.[38] Bell's essay "The Study of the Future," in the first issue of the *Public Interest* in 1966, regarded future research as a contribution to planning that would improve governmental efficacy and the quality of decisions by integrating a kind of informed speculation about the consequences of decisions.[39]

Planning with the future in view was a way of increasing societal options and avoiding bad decisions. With Dewey in mind, Bell seems to have intended an essentially qualitative social science discussion that would reflect on the value-laden character of social problems and present options to politicians and public opinion. This was also the guiding idea behind the Commission on the Year 2000, which was basically a congregation of Cold War intellectuals, wise men (only one woman, Margaret Mead, was involved, and she was not a member of the commission), and friends of Bell. The commission was introduced in "Government by Commission," another essay in *The Public Interest*, as a forum that would help plan long-term decisions. Importantly, the essay picked up on de Jouvenel's notion that long-term forecasting should not take place on presidential orders, but rather should have a measure of independence from the locus of decision because growing political power was in itself one of the drivers of change.[40]

This was a noteworthy comment in 1966, the year in which the criticism of the Great Society programs, and the community-action program in particular, really began—not least in the pages of *The Public Interest*. Justin Vaisse includes Bell in what he qualifies as the first generation of neoconservatives, the former progressives who, like Irving Kristol, Daniel Patrick Moynihan, and Bell, had applauded the Great Society programs but now thought that growing public responsibility for welfare was transforming the American social contract and had set in motion a new set of group claims on the state.[41]

The same pages carried a critique of a growing centralization of presidential power, precisely due to its dislocation of decision from the marketplace and the individual to an unchecked "public choice." These debates marked a new strand of American social science from this moment on, as Chicago school theorists identified public choice as the central factor in politics.[42] As Bell completed the chapter on social forecasting in *Post-Industrial Society*, the argument also revealed the conflict between the social democrat, who thought that future research could achieve a planning function for communal welfarist purposes, and the neoconservative, who thought that forecasting could perform a kind of correction to a spiraling logic of growing public power and group claims.

In the book, Bell presents social forecasting as a solution to Kenneth Arrow's social choice theorem, also known as the "impossibility" theorem, according to which a planner cannot move from the individual ranking of preferences to a collective ranking without violating the former (in other words, individual freedom). In a communal society with welfare ambitions, this dilemma somehow had to be resolved, and Bell's suggestion in 1973 is a quantitative application of social indicators in order to ex ante evaluate the costs and benefits of social programs and their desirability over time. In the 1973 book, this is no longer a question of a qualitative social science speculation on the future; rather, it concerns the need to apply a new "calculus" to the problem of social choice and resolve those issues that arise because "men have different valuations."[43] The role of this technicist ex ante evaluation is to mediate between competing social claims, solve the problem of social choice, and thereby contribute to managing post-industrialism by turning value-laden social analysis into a problem of rational scrutiny.

In the end, the definition of post-industrialism in the book is one that has fallen by the wayside in retrospective readings—namely, the idea that a post-industrial society is one in which the key form of social struggle is no longer labor–capital conflict but rather the struggle over social choice, hence transforming the locus of decision into the key point of social struggle in society. Bell says, "There is visible change from market to non-market, political decision making. The market disperses responsibility. The political center is visible, the question of who gains and loses is clear, and government becomes a cockpit."[44] The act and site of political decision, the "cockpit," then becomes a space where political power bargains with interest groups in ways that Bell thought were detrimental to the form. He argues, "One of the issues of a Great Society—one which can be defined as a society that seeks to become conscious of its goals—is the relationship, if not the clash, between 'rationality' and 'politics.' "[45] A society caught in a logic of growing social claims on behalf of interest groups depended, in Bell's view, on a new capacity to manage political decisions so that conflicts between groups could be settled rationally. The chapter on social forecasting in the 1973 book, therefore, was devoted to the problem of how to transform social choice into a "rational social choice," which Bell defines as a social choice mediated through forecasting expertise and a systematic application of quantitative judgment in evaluation of costs and benefits, so the best priorities for spending can be achieved.[46]

FINAL REMARKS

Whether this was a plea for technocracy, in our understanding of the term, is in some ways a different question, and Bell used many pages in both *The End of Ideology* and *Post-Industrial Society* to warn against the fallacies and dangers of a new technocratic society governed by systems engineers. But Bell increasingly thought, from the late 1960s on, that post-industrial society was a society in which the relationship between groups and the political order was marked by a latent dissatisfaction resulting from growing claims. He also clearly thought that these were to some extent irrational, and they sidelined social science expertise. In both *The End of Ideology* and *Post-Industrial Society*, there is therefore a kind of legacy with the skepticism of conservative theories of mass society—looking forward perhaps to the argument in *Cultural Contradictions*.[47]

Bell's insistence on the mobilization of social scientists and systems engineers for social problem-solving reflects a worry about how to avoid a return of the politics of passion, and he thought that the application of decision technology could help rationalize decisions and create a basis of legitimacy for an at least limited welfare state in American society. As such, it would help mediate and correct the return of contestation in American society. Some of the tools that he mobilized for this—in particular, the notions of rationality and public choice—were also the tools and concepts that formed the epistemological cornerstone of the great backlash to the welfare state in the subsequent decades.[48]

Here, Bell operated yet another central act of translation, which links the progressivist ideals of the early 1960s to the mounting critique of the welfare state in the years to come.

NOTES

1. Daniel Bell, *The Coming of Post-Industrial Society: A Venture in Social Forecasting*, 2nd ed. (Cambridge, MA: Harvard University Press, 1999), xxv–xxx.

2. Bell's notes from a trip to Poland, 1956, in the Bell archives, Harvard. See also Daniel Bell, "Foreword," *The Coming of Post-Industrial Society*, ix–lxxxv.

3. Radovan Richta, *Civilization at the Crossroads: Social and Human Implications of the Scientific Revolution* (White Plains, NY: International Arts and Science Press, 1969); Viteszlav Sommer, "Forecasting the Post-Socialist Future: From Futurology to Prognostika," in *The Struggle for the Long Term in Transnational Science and Politics. Forging the Future*, ed. Jenny Andersson and Eglė Rindzevičiūtė (London: Routledge, 2015), 144–168.

4. Nils Gilman, *Mandarins of the Future: Modernization Theory in Cold War America* (Baltimore: John Hopkins Press, 2003).

5. Malcolm Waters, *Daniel Bell* (New York: Routledge, 1996), 69.

6. Howard Brick, *Daniel Bell and the Decline of Intellectual Radicalism: Social Theory and Political Reconciliation in the 1940s* (Madison: Wisconsin University Press, 1986); Howard Brick, *The Age of Contradiction: American Thought and Culture in the 1960s* (Ithaca, NY: Cornell University Press, 2000); Daniel Horowitz, *The Anxieties of Affluence: Critiques of American Consumer Culture, 1939–1979* (Amherst: University of Massachusetts Press, 2004).

7. Note dated 1959, box 3, folder 14, Bell archives, Harvard.

8. See Jenny Andersson, *The Future of the World: Futurology, Futurists and the Struggle for the Cold War Imagination* (New York: Oxford University Press, 2018), 49–57.

9. See Pierre Gremion, *L'intelligence de l'anticommunisme: Le congrès de la liberté de la culture à Paris, 1950–1975* (Paris, Seuil, 1995).

10. Brick, *Age of Contradiction*; Waters, *Daniel Bell*.

11. See David Engerman, "Social Science in the Cold War," *Isis* 2 (2010): 393–400.

12. See Waters, *Daniel Bell*, 150.

13. Daniel Bell, "Ten Theories in Search of Reality: The Prediction of Soviet Behavior in the Social Sciences," *World Politics* 10, no. 3 (1958): 327–365.

14. Daniel Bell, *The End of Ideology*, 3rd ed. (Glencoe, IL: Free Press, 1960), 66f.

15. Zeev Sternhell, *Ni droite ni gauche: L'ideologie fasciste en France* (Paris: Seuil, 2013); Francois Denord, *Néolibéralisme version française: Histoire d'une idéologie politique* (Paris: Demopolis, 2007); Olivier Dard, *Bertrand de Jouvenel* (Paris: Seuil, 2008).

16. Andersson, *The Future of the World*, 70.

17. See Bell, "Mass Society—A Critique," *The End of Ideology: On the Exhaustion of Political Ideas in the 1950s* (Cambridge MA: Harvard University Press, 2000), 21–39, and Bell, "Coda: An Agenda for the Future," *The Coming of Post Industrial Society*, 371–488.

18. CCF seminar on the future, 1965, box 3, Bell archives, Harvard.

19. Giles Scott Smith, "The Congress for Cultural Freedom, the End of Ideology, and the Milan Seminar of 1955," *Journal of Contemporary History* 37, no. 3 (2002): 437–455.

20. These were the notes that became "The Breakup of Family Capitalism," in *The End of Ideology*, 2000, 39–46.

21. Bell, *The End of Ideology*, 2000; see also "Preface" (written in 1976), *The Coming of Post-Industrial Society*, cii.

22. Bell, *The End of Ideology*, 31.

23. Bell, *The End of Ideology*, 38.

24. Bell, *The End of Ideology*, 36–38, 38.

25. Elena Aronova, "The Congress for Cultural Freedom, Minerva, and the Quest for Instituting Science Studies in the Age of Cold War," *Minerva* 50 (2012): 307–337.

26. Bell, *The End of Ideology*, 405.

27. Bell, *The End of Ideology*, 32.

28. Bell, *The Coming of Post-Industrial Society*, 34.

29. See Bell, *The Coming of Post-Industrial Society*, xxv f.

30. Sommer, "Forecasting the Post Socialist Future."

31. See Jennifer Light, *From Warfare to Welfare: Defense Intellectuals and Urban Problems in Cold War America* (Baltimore: John Hopkins University Press, 2003), 166.

32. See, for instance, Bell, *The Coming of Post-Industrial Society*, 203.

33. Bell, *The Coming of Post-Industrial Society* (for instance, pp. 307, 326, 357), and also Bell, lecture notes on forecasting as "goalsetting," dated 1967, Bell archives, Harvard, box 3.

34. Bell, *The Coming of Post-Industrial Society*, 301; see also Daniel Bell, "Preliminary Memorandum," in *Toward the Year 2000: Work in Progress*, ed. Daniel Bell and Stephen R. Graubard (Cambridge, MA: MIT Press), 17–21.

35. Bell, *The Coming of Post-Industrial Society*, 301–304.

36. Daniel Bell, "The Trajectory of an Idea," in *The Year 2000: Work in Progress*, ed. Daniel Bell and Stephen R. Graubard (Cambridge, MA: MIT Press), 1–17.

37. Otis Graham, *Toward a Planned Society: From Roosevelt to Nixon* (New York: Oxford University Press, 1976), 110f.

38. Daniel Bell, "Twelve Modes of Prediction. A Preliminary Sorting of Approaches in the Social Sciences," in *Daedalus* 3 (1964): 845–880; Bell,

"Preface," *The Coming of Post-Industrial Society*, ci–cv, ciii. On Dewey, see Dorothy Ross, *Origins of American Social Science* (Cambridge, MA: Harvard University Press, 1991), and John Dewey, *Liberalism and Social Action* (New York: G. P. Putnam, 1935).

39. Daniel Bell, "The Study of the Future," *The Public Interest* 1 (1966): 119–131.

40. Daniel Bell, "Government by Commission," *The Public Interest* 5 (1966): 3–10. See also Bell's discussion of Bertrand de Jouvenel's essay "The Principate," in *The Coming of Post-Industrial Society*, 312.

41. Justin Vaisse, *Neoconservatism: The Biography of a Movement* (Cambridge, MA: Harvard University Press, 2010), 43–55; Michael Katz, *The Undeserving Poor: From the War on Poverty to the War on Welfare* (New York: Pantheon, 1990).

42. Daniel Rodgers discussion, *Age of Fracture* (Cambridge MA, Harvard University Press, 2011), 86.

43. Bell, *The Coming of Post-Industrial Society*, 305, 358.

44. Bell, *The Coming of Post-Industrial Society*, 298.

45. Bell, *The Coming of Post-Industrial Society*, 307.

46. Bell, chapter 6, "Who Will Rule? Politicians and Technocrats in the Post Industrial Society," in *The Coming of Post-Industrial Society*, 339–369.

47. See Peter Murphy, "Daniel Bell, Conservative," *Thesis Eleven* 118, no. 1 (2013): 72–82.

48. Waters does point to these elements, as well as to Bell's idea of the public as a household, which became a key element of neoliberal thinking, Waters, *Daniel Bell*, 83f.

PART IV

CAPITALISM, CULTURE, AND THE PUBLIC HOUSEHOLD

10

THE CULTURAL CONTRADICTIONS
OF CAPITALISM, THEN AND NOW

FRED TURNER

I n 1976, Daniel Bell was a worried man. A few years earlier, in *The Coming of Post-Industrial Society*, he had proclaimed the rise of a new social order. In the industrial era, when men made their money by making things, he'd argued, the brute strength of muscles and machines ruled the day. Now, thanks to the acceleration of scientific research and the rise of new information technologies, "theoretical knowledge" would drive innovation; the economy would shift from making things to providing services; and a "new class" of well-educated technocrats would manage the system.[1] Yet, when he looked out the window of his Harvard office, Bell saw young, long-haired students who seemed to care little for reason or technology and to worry only about finding themselves. When he went to the magazine stand or the movies, he saw what he called a "porno-pop culture," swamped in hedonism and utterly preoccupied with individual desire.[2] How was it, he wondered, that the rise of an economic and technological order, driven by reason, should be accompanied by the rise of a culture that celebrated the irrational, the sexual, the very Dionysian forces against which reason had always struggled?

In *The Cultural Contradictions of Capitalism*, Bell tried to answer this question by repurposing the analytical framework that he had developed for *The Coming of Post-Industrial Society*. The cultural conditions he saw around him could best be imagined as products of the interplay of three distinct realms, he explained: the technical-economic, the political, and the cultural, each governed by its own core principle. The techno-economic sphere embraced rationalization; the political, the search for equality; and the cultural, the desire for symbolic expression. The central contradiction of capitalism, he argued, was that a techno-economic realm driven by the search for "efficiency and functional rationality" had produced a modernist culture that was "prodigal, promiscuous, dominated by an anti-rational, anti-intellectual temper in which the self is taken as the touchstone of cultural judgments, and the effect on the self the measure of the aesthetic worth of experience."[3]

Bell was hardly alone in critiquing Americans' obsession with the self in the late 1970s.[4] What made Bell's analysis distinct, however, was the way that he lifted Americans' inward turn in the wake of the Vietnam War out of its proximate historical context and relocated it along a historical arc that stretched from the middle of the eighteenth century to the end of the twentieth. Prior to the age of mass production, he argued, the Protestant ethic had united the cultural and the techno-economic spheres and provided a moral rationale for good government too. But since the advent of industrialization in eighteenth-century Europe, the rise of marketing and the mass production of consumer goods had corroded the ethos of delayed gratification and the ostensibly abstemious habits of workers. This corrosion in turn helped spark the rise of modernism, a cultural movement that Bell defined by its constant search for the new, the disruptive, and the dangerous. In his view, it was not just post-Vietnam malaise that afflicted Americans. It was also the fact that the chaotic, narcissistic culture of modernism had begun to swamp the rational ethos on which techno-economic development and American democracy depended.

Today, we might be tempted to agree. Irrationality is everywhere triumphant. From Instagram to Facebook to Twitter, the individual self has become ground zero for assessing the value and meaning of experience. But if that's true, it's not because the antinomian impulses of American culture somehow overwhelmed the more rational, progressive impulses of the technological and economic spheres. Rather, it's because the two worlds were entwined from the beginning. By artificially dividing American society into three spheres—the techno-economic, the political, and the cultural—Bell was able to identify the technological and cultural forces that continue to shape our moment. Yet, when he asserted that each sphere moved to its own music, he blinded himself to the ways that much of the culture he decried in fact embraced and even grew out of the techno-economic changes he described. Within Bell's intellectual framework, culture and technocracy appear to be at odds, but in the world outside his office, they were deeply in synch. And it is that synchrony that has brought us to where we are today.

WHAT DANIEL BELL GOT WRONG

The Cultural Contradictions of Capitalism takes aim not only at tendencies in modernism, but at the counterculture of the 1960s in particular. To understand why, we need to return to the spring of 1968. That April, Bell was teaching at Columbia University when the campus erupted. Driven by fears that Columbia was expanding into Harlem against the will of its African American residents, as well as by anger at the university's role in U.S. Defense Department research, students had seized a handful of campus buildings, taken a dean hostage for twenty-four hours, and brought university life to a standstill for a week. Bell tried to help mediate the dispute as a member of an ad-hoc faculty committee, but to no avail. At 2:30 in the morning on April 30, a thousand helmeted, baton-wielding New York City policemen launched a violent assault on the student occupiers, arresting nearly seven hundred and injuring more than a hundred as well.[5]

The student uprising at Columbia was one of hundreds of explosive events that spring, including the Tet Offensive in February, the assassination of Martin Luther King, Jr., and subsequent rioting in April, and the violent marches that overwhelmed Paris in May. For Bell, the revolt at Columbia came to stand in for them all. In a long account of what he had seen at Columbia written soon after the crackdown, Bell described the university as a "moral community" and the student strikes as a threat to its moral order. What's more, wrote Bell, the university was "*the* paramount institution" in "the post-industrial societies of tomorrow."[6] When students called for participation in university governance and challenged the logic of American technocracy, Bell implied, they challenged their own future. And when they imagined themselves as rebels in the mold of Che Guevara or Malcolm X, they were simply acting out a logic born hundreds of years earlier. Their guerrilla tactics, wrote Bell, were "the guttering last gasps of a romanticism soured by rancor and impotence."[7]

In the fall of 1969, while at the Russell Sage Foundation, Bell drafted the essay that would become the first chapter of *The Cultural Contradictions of Capitalism*. There and throughout the rest of the book, Bell depicted the kinds of students who marched at Columbia as disappointed idealists and unwitting descendants of the modernist artistic rebels of a hundred years before, as well as of their Romantic predecessors. To the modernist mindset, he wrote, "the sensibility of the 1960s added something distinctly its own: a concern with violence and cruelty; a preoccupation with the sexually perverse; a desire to make noise; an anti-cognitive and anti-intellectual mood; an effort once and for all to erase the boundary between 'art' and 'life'; and a fusion of art and politics."[8] Today, we might see through Bell's worries about sexual perversion to the early stirrings of lesbian, bisexual, gay, transgender, and queer/questioning (LBGTQ) rights and feminism, and through his concern with violence to a younger generation's entirely appropriate rage at America's obscene adventure in Vietnam. But by his own lights, these were all features of a modernist preoccupation with the "demonic" now manifesting in a single social movement called the *counterculture.*[9]

According to Bell, the counterculture was a "counterfeit culture," one that wanted to dissolve a "shared moral order."[10] It sought to tear down orderly bureaucratic institutions and the meritocratic ideals that sustained them, replacing both with a celebration of individual experience. Even as he saw the worlds of technology and economics becoming more rationalized—and demanding a new class of more rational workers—Bell feared that the counterculture's preoccupation with the ecstatic would dissolve the desire to work. "The rise of a hippie drug rock culture on the popular level . . . undermines the social structure itself," he argued, "by striking at the motivational and psychic-reward system which has sustained it."[11] Perhaps even more dangerous, in Bell's view, was the countercultural preoccupation with consciousness. Attempting to sum up the threat posed by the counterculture to post-industrial society, Bell quoted the book that more than other defined the counterculture's aspirations at the time: Theodore Roszak's 1968 volume *The Making of a Counter Culture*:

> Nothing less is required than the subversion of the scientific world-view with its entrenched commitment to an egocentric and cerebral mode of consciousness. In its place there must be a new culture in which the non-intellectual capacities of personality—those

capacities that take fire from visionary splendor and the experience of human communion—become the arbiters of the true, the good, and the beautiful.[12]

Wedded to his tripartite model of society, Bell had already declared the counterculture a descendant of an antinomian modernism and, by definition, structurally distinct from the techno-economic sphere. Thus, he had no way of interpreting Roszak's critique of the scientific worldview. For Roszak and others like him, science as a whole was not the problem. Rather, what horrified the counterculture was the way that the rationality of science had fueled the madness of atomic warfare and the fighting in Vietnam. Even as he and others rejected the egotism of America's generals and chief executive officers and their faith in the military-industrial complex, the counterculture that Roszak described actually *celebrated* the collaborative style of the scientific research world, its faith in technology and engineering, and its vision of a social world interlinked by invisible systems of communication.

At Columbia, Bell had seen the New Left's concern with cultural style and assumed that within the movement, culture and politics were one. Yet, across the United States, and particularly in northern California where Roszak lived and worked, there were at least two distinct social movements—the New Left and another that I have elsewhere called the "New Communalists."[13] Born of the civil rights movement, led by Students for a Democratic Society, and anchored in Berkeley, the New Left sought to do politics to change politics. Its members may have smoked pot and grown out their hair, but by and large, they trusted in the power of political action to make social change. The New Communalists, on the other hand, eschewed politics. Gathered in the Victorian townhouses of San Francisco's Haight-Ashbury district, they dropped acid, lived communally, and tried to build a new kind of intimacy around their shared mindsets—that is, consciousness.

In the fall of 1967, after San Francisco's fabled Summer of Love, the hippies of the Haight had become a media spectacle, and some were getting tired of it. They began to leave the city for the hills, heading "back to the land," as the saying went. When they did, they joined the largest wave of commune-building in American history. Between 1965 and 1972, analysts estimate that as many as 10,000 communes were formed, and they were inhabited by as many as three-quarters of a million Americans.[14] To Daniel Bell, the scruffy back-to-the-landers must have looked like living antitheses to the research scientists of the Cold War. Yet, despite their desire to get back in touch with nature and their self-imposed poverty, the New Communalists were very much the children of American technocracy. Most were white and middle or upper-middle class. Many had college educations. Some, like Apple Computer cofounder Steve Jobs, were already on their way to membership in Bell's "new class."

The commune dwellers of the 1960s had grown up in the United States of the 1950s, and as such, they faced a generational dilemma with regard to technology. They did not want to become the white-collar men and stay-at-home mothers of the period sit-com *Father Knows Best*, nor did they want to become the kind of scientists who produced the atom bomb. At the same time, they enjoyed a postwar scientific and industrial boom that had brought them a national highway system and cheap cars to travel it, not to mention affordable amplifiers and electric guitars, the Pill and LSD. How could they escape the militarized world of big technology and big bureaucracy and at the same time keep hold of the glorious consumer technologies that world had provided?

In a 1963 paperback called *Ideas and Integrities* that was read across the counterculture, the peripatetic architect Buckminster

Fuller gave them an answer. Fuller argued that the young should take the technological world they had inherited and repurpose it, as he put it, "from killingry to advanced livingry—adequate for all humanity."[15] Like pirates, they should capture everything, from new building materials to new machines to the kinds of new ideas that Daniel Bell called "theoretical knowledge," and put it to work to improve their individual lives at home. Commune dwellers took him at his word, turning the geodesic domes that Fuller had once sold to the U.S. Army as housing for radar installations into housing for themselves.

In the fall of 1968, Fuller's writings helped inspire the creation of what would become the flagship publication of the New Communalist movement, the *Whole Earth Catalog*. Its publishers, entrepreneur and multimedia artist Stewart Brand and his then-wife, Lois, created the *Catalog* to be an "access device" for people who had moved back to the land.[16] The *Catalog* appeared twice a year until 1972, sold more than a million copies, and even won a National Book Award. It presented descriptions of tools that Brand and his readers thought would be useful to commune dwellers and explained how to acquire them. Although the tools on display did include the occasional windmill or woodstove, the vast majority were books. And many of those were titles that synthesized the systems theories and cybernetics that had dominated the military-industrial world since World War II.

The *Catalog*'s first and most prominent section was called "Whole Systems." Alongside the writings of Fuller, it featured such classics of the military-industrial research world as Herbert Simon's *Sciences of the Artificial* and Norbert Wiener's *The Human Use of Human Beings*. Clearly the New Communalists were not antiscience. But to understand why hippies on farms in Tennessee and Colorado would want to be reading the founding documents of artificial intelligence and cybernetics, we have to let go of a second piece of Bell's analytical framework. According to him, the core principle driving technological and scientific innovation was rationality. If you think of science and engineering at the level of experiment and device design, it's hard to disagree: irrational procedures don't tend to produce systematic knowledge or machines that work. Yet, in the 1960s and 1970s, the members of Cold War research communities were often invested in the same search for alternative systems of meaning and new ways of living that drove the New Communalists. Physicists embraced the Tao; chemists helped grow organic foods; psychologists celebrated human potential and the wonders of LSD; biologists established semicommunal research centers such as the New Alchemy Institute and Biosphere II, in which to contemplate the fate of the species as a whole.[17]

The New Communalists in turn embraced the works of Simon and Wiener because they offered a vision of a world in which politics could be replaced by invisible systems of communication. In *The Human Use of Human Beings*, for instance, Wiener imagined that the organic, social, and mechanical worlds could all be seen as a single system of information exchange. Like computers, he wrote, human beings simply moved through their lives seeking feedback from one another, and from that process, order emerged. For commune dwellers who were seeking to escape the kinds of political conflicts then tearing American public life apart, Wiener's vision presented an appealing alternative: just do want you want to do, and the world will teach you what you need to know. Do it together, and society will organize itself.

In *The Coming of Post-Industrial Society*, Bell had argued that "a technocratic society is not ennobling . . . a post-industrial society cannot provide a transcendent ethic."[18] In *The Cultural Contradictions of Capitalism*, he explained why: the hedonistic cultures that arose alongside post-industrial society had undercut the Protestant ethic. What Bell couldn't see was that as they emerged

together, post-industrial technocracy and countercultural ideal-
ism were legitimating one another and producing a new ethos.
To the readers of the *Whole Earth Catalog* and cyberneticists alike,
a good world was one in which domination and hierarchy had
largely been replaced by collaboration and information exchange.
Individuals were to seek their own happiness, to express their
inner being, and to adjust themselves to one another as they did.
Technologies would assist in this process. As the *Catalog* demonstrated, information technologies could create visible social
worlds, interlink individual ambitions, and provide a forum for
self-expression and personal growth.

This new ethos did indeed have the self at its center, as Bell
feared. But so did the Protestant ethic. And like that ethic, the
new ethos had a religious tinge. Where a preindustrial Protestant
might have forestalled personal gratification so as to accumulate
wealth, and thereby evidence of his or her upcoming admission
to heaven, a post-industrial reader of the *Whole Earth Catalog* or
The Human Use of Human Beings would have sought to express himself or herself in that very moment, to self-actualize, as many said
at the time. But in a post-industrial world of collaboration and
knowledge sharing, technology-enabled self-expression opened
the door to the same wealth that once rewarded the self-denying
Protestant. Moreover, in the 1960s and 1970s at least, it promised
something of a heaven on Earth—that is, a world watched over not
by radar operators and missile stations, nor even by traditional
politicians, but by individuals themselves, seeking feedback from
one another and living in mutual harmony.

THE COMING OF BOHEMIAN TECHNOCRACY

In *The Cultural Contradictions of Capitalism*, Bell suffered as he
watched what he thought might be the overthrow of a once

well-ordered America. He was plagued by the fear that the children of the industrial and scientific establishments had turned their backs on its gifts. Just at the moment when science and engineering were beginning to create a world in the image of the university, a moral system in which knowledge and collaboration would drive social change, the countercultural young seemed to have rushed to "the psychedelic extremes—in sexuality, nudity, perversions, pot, and rock."[19] Reading the book today, you can almost see Bell sitting at his desk, head in his hands. "Who today defends tradition?" he exclaimed. "And where is the power of the past to hold back any tides of the new?"[20]

Bell might have been comforted if he had traveled to Silicon Valley. There, he would have seen a region migrating from large-scale military-industrial production toward small-scale start-ups and consumer technology. And he would have caught a glimpse of the ways that the culture that he thought would undermine the techno-economic sphere was in fact coming to sustain it. Since the early 1970s, in Silicon Valley and beyond, the counterculture of the 1960s, and especially its New Communalist wing, have provided a rich set of resources with which members of Bell's new class have in fact built out much of the post-industrial society he foresaw. In the 1980s and 1990s, Americans saw wave after wave of outsourcing, corporate disaggregation, and radical deindustrialization. Culture—and specifically counterculture—began to do some of the work that bureaucracy itself had once done. The language of self-actualization provided a new management ethos. Communal modes of gathering provided new models for project-based teams. And even cities themselves, under pressure to attract ostensibly valuable high-tech industries, began to cultivate artists and hipsters in the hope that their countercultural habits would draw industrial entrepreneurs. Far from undoing the Protestant ethic, the ideals of the counterculture helped organize and legitimate today's digital capitalism.

The process began at about the same time that Bell's book was heading into print. Over the preceding decade, the computer industry on both coasts had been busily developing desktop computers, primarily for business applications. In 1976, Steve Jobs and Steve Wozniak founded Apple Computer and began to market computer miniaturization as a species of countercultural change. Jobs had lived on the communal All One Farm for about a year and would later call the *Whole Earth Catalog* "one of the bibles of my generation."[21] He and Wozniak presented their small, user-centered computers as "personal" devices much in the tradition of the *Catalog*. They were tools of personal empowerment, all-purpose information machines designed to help you become ever more the person you wanted to be. Despite Silicon Valley's deep roots in the military-industrial firmament, Apple computers were meant to be tools of personal liberation. In 1984, Apple's marketing team drove the point home in a TV ad for the Super Bowl: the Macintosh computer, they intoned, "was the reason 1984 wouldn't be like *1984*."[22]

Jobs and Wozniak were hardly the only young programmers to draw inspiration from the counterculture or the *Whole Earth Catalog*. Alan Kay and his colleagues at Xerox PARC mined the *Catalog* for interface design ideas. Ted Nelson, a visionary programmer whose designs foreshadowed the linked world of the internet, wrote a book called *Computer Lib! You Can and Must Understand Computers Now!* that was designed to resemble the *Catalog*. And Brand himself would go on to stage the first Hackers' Conference in 1984, found one of the most influential online communities, the Whole Earth 'Lectronic Link, in 1985, and help *Wired* magazine get off the ground in 1993.[23] In the 1970s and 1980s, the legacy of the Bay Area counterculture permeated Silicon Valley's computer industry. Brand even went so far as to suggest that the computer might be a new LSD—that is, the kind of technology that might finally bring about the kind of community that so many New Communalists had dreamed of.[24]

Beyond the Valley, though, the landscape of the American economy was changing dramatically. As sociologist Gerald Davis shows in his gut-wrenching historical analysis, *The Vanishing American Corporation*, the 1970s marked the beginning of the end of the postwar corporate order.[25] In the wake of World War II, corporations like General Electric and General Motors employed vast numbers of workers and sustained whole regions with their profits. Thanks to agreements with unionized labor, as well as a broad cultural consensus that corporations should serve the public good, firms offered stable, long-term employment and held executive compensation in check. In the 1970s, a recession driven by the Organization of the Petroleum-Exporting Countries (OPEC) triggered a wave of layoffs, and in the early 1980s, Reagan-era deregulation led to hostile takeovers, the rise of activist investors, and a new way of understanding the corporation among the public at large. By the end of the decade, the corporation was no longer a vehicle for providing long-term employment or sustaining American communities; it was a mechanism for generating profits for shareholders.

In the early 1990s, this newly financialized corporation met the internet and the World Wide Web.[26] Increasingly ubiquitous digital networks helped make it easy and inexpensive to outsource functions that had once had to be gathered under a single corporate roof.[27] As a result, corporations became free to break up their supply chains, to seek the lowest-cost providers anywhere in the world, and to abandon the kinds of regions and communities that had animated the corporations of the 1950s. Journalists and scholars began to describe these new corporate forms in language supplied by the internet sector, as "networked" and "virtual." A 1993 cover story for *Business Week* magazine, for instance, explained that "the virtual corporation is a temporary network of independent companies—suppliers, customers, even erstwhile rivals—linked by information technology to share skills, costs, and access to one another's markets." It had no "central office," no "organization chart," "no hierarchy, no vertical integration."[28] Like the internet itself, the newly disaggregated corporation could be everywhere and nowhere at the same time. It became the heart of what analysts began to call the "new economy," and even "the network society."[29]

These developments were disastrous for many Americans. From the late 1970s on, corporate financialization, globalization, and virtualization helped drive a wave of deindustrialization whose consequences can still be seen in the run-down houses of Flint, Michigan, or the empty textile mills of Dan River, North Carolina.[30] Although Daniel Bell would likely have paled at this outcome, he had in part predicted it. The rational, economizing impulses that he saw at the center of the techno-economic realm had allowed this decentralized model of manufacturing to emerge. What Bell did not predict was that the antinomian style of the counterculture would become a structuring resource for managers and workers in this new environment. Networked organizations required temporary, project-based, hyperflexible modes of work and a kind of person comfortable with frequent changes of employment.[31] Workers in turn needed to build rich social and professional networks to help them find projects quickly and easily. As the French sociologists Luc Boltanski and Eve Chiapello have shown, memories of the 1960s counterculture provided a rich set of tools with which to keep body and soul together in this new environment.

In 1999, Boltanski and Chiapello published a large-scale study of management literature in the United States and France, entitled *Le nouvel esprit du capitalisme* (The new spirit of capitalism).

They focused on two periods: 1959–1969 and 1989–1984. Like other scholars, they noted the disaggregation of the corporation in the 1980s and 1990s. They called out the rise of project-based networks, inside firms and among them; and the power of digital technologies to make those networks function. They also showed that the rise of this rational, economizing organizational structure was accompanied by the rise of a managerial ideology grounded in the events of May 1968. They began by articulating two critiques of bourgeois society leveled in the 1960s, the "social critique" and the "artistic critique."[32]

In the United States, these critiques corresponded to those put forth by the New Left and the New Communalists. The social, or New Left, critique was fundamentally structural. Its advocates attacked bureaucracy and favored decentralization and the devolving of power onto individuals. The artistic, or New Communalist, critique celebrated the creation of a "Bohemian lifestyle" and put individuality, creativity, and personal authenticity at the center of its ideal society.[33]

In the late 1980s and early 1990s, management theorists on both sides of the Atlantic turned the workplace into a site of counter-cultural change. Building on the social critique of the 1960s, they advocated the leveling of corporate bureaucracies, the decentralization of firms, the end of laborious planning processes, and the empowering of workers within corporate decision-making.[34] Building on the artistic critique, they urged workers and managers to see themselves as creative, self-actualizing individuals and to view the workplace as a site for self-expression. Both critiques provided a clear justification for the corporate disaggregation already under way. And both gave workers and managers a new language and a new set of frameworks with which to imagine their roles in the economy. Suddenly, the office could become a way station in a lifelong journey toward the creation of a self. Even if states retained their military-bureaucratic structures, entrepreneurs could turn companies into places where hierarchy disappeared, where the social and the professional seamlessly blurred—where, in fact, the ideals of the 1960s communes might actually obtain.

The technology firms of Silicon Valley and New York's "Silicon Alley" became poster children for this fusion of techno-economic rationality and countercultural self-development.[35] Collaborative and playful, their offices stocked with bean bag chairs and cappuccino machines, these new digital companies lauded their programmers as creative artists and promised them the kind of freedom once claimed by those who headed back to the land. Across the United States and Western Europe, the leaders of recently deindustrialized regions wanted to catch what journalists and scholars clearly agreed was the wave of the post-industrial future.[36] Many turned to management consultant Richard Florida for advice on how to do it. Florida had recently dubbed programmers and other knowledge-workers members of the "creative class."[37] Such workers represented "a new resolution of the centuries-old tension between . . . the Protestant work ethic and the bohemian ethic," he argued.[38] Thus, they required the presence of an active bohemia to be successful. He and his colleagues began to measure American cities using a tool of their own invention, the Bohemian Index. The more artists and social activists you could cluster, he argued, the more likely you were to attract high-tech talent.

Had he worked for Richard Florida, Daniel Bell would have been quick to recognize the professionals of the "creative class" as members of his own post-industrial knowledge elite, the "new class." Unlike the technocrats of the early 1970s, though, these new workers had to make their way outside the safe, hierarchical pyramid of the midcentury American corporation. As they did, they leaned on the legacy of the counterculture to make sense of their lives. From Florida and others, they learned to celebrate the Dionysian aspects of the new economy, to cheer Joseph Schumpeter's creative destruction, and to imagine that it was not their skills or training that would allow them to flourish, but the ineffable essence of their inner lives, their creativity. As they took on board the risks formerly borne by their employers, they could imagine themselves as settlers of a new techno-economic landscape. They could seek out fellow travelers, recognize them by their Bohemian styles, and so move from network to network, seeking projects, earning money, and acquiring new skills as they went. By the late 1990s, it was hard to find an analyst anywhere who would have seen a contradiction between the search for countercultural self-expression and the drive for entrepreneurial success. As Boltanski and Chiapello put it, this new "spirit of capitalism . . . offered itself both as a way of achieving self-fulfillment by engaging in capitalism, and as a path of liberation from capitalism itself, from what was oppressive about its early creations."[39]

From a distance of fifty years, the fusion of the expressive impulses of the counterculture and the rational, economizing practices of technology-enabled economic life might well look like a peaceful resolution of what Bell believed to be the core cultural contradiction of capitalism. But if we see that the bohemian and the technocratic have shaped one other at least since the invention of digital computing, if not long before, then the personalization of labor, the decentralization of the firm, and the ostensible humanizing of economic life begin to look a lot like stages in a species of class warfare. The young rebels at Columbia may have dreamed of revolution, but once the fighting was done, many were on their way to the top of the economic ladder. As corporations disaggregated and as work required new levels of flexibility, those who had access to the financial and cultural resources that allowed one to float from project to project and to speak the cultural language of those in charge enjoyed a ferocious advantage over those who did not. Farmers, small retailers, local contractors, workers with aging parents or small children, or even a heavy regional accent—anyone wedded to a particular place and unable to leave it, physically or culturally—would be barred from full participation in the network economy. Moreover, the computer hardware and software industries provided nothing like the high levels of employment seen in the 1950s. As Gerald Davis has pointed out, almost 2 million Americans graduated with a bachelor's degree in 2015; that year, Facebook planned to hire only about 1,200 new personnel.[40] In 2016, Google had only 53,000 employees worldwide. As Davis puts it, "The modal job at Apple is not a high-end software engineer but a sales clerk in a blue T-shirt at the mall."[41]

In many ways, the counterculture of the 1960s has supplied the lingua franca for today's ruling class. The buttoned-down world of the WASPy, reserved executive can still be found, but among the frequent flyers of the virtual corporation, the search for self-expression and the performance of cool are what count. This is especially true in the technology sector. Just think of Steve Jobs's famous turtleneck and jeans, or Mark Zuckerberg's carefully selected t-shirts. Even as they launch their commercial products, figures like Jobs and Zuckerberg symbolically assert their membership in a disruptive, antinomian, countercultural caste.

Daniel Bell may have feared perversion, but the celebration of homosexuality, and more generally individual differences in sexuality, has become central to corporate life. On its recruiting website, for instance, Facebook tells potential employees to "BE YOURSELF": "Be *unique*. Be authentic. However you prefer to say it, we really mean it. Our culture embraces people's diverse perspectives and creates a positive environment where everyone belongs."[42]

A NEW KIND OF CAPITALISM AND
A NEW CONTRADICTION

At Facebook, of course, everyone belongs—just differently. Those with elite computer programming skills or the kinds of education and life experiences that produce a smooth-talking marketer can work at Facebook. They can channel their creativity through their structural or cultural advantages and profits. The rest of us can work *for* Facebook. At one level, Facebook resembles the latest iteration of the *Whole Earth Catalog*. It too hosts a range of geographically distributed users, and it too promotes itself as the home of a community. Like *The Catalog*, its value comes from user contributions. Thanks to the nature of digital media, however, it can track those contributions in real time, match patterns of interaction on the platform to patterns of interaction elsewhere, and use that analysis to make money—all without the average user's knowledge. Facebook is less a platform for the establishment of community than a system for mining and monetizing the social world.

And Facebook is hardly unique. In her monumental study of the business models driving social media, *The Age of Surveillance Capitalism*, Shoshana Zuboff describes Facebook as simply one example of a new mode of capital accumulation. Surveillance capitalism, she explains, has two aspects: it is both "a new economic order that claims human experience as free raw material for hidden commercial practices of extraction, prediction, and sales" and "a parasitic economic logic in which the production of goods and services is subordinated to a new global architecture of behavioral modification."[43] It depends on the distribution of devices such as cell phones and home monitoring systems, on the development of apps that let us take pictures of ourselves and send them instantly to friends, and on platforms that offer us services from web searching to pornography. In all these cases, and in keeping with the ideals of the counterculture, digital technologies and the companies behind them offer us a chance to express ourselves, to seek feedback from the world around us, and to shape our lives as we see fit. At the same time, in keeping with the rationalized profit-seeking of the economic sphere, they harvest and resell our patterns of self-expression and interaction and use them to change our behavior, to make us buy more, and even to change our political views.

Here, we come full circle. In 1976, Daniel Bell feared that the counterculture's attention to the self would do away with the Protestant ethic, and so perhaps with capitalism itself. But with Facebook and the rise of surveillance capitalism, we can see that the opposite has occurred. The expressive individualism of the counterculture thrives on social media. And the computational technologies of social media, together with the profit motive, solicit, amplify, and interconnect everything we say. From the perspective of social media, the more outrageous we are, the better: Outrage keeps users on the site and the ad dollars rolling in.

And perhaps this is the central cultural contradiction of capitalism today. Since the Protestant Reformation, Westerners have sought political, religious, and psychological liberation by exploring their inner lives and expressing what they found there in public. To do that today, however, is to help build a web of techniques, devices, services, and institutions that seek in return to corral our behavior, to make us more efficient consumers and angrier citizens, and so to generate ever higher profits. Much like the students at Columbia in 1968, we confront a world in which the forces of technological and economic rationalization have gone awry. But this time, thanks to the unique affordances of digital technology, the system will *embrace* our rage—in fact, any feeling that we might have—and use it to calm us down, help us adjust to things as they are, or maybe give us a chance to buy ourselves a treat online. Thanks to the fusion of countercultural rebellion and techno-economic innovation, we will no longer be alienated in the ways that so disturbed Daniel Bell. We might even be sort of happy, in a way.

NOTES

1. Daniel Bell, *The Coming of Post-Industrial Society; A Venture in Social Fore-casting* (New York: Basic Books, 1973), 13, 118

2. Daniel Bell, *The Cultural Contradictions of Capitalism* (New York: Basic Books, 1996), 51.

3. Bell, *Cultural Contradictions*, 37.

4. For prominent examples, see Richard Sennett, *The Fall of Public Man: The Forces Eroding Public Life and Burdening the Modern Psyche with Roles It Cannot Perform* (New York: Knopf, 1977), and Christopher Lasch, *The Culture of Narcissism: American Life in an Age of Diminishing Expectations* (New York: Norton, 1978).

5. Blake Slonecker, "The Columbia Coalition: African Americans, New Leftists, and Counterculture at the Columbia University Protest of 1968," *Journal of Social History* 41, no. 4 (2008): 967–996. For more on the strikes and the police response, see Jerry L. Avorn et al., *Up Against the Ivy Wall: A History of the Columbia Crisis* (New York: Atheneum Press, 1970), 181–199, and "University Calls in 1,000 Police to End Demonstration as Nearly 700 Are Arrested and 100 Injured; Violent Solution Follows Failure of Negotiations," *Columbia Daily Spectator*, April 30, 1968, 1. For Bell's own account, see Daniel Bell, "Columbia and the New Left," in *Confrontation: The Student Rebellion and the Universities*, ed. Daniel Bell and Irving Kristol (New York and London: Basic Books, 1968), 67–107.

6. Bell, "Columbia and the New Left," 107.

7. Bell, "Columbia and the New Left," 106.

8. Bell, *Cultural Contradictions*, 121.

9. Modern culture, wrote Bell, "took over the relation with the demonic. But instead of taming it, as religion tried to do, the secular culture (art and literature) began to accept it, explore it, and revel in it, coming to see it as a source of creativity." Bell, *Cultural Contradictions*, 19.

10. Daniel Bell, "Introduction (1978)," in Bell, *Cultural Contradictions* (New York: Basic Books, 1996), xxvii.

11. Bell, *Cultural Contradictions*, 54.

12. Theodore Roszak, *The Making of a Counter Culture: Reflections on the Technocratic Society and Its Youthful Opposition* (Berkeley: University of California Press, 1995), 50, quoted in Bell, *Cultural Contradictions*, 143.

13. Fred Turner, *From Counterculture to Cyberculture: Stewart Brand, the Whole Earth Network, and the Rise of Digital Utopianism* (Chicago: University of Chicago Press, 2006), 4–5.

14. For a full discussion of the number of communes and commune-dwellers, as well as related sources, see Turner, *From Counterculture to Cyberculture*, 32.

15. R. Buckminster Fuller, *Ideas and Integrities: A Spontaneous Autobiographical Disclosure* (Englewood Cliffs, NJ: Prentice-Hall, 1963), 249.

16. Stewart Brand, "Function," *Whole Earth Catalog* Spring, 1969 (Menlo Park, CA), inside front cover.

17. Over the last fifteen years, a substantial literature has grown up around the intersection of American science and the counterculture. Key works include Andrew G. Kirk, *Counterculture Green: The Whole Earth Catalog and American Environmentalism* (Lawrence: University Press of Kansas, 2007); David Kaiser, *How the Hippies Saved Physics: Science, Counterculture, and the Quantum Revival* (New York: Norton, 2012); Andrew Blauvelt, Greg Castillo, Esther Choi, Alison Clarke, et al., *Hippie Modernism: The Struggle for Utopia*, ed. Andrew Blauvelt (Minneapolis: Walker Art Center, 2015); and David Kaiser and Patrick McCray, *Groovy Science: Knowledge, Innovation, and American Counterculture* (Chicago: University of Chicago Press), 2016.

18. Bell, *Coming of Post-Industrial Society*, 480.

19. Bell, *Cultural Contradictions of Capitalism*, 74.

20. Bell, *Cultural Contradictions of Capitalism*, 170.

21. Steve Jobs, commencement address, Stanford University, June 12, 2005, https://news.stanford.edu/2005/06/14/jobs-061505/.

22. Margaret Pugh O'Mara, *The Code: Silicon Valley and the Remaking of America* (New York: Penguin Press, 2019), 243.

23. For the full history of Brand's relationship to the computer industry, see Turner, *From Counterculture to Cyberculture*.

24. Stewart Brand, "Spacewar: Fanatic Life and Symbolic Death Among the Computer Bums," *Rolling Stone*, December 7, 1972, 50–58, 50. The article opens thus: "Ready or not, computers are coming to the people. That's good news, maybe the best since psychedelics."

25. Gerald F. Davis, *The Vanishing American Corporation: Navigating the Hazards of a New Economy* (Oakland, CA: Berrett-Koehler, 2016), 4–54; my account summarizes his.

26. The first few nodes of the internet were connected in 1969; by 1991, the internet included a wide array of public and private computational networks, many interlinked, and Tim Berners-Lee had created the protocols that would drive the World Wide Web. See Janet Abbate, *Inventing the Internet* (Cambridge, MA: MIT Press, 1999), 197–198; 214.

27. Davis, *Vanishing American Corporation*, 69.

28. John Byrne, "The Virtual Corporation," *Business Week*, February 7, 1993; quoted in Davis, *Vanishing American Corporation*, 70.

29. Kevin Kelly, *New Rules for the New Economy: 10 Radical Strategies for a Connected World* (New York: Viking, 1998); Manuel Castells, *The Rise of the Network Society* (Cambridge, MA: Blackwell, 1996).

30. Barry Bluestone and Bennett Harrison, *The Deindustrialization of America: Plant Closings, Community Abandonment, and the Dismantling of Basic Industry* (New York: Basic Books, 1982).

31. Gina Neff, *Venture Labor: Work and the Burden of Risk in Innovative Industries* (Cambridge, MA: MIT Press, 2012); Ilana Gershon, *Down and Out in the New Economy: How People Find (or Don't Find) Work Today* (Chicago: University of Chicago Press, 2017).

32. Luc Boltanski and Eve Chiapello, *The New Spirit of Capitalism* (London: Verso, 2005), 38.

33. Boltanski and Chiapello, *New Spirit of Capitalism*, 38.

34. Boltanski and Chiapello, *New Spirit of Capitalism*, 65–71.

35. Neff, *Venture Labor*; Andrew Ross, *No-Collar: The Humane Workplace and Its Hidden Costs* (New York: Basic Books, 2003).

36. Richard L. Florida, *The Rise of the Creative Class: And How It's Transforming Work, Leisure, Community and Everyday Life* (New York: Basic Books, 2002); Richard Florida, *Cities and the Creative Class* (New York: Routledge, 2005); Charles Landry, *The Creative City: A Toolkit for Urban Innovators* (London: Earthscan Publications, 2000); Andrew Ross, *Nice Work If You Can Get It:*

Life and Labor in Precarious Times (New York: New York University Press, 2009), 15–52; Andreas Reckwitz, *The Invention of Creativity: Modern Society and the Culture of the New* (Malden, MA: Polity, 2017), 173–200.

37. Florida, *Rise of the Creative Class*, 328.

38. Florida, *Rise of the Creative Class*, 192.

39. Boltanski and Chiapello, *New Spirit of Capitalism*, 425.

40. Davis, *Vanishing American Corporation*, 147.

41. Davis, *Vanishing American Corporation*, 147.

42. Facebook Careers website: https://www.facebook.com/careers/; accessed February 17, 2017, and quoted in Fred Turner, "The Arts at Facebook: An Aesthetic Infrastructure for Surveillance Capitalism," *Poetics* 67 (2018): 53–62, 56.

43. Shoshana Zuboff, *The Age of Surveillance Capitalism: The Fight for a Human Future at the New Frontier of Power* (New York: Public Affairs, 2018), frontispiece.

11

THE DOUBLE BIND
Daniel Bell, the Public Household,
and Financialization

STEFAN EICH

During the 1970s, Daniel Bell famously prophesized the arrival of a post-industrial service economy. The new services, he explained in the 1976 foreword to *The Coming of Post-Industrial Society*, would be "primarily human services (principally in health, education and social services) and professional and technical services (e.g., research, evaluation, computers, and systems analysis)."[1] While Bell acknowledged finance in the same foreword, he saw it primarily as an auxiliary function within the production of industrial goods.[2] The prospect that finance might become a major post-industrial service in its own right was still alien to his line of thought.

But if Bell failed to anticipate financialization, he was extraordinarily prescient in detecting the underlying political pressures behind it.[3] In *The Cultural Contradictions of Capitalism* (1976), he not only posited a fundamental tension between capitalist production and hedonistic consumption, but also sketched a subtle political double bind facing democratic states.[4] Modern economies needed governing, but they failed to provide legitimacy to the institutions of economic governance. As a result, the state was caught up in contradictory demands since it was no longer clear how it could aid capital accumulation and growth while simultaneously meeting the rising claims of citizens for social well-being. Economic success depended more than ever on the state's economic management, but its ability to legitimate economic policy and finance expenditures was under threat.

The resulting "contradictory havoc," Bell observed in 1977, was evident in the clash between a desire for more spending for one's own collective projects and simultaneous demands for lower taxes and less interference by the government.[5] This double bind had become an inherent feature of any "democratic or responsive polity."[6] Thus, the only two ways left open to states to finance desired expenditures were borrowing and inflation. The politics of money and credit consequently emerged as a key site for how the structural double bind of advanced societies would play out. This was prescient—and yet Bell's diagnosis still underestimated the extent to which financialization would emerge over the next decade as simultaneously a product of the double bind and, for a while, a seeming escape from it.

Although Bell had originally not conceived of finance as being integral to post-industrial societies, by the end of the 1980s he had made room for it. In 1987, after the first big wave of financial deregulation had swept across Wall Street and the City of London, Bell offered a clarificatory correction. "The word 'services'," he explained, "conjures up images of fast-food, low-wage employments. This is misleading. The major services are financial services; professional and design services; human services (health, education, and social services); and, at the low end of the scale, personal services."[7] Finance now stood at the top of the services pyramid, even ahead of health and education.

Today, historians recognize these years, at the turn of the 1970s and the 1980s, as crucial to the origins of contemporary financialized capitalism. Bell can serve as a rewarding guide through these developments and the corresponding historiography. In this essay,

I trace Bell's commentary on deficits, debts, and financialization in light of his account of the double bind and his notion of the "public household," as developed in *The Cultural Contradictions of Capitalism*. The emergent shape of our financialized post-industrial society both surprised Bell and at the same time confirmed his prognosis. Despite failing to anticipate the rise of finance, Bell continues to provide one of the most acute accounts of the political dilemma from which financialization was once thought to offer an escape.

THE POLITICAL CONTRADICTION OF CAPITALISM

In 1976, the same year he published *The Cultural Contradictions of Capitalism*, Bell became the U.S. representative on the advisory panel of the Interfutures project by the Organisation of Economic Co-operation and Development (OECD). Initiated by the Japanese government and supported by the Toyota Foundation, as well as the Ford Foundation and the German Marshall Fund, the project was meant to explore alternatives to the forecast set out shortly before by the Club of Rome and the Global South's vision of a New International Economic Order.[8] For Bell, the project became an international laboratory and testing ground for some of his own prognoses in *The Cultural Contradictions of Capitalism*. In a 1977 briefing paper for the project, Bell sketched four structural problems facing advanced economies.[9] One touched on global wealth inequalities between rich and poor nations, while another concerned demographic trends. But the first two captured a peculiar domestic double bind of economic governance that Bell identified across advanced societies. "When the economic realm had greater autonomy," he recounted, the shocks and dislocations generated through the market could be walled off, or even ignored—though the social consequences were often enormous. But now all major shocks are increasingly *systemic*, and the political controllers must make decisions not for or against particular interests, powerful as these may be, but for the consequences of the system itself. Yet that very fact increases the inherent double bind in the nature of democratic or responsive polity. For the state increasingly has the double problem of aiding capital formation and growth (*accumulation*, in the Marxist jargon) and meeting the rising claims of citizens for income security, social services, social amenities, and the like (the problem of *legitimation*, in Max Weber's terminology).[10]

While Bell expressed his diagnosis in the Weberian language of legitimacy, he credited Marx with anticipating the double bind.[11] The 1970s, Bell argued, witnessed the belated fulfillment of Marx's prediction concerning the consequences of the democratic revolution. This democratic double bind of economic governance now found its expression in the form of growing deficits, both financial and political.[12]

According to Bell's better-known argument, advanced Western capitalism had become entangled in a fateful cultural contradiction. The postwar boom and the counterculture of the 1960s had entrenched a consumerist ethic of immediate gratification and self-realization that undermined the Protestant virtues of frugality and modesty, which Bell—following Weber—considered the pillars of capitalism's historical success. As Bell had put it already in October 1970, all social systems rely on the acceptance of a "moral justification of authority" by the population.[13] But the new capitalism of abundance lacked any such moral grounding. Instead, its character was oddly split between traditionalist values of restraint and a consumerist celebration of self-realization. The former emphasized a "Protestant sanctification of work" based on norms of efficiency and functional rationality. The latter engendered "apocalyptic moods" and "antirational modes of behavior," which culminated in hedonism. Far from entrenching conservative values, the corporate capitalism of the postwar years had unwittingly produced a hedonistic consumer society. The 1960s had thus given rise to a deep cultural transformation that constituted a profound challenge to the very "moral temper" of society and its existing norms of reward. As Bell put it, "Call it psychedelic or call it, as its own protagonists have, a 'counter-culture.' It announced a strident opposition to bourgeois values and to the traditional codes of American life."[14] This disjunction, Bell warned, was a historic crisis of Western society.[15] The corporate revolution was being devoured by its own children.

Like Bell's two previous books, *The Cultural Contradictions of Capitalism* quickly became a key prism for understanding the spirit of the times, in this case the political and cultural crisis of the 1970s.[16] The book rapidly acquired the status of, in Daniel Rodgers's words, "one of the mid-1970s' most important books of social theory," exercising a hold on the intellectual imaginary of the late 1970s.[17] Its influential reception ranged widely from neoconservatives to critical theorists. In the late 1970s, Jürgen Habermas repeatedly stressed the convergence between Bell's account and his own diagnosis of an entwined legitimation and cultural crisis.[18] When in 1995, the *Times Literary Supplement* compiled the 100 most influential books since World War II, it featured Bell's book prominently.[19]

While *The Cultural Contradictions of Capitalism* came to be seen as capturing the spirit of stagflation of the 1970s, the crisis that Bell originally had had in mind was the paradox of material abundance, not economic slump. The kernel of the book (initially titled *The Divided Society*) originated during a sabbatical year in 1969–1970, when Bell was a fellow in residence at the Russell Sage Foundation in New York, where he had originally been planning to write a book on Charles Fourier characterizing him as the prophet of the "orgiastic chiliasm" of the student protests and the sexual revolution.[20] Instead, Bell began to bring together his understanding of countercultural developments with his analysis of the changing industrial nature of advanced capitalism. Connecting the two, Bell detected, was an increasing questioning of material growth. This was not merely a narrow economic matter, for growth had become, as Bell put it, "the secular religion of advancing industrial societies."[21] The promise of growth had functioned as the theodicy of postwar liberalism, and it was all the more concerning that countercultural currents now took direct aim at this central pillar of political legitimacy. "The idea of growth," Bell, explained in 1972,

> has become so fully absorbed as an economic ideology that one realizes no longer how much of a liberal innovation it was. The liberal answer to social problems such as poverty was that growth would provide the resources to raise the incomes of the poor. . . . And yet, paradoxically, it is the very idea of economic growth that is now coming under attack—and from liberals. Affluence is no longer seen as an answer. Growth is held responsible for the spoliation of the environment, the voracious use of natural resources, the crowding in the recreation areas, the densities in the city, and the like.[22]

But without growth, Bell asked, what was the raison d'être of capitalism? What would undergird its political legitimacy?[23]

When he first posed this question, Bell still had in mind the conscious rejection of the imperative of economic expansion by young Americans in the late 1960s and early 1970s. But soon that choice was out of reach. Growth came to an abrupt halt in 1973, as the U.S. economy settled into the worst recession since the 1930s. Despite the malaise, Bell continued to assert confidently that the economic crisis could be managed; it was the cultural crisis that was deeper and more lasting. The real problem was not a temporary hiccup in quarterly economic performance, but rather the questioning of the very desirability of growth.

The religious foundations of American capitalism, its sources of motivation and legitimacy, were eroding, as the secular religion of the postwar period growth had been a powerful "political solvent."[24] Widely dispersed and growing affluence had disguised the vastly increased role of the administrative welfare state in economic outcomes. According to Bell's diagnosis, the distinction between state and economy that had structured classical liberalism became obsolete in the twentieth century. Although rhetorically opposed to planning, the modern capitalist economy nonetheless depended on constant measuring, managing, and steering. While upholding an empty idol of the market, advanced capitalism had in fact "begun to center the crucial decisions about the economy and the society in the political cockpit, rather than in the diffused, aggregated market."[25] This erosion of the classic liberal distinction between state and market raised profound questions of legitimacy. Unlike conservative critics, who sought to reverse the growing role of the state, Bell regarded the change as an inherent feature of advanced capitalism. There was no going back.

While growth had helped to stabilize and legitimate technocratic economic government during the postwar period, the economic crisis and inflation of the 1970s made governmental interventions more visible and contestable. Political leaders would now inevitably have to base policies and interventions on contentious distributive judgments that would be certain to provoke resentment from those on the losing side. The political system would struggle under the weight of these conflicting demands.

"[D]ecision-making has become 'politicalized'," Bell explained in 1976, by now being subject to multiple direct and indirect pressures.[26] Group conflicts would inevitably intensify. Instead of attributing their problems to the anonymous naturalized market, citizens would direct their frustrations at the administrative state that had failed them. Now they would know whom to blame.

The inflation of the 1970s thus revealed a potent combination of rising material expectations and intensified democratic fiscal and welfare politics that had come to bind states, preventing them from either reducing governmental expenditures or cutting wages by way of "traditional modes of restraint or 'discipline' (in the archaic use of the term)," as Bell put it.[27] By this account, inflation emerged as the inevitable price that a polity had to pay for social peace. Bell concluded that it was unlikely that any democratic state could abolish inflation without disastrous political consequences. In the final chapter of *The Cultural Contradictions of Capitalism*, he argued instead that democratic capitalist politics after the boom were stuck between the economic imperatives of intervention and the devastating effect that those very acts of intervention had on political legitimacy.[28]

THE PUBLIC HOUSEHOLD

At the time of writing *The Cultural Contradictions of Capitalism*, Bell's own preferred solution to the double bind was emphatically *not* the liberalized market. The only true answer, he argued in the book's closing section, consisted in squarely confronting the question as a supremely political challenge.[29] The way out of the double bind without a class war would be a combination of strong wage-price controls, a redistributive incomes policy to adjust the resulting inequities, and strict governmental regulation of investment to deter evasions.[30] As Bell acknowledged, this implied direct interventions in the capital markets that were certain to provoke opposition and resentment. Although governments would struggle under the weight of conflicting demands, they somehow had to learn how to live with the resulting dilemmas of legitimacy now forced into the open.

Crucially, difficult distributive decisions could avoid jeopardizing the legitimacy of the state if they were based on a public philosophy that accepted the economy as a contested arena to be politically managed. It would be necessary, therefore, to develop a widely accepted set of public norms about how to share economic gain and pain fairly. Bell dubbed this a political philosophy of "the public household." While tracing the term back to Joseph Schumpeter's sociology of taxation, Bell saw the public household as primarily an attempt to make legible the public underpinnings of seemingly private economic decisions. In provocatively combining the fiscal budget and the private home under the term "public household," Bell sought to take seriously the *political* in political economy.[31]

The need for a distributive public philosophy that could guide policy decisions and adjudicate between conflicting demands was not meant as a rebuke of liberalism. Bell argued that, on the contrary, only such a philosophy could ensure the preconditions for a liberal society. "A new public philosophy will have to be created," he concluded, "in order that something we recognize as a liberal society may survive."[32] The failure to develop such a philosophy, Bell prophesized, would lead to an endless spiral of tax revolts, growing indebtedness, and extremist politics on the right that would eventually put the entire system in question. *The Cultural Contradictions of Capitalism* thus ended with a call for a renovation of political thought.

To political theorists and intellectual historians, this conclusion might seem paradoxical. After all, the 1970s have come to be seen as the decade when John Rawls's *Theory of Justice* (1971) revived American liberal political theory.[33] Bell, in contrast, saw a precarious philosophical void. "We are groping for a new vocabulary," he despaired.[34] While mockingly predicting that "in Sweden, Rawls's philosophy of 'fairness' is likely to become the quasi-official philosophy," Bell thought that Rawls's "socialist ethic" and rejection of meritocracy were ill suited for American mores.[35]

But this insistence on the value of meritocracy left Bell in a difficult position. While pointing out that American society continued to be built on faith in a meritocratic value system, he simultaneously insisted that advanced capitalism had rendered obsolete any notion of prepolitical market merit. Bell hoped to address the resulting problem through his notion of the public household. The public household was not a moral order in its own right, but it did express Bell's hope that it might be possible to guide capitalist decision-making in a way that would restrain the threat of hedonism while acknowledging the political dimension of market outcomes.

THE SHOCK

At first sight, the 1980s seemed to prove Bell spectacularly wrong. Instead of a cultural contradiction between hedonism and discipline, the decade explosively fused the two. Rather than a capitalist identity crisis, what emerged was an intense commodification of the counterculture, harnessed to a rhetoric of self-realization, a proliferating self-help industry, and a human resources revolution within corporations. The hedonistic licentiousness and irrational exuberance that Bell had painted as antagonistic to capitalism instead became the driving forces of a new, debt-fueled, and financialized service economy, later embodied symbolically by

the figure of the yuppie bond market trader. The newly empowered financial markets soon internalized both the hedonism of
the counterculture and its identity-shifting fluidity.[36] Instead of
learning how to live with the "insoluble problem" of inflation,
the economy had been brutally disinflated by the middle of the
decade.[37] Instead of turning their back on the rat race, baby boom-
ers worked longer hours than ever. Instead of "tune in, drop out,"
we got *Prozac Nation* and "Generation Adderall."

The origins of this brave new world can in many ways be dated
to October 6, 1979, when the then–recently appointed chairman
of the Federal Reserve Board, Paul Volcker, declared at an unusual
late-night press conference that it would no longer attempt to stabilize prices through short-term interest rates. Instead, it would
adopt a monetarist target of the size of reserves held within the
Federal Reserve system.[38] Instead of a new public political philosophy of fair burden sharing, the Fed under Volcker violently disinflated the U.S. economy by intentionally creating a recession, with
accompanying unemployment. In August 1981, the new U.S. president, Ronald Reagan, came to Volcker's aid when he crushed an
air traffic controllers' strike by summarily firing more than 10,000
federal workers with devastating symbolic force.[39] Soon inflation
was conquered, and central bankers took up their reign as the
maestros of the "Great Moderation."

It is tempting to conclude that just as the 1980s proved Bell's
account of cultural contradiction wrong, so did that decade negate
his fears of a class war and an erosion of the state's legitimacy. But
in an important sense, Bell's nightmare of tax revolts and indebtedness, accompanied by a systematic dismantling of the American
labor union movement and an implosion of the state's legitimacy
(particularly on the right), did come to pass. Indeed, it became the
new normal. The class war ended quickly, precisely because capital
was able to extract such a remarkable victory.

In an ironic twist, Bell's prognosis of a cultural contradiction seemingly failed in the 1980s because his diagnosis of the political double bind had been so acute. Rather than misdiagnosing the problem, he underestimated the lengths to which politicians and other actors would go to evade it. As Greta Krippner has shown in her pathbreaking work on the financialization of the U.S. economy, Bell put his finger on the central pressure point that eventually motivated the turn toward a new politics of depoliticization.[40] Consequently, his account of the central double bind of advanced capitalism has justly reemerged as a productive theoretical frame in which to understand the politics of deregulation and financialization since the 1970s.

GOVERNING IN THE DARK

In *The Cultural Contradictions of Capitalism*, Bell already had observed that "the virtue of the market is that it disperses responsibility for decisions and effects."[41] To be sure, markets did not disperse power itself. Instead, what Bell had in mind was the market's ability to disperse responsibility by dispersing the *appearance* of coercion. Where the administrative state concentrated decisions and exposed the legitimacy of the state, markets disguised political choices and distributive decisions. This did not mean that Bell endorsed a turn to the market. However, only too aware of the market's political attractions as a diffuser of the appearance of power, he was pointing to its potential use as a safety valve or temporary escape from the double bind. Market-based interventions could serve as a convenient tool for hiding the all-too-visible hand of the state.[42]

Bell closed his 1977 OECD briefing paper in this spirit by remarking on the increasing attractiveness of the market as a diffuser of political responsibility.[43] Instead of direct welfare payments, governments could intervene indirectly through the price mechanism. Instead of providing services directly, governments could use vouchers or cash payments to allow recipients to make their consumption choices according to their own preferences. Deploying the hiding hand of the market, Bell conjectured, might offer a chance to break out of the stale debate between liberal calls for state action and conservative pleas for free enterprise. Instead, he argued, "one can use the market for social purposes."[44] This did not mean that Bell had abandoned his earlier affirmation of the need for a public household, with its political vocabulary of fair sharing of benefits and burdens.[45] But in the absence of such a public philosophy, markets could at least help to reduce some of the resulting pressures. Indirect steering via the market offered in this light the prospect of shielding the legitimacy of at least some institutions of economic governance from the public glare, while leaving more consumption choices to citizens.

Bell's reflections concerning a tension between the imperative need for the state and a simultaneous desire to render its interventions less visible soon found echoes at other levels of public policy, perhaps most lastingly in the realm of monetary policy. By deploying "the market" as a shield against responsibility, Volcker's Fed began to do what governments had been seemingly unable to stomach in the 1970s: consciously induce an artificial recession in order to disinflate the economy.[46] But what allowed this to work politically was that, as Krippner put it, the market turned out to be "not the strict disciplinarian imagined by neoliberal visionaries, operating with the blunt force of unforgiving nature," but instead a "surprisingly lax master."[47] In particular, the proliferation of private credit—especially newly available forms of consumer credit—initially seemed remarkably effective at diffusing, disguising, and delaying the divisive distributive conflicts that Bell had feared. By unleashing a credit card–fueled return to material abundance, policymakers appeared to have found a tempting substitute for the disappearance of wage growth and a way to evade haunting distributive challenges.[48] Even when politicians realized that these solutions were only temporary stopgaps, they saw, in Wolfgang Streeck's evocative language, that financialization could "buy time."[49]

This did not mean that Bell's diagnosis of a fundamental political double bind of economic governance had become obsolete. The economy remained as entangled with the state as it had been before. Economic steering continued to be necessary for the functioning of advanced capitalism. As a result, new tools had to be found in order to move economic steering once more behind the scenes. A new, depoliticized conception of monetary policy was fundamental to this orchestration of disinflationary discipline and effervescent private credit. Now newly independent central banks became the irreproachable agents of indirect steering, guiding the economy with a firm, but once more invisible hand. If Bell became convinced that the active management of capital was both economically unavoidable and politically explosive, what he underestimated was the ability of central banks to operate—at least for a while—beyond the double bind of democratic political legitimation. Independent central banks turned out to be remarkably effective at governing in the dark.

Bell's initial neglect of the ability of central banks to govern by stealth did not derive from a lack of familiarity with monetary economics and central banking. He had closely followed the way in which the 1970s inflation had broken the postwar consensus in economic theory. Already, in his OECD briefing paper from 1977, he had provided a panoramic tour of debates about money and credit, from Abba Lerner's "functional finance" to the more recent fad of monetarism and the emerging rational expectations revolution.[50] Over the following years, he delved even more deeply into recent developments in monetary economics. He came to appreciate both the paradoxical need for the state to intervene in ways that confounded people's expectations and the corrosive effects of such surprise shocks for the level of societal trust in a polity.[51] He flagged the ambivalent role of growing international indebtedness as offering both a temporary escape from existing constraints and a new kind of discipline in its own right.[52] As Bell was only too aware, what would come to be known as "financialization" was emerging clearly as both a symptom of and a response to the double bind that he had diagnosed earlier.

CONCLUSION

Looking back in 1987 to his own diagnosis a decade earlier, Bell flagged his account of the double bind and his related discussion of the politics of debt as "somewhat prescient."[53] Both aspects had only intensified since, and came to be entwined with an internationalization of capital on the back of "the vast hoard of 'stateless' Eurodollars," beyond the reach of U.S. financial regulation.[54] As a result, multinational banks and corporations could now pursue higher returns by directing their capital anywhere in the world, even when such actions undermined the interests of individual countries. Governments therefore were losing control over their own currencies, one of their main levers of power and influence.[55] "Though capital is able to move freely," Bell observed, "most people do not." This mismatch was the true "hidden iceberg."[56]

The safety valve of financialization may have temporarily alleviated the political pressures that weighed on domestic policymakers, but it did so by compounding the international mismatch between global capital and national politics. Not least due to the special status of the U.S. dollar, the pressures resting on the international monetary system that had haphazardly emerged out of the collapse of Bretton Woods were building up. Eventually, Bell insisted, "some new international monetary systems will have to emerge to form the backbone of the new international economy."[57] But until then, the fickle contradictions of the existing system would only further expose the fragmented nature of political institutions. While international supply chains and corporate balance sheets were integrated into a world economy, polities remained deeply fractured along national or even regional lines. Indeed, intensified economic integration had paradoxically deepened political and cultural fragmentation within countries, while largely failing to produce new institutions of governance on a global level.[58] This mismatch between economic and political institutions was nothing less than a "structural time bomb."[59]

If private credit had once held the promise of diffusing difficult political choices, the financial crisis of 2008 revealed it to be an exceedingly poor substitute for public goods, rising wages, and a political philosophy of economic burden sharing. Consumer debt never constituted a solution to Bell's double bind; it was at best another instance of "buying time."[60] Indeed, private credit turned out to be vastly more fickle and unsustainable than public debt.[61] States are able to step into the breach, after all, thanks to the sovereign's ability to create its own reserves. In 2008, and once more during the COVID-19 pandemic in the spring of 2020, states responded with vast emergency interventions. But the past decade has only served to further illustrate the validity of Bell's worries about the contradictions of the global monetary system and the toxic mismatch between national political systems and transnational corporate balance sheets.[62] Finally, the aftermath of the global financial crisis has served as a reminder that private credit remains an enormously regressive force that compounds

inequalities rather than acting as a sustainable political solvent.[63]
Even where barriers to credit were lowered, those with collateral
were able to get more and better credit than those without. Even
worse, the crisis revealed what happens when credit stops and
liquidity support fails to trickle down the unequal hierarchy of
the credit pyramid. While banks received bailouts, those people
who were behind on their mortgages or consumer loans, especially in poorer neighborhoods, suffered foreclosures and personal
bankruptcies.

Bell's argument for a shared public political philosophy to guide
economic policy, as the only sustainable response to the double
bind, resonates today once more, if only because it is more out of
reach than ever in the face of a proliferation of global crises. But as
Bell insisted, the underlying double bind of legitimacy cannot be
permanently evaded. Consumer credit turned out to be a mighty
conjurer of time and desires, but today the evasive political strategies of financialization have run their course. Private credit cannot be the solution to contemporary problems of inequality and
legitimacy. Capitalism is nonetheless more financialized than ever.
Americans owe nearly a trillion dollars in credit card debt—an
all-time high—and delinquencies are rising rapidly.[64] Student loan
debt in the United States has doubled since the 2008 financial crisis. As a result, demands for a more egalitarian public provision
of credit have begun to emerge. Central banks and the process of
money creation have come into focus as neglected sites of democratic governance.

Bell cannot tell us what a possible solution might look like. But
he can help see us more clearly what the question is. Recognizing
the double bind—and understanding temporary evasions of it for
what they are—requires structural thinking of the kind that Bell
championed and practiced, despite the intellectual risks involved.
Precisely because of his own prescience, he was only too aware of

the limits of forecasting. "As one reflects back to the kinds of predictions made by our rash forebears," he wrote somberly in 1987, "one is mindful . . . of the dashing of hopes."[65] Yet he nonetheless insisted on the need to identify structural trends, with all their flaws. To make predictions was akin to "holding a small candle in a hurricane to see if there are any paths ahead and how to go forth. But if one cannot light and hold even a small candle, then there is only darkness before us."[66]

NOTES

1. Daniel Bell, "Foreword: 1976," in *The Coming of Post-Industrial Society. A Venture in Social Forecasting* (New York: Basic Books, 1999), xciv.

2. Bell, "Foreword: 1976," xciv.

3. Bell serves in this sense as Greta Krippner's guide in her account of the rise of finance. Greta Krippner, *Capitalizing on Crisis: The Political Origins of the Rise of Finance* (Cambridge, MA: Harvard University Press, 2011).

4. Daniel Bell, *Cultural Contradictions of Capitalism* (New York: Basic Books, 1976).

5. Daniel Bell, "The Future World Disorder: The Structural Context of Crisis," in *The Winding Passage: Essays and Sociological Journeys, 1960–1980* (Cambridge, MA: Abt Books, 1980), 227. First published as Daniel Bell, "The Future World Disorder: The Structural Context of Crisis," *Foreign Policy*, no. 27 (1977), 109–135.

6. Bell, "The Future World Disorder," 215.

7. Daniel Bell, "The World and the United States in 2013," *Daedalus* 116, no. 3, *Futures* (Summer 1987), 2n1.

8. Jenny Andersson, "The Future of the Western World: The OECD and the Interfutures Project," *Journal of Global History* 14, no. 1 (March 2019): 126–144.

9. Bell, "The Future World Disorder," 210–227.

10. Bell, "The Future World Disorder," 215. Original emphasis.

11. Bell also pointed his readers in this context to James O'Connor's Marxist analysis of fiscal politics in *The Fiscal Crisis of the State* (New York: St. Martin's, 1973).

12. Bell, "The Future World Disorder," 215.

13. Daniel Bell, "The Cultural Contradiction," *New York Times*, October 27, 1970, L45.

14. Daniel Bell, "The Cultural Contradictions of Capitalism," in "Capitalism, Culture, and Education," ed. Ralph A. Smith, *Journal of Aesthetic Education* 6, no. 1/2, (January–April 1972—special issue), 35.

15. Bell, "The Cultural Contradiction."

16. In this section, and the opening of section three of this essay ("The Shock"), I draw on the account published in Stefan Eich, "Financialization, Family Values, and Their Discontents," *Capitalism: A Journal of History and Economics* 1, no. 1 (Spring 2020), 241–258.

17. Daniel T. Rodgers, *Age of Fracture* (Cambridge, MA: Harvard University Press, 2011), 75.

18. Jürgen Habermas, "Ideologies and Society in the Post-war World," in *Autonomy and Solidarity: Interviews with Jürgen Habermas*, ed. Peter Dews (London: Verso, 1992), 51.

19. *Times Literary Supplement* (October 6, 1995), https://www.the-tls.co.uk/the-hundred-most-influential-books-since-the-war/.

20. Daniel Bell, "Charles Fourier: Prophet of Eupsychia," *The American Scholar* 38, no. 1 (Winter 1968–69): 41–58; reprinted as Daniel Bell, "Charles Fourier: Prophet of Eupsychia [1968]," in *The Winding Passage. Essays in Sociological Journeys, 1960–1980* (Cambridge, MA: Abt Books, 1980), 91–104.

21. Bell, *Cultural Contradictions of Capitalism*, 237–238.

22. Bell, "The Cultural Contradictions of Capitalism," 36–37.

23. Bell, "The Cultural Contradictions of Capitalism."

24. Bell, *Cultural Contradictions of Capitalism*, 237.

25. Bell, *Cultural Contradictions of Capitalism*, 24.

26. Bell, *Cultural Contradictions of Capitalism*, 197.

27. Bell, *Cultural Contradictions of Capitalism*, 239.

28. Bell, *Cultural Contradictions of Capitalism*, chapter 6 ("The Public Household: On 'Fiscal Sociology' and the Liberal Society"), 243.

29. Bell, *Cultural Contradictions of Capitalism*, 220–282. For another contemporary call for a public philosophy of equality in sharing the burden of disinflationary austerity, see Michael Walzer, "Socialism and Self-Restraint: The Moral Equivalent of War Requires the Moral Equivalent of Wartime Equality," *New Republic* 181 (July 7, 1979); reprinted as Michael Walzer, "Socialism and Self-Restraint [1979]," in *Radical Principles: Reflections of an Unreconstructed Democrat* (New York: Basic Books, 1980), 291–303.

30. Bell, *Cultural Contradictions of Capitalism*, 240–242.

31. As Melinda Cooper has recently shown in her account of "family values" in the economic debates of the 1970s, to frame economics through the household was at the same time an intentionally symbolic and emotional attempt to link it to "family values." Melinda Cooper, *Family Values: Between Neoliberalism and the New Social Conservatism* (New York: Zone Books, 2017). For Bell, after all, not only was the family the key institution of the civilized state, but it had been precisely the breakdown of family mores and their replacement by "hedonism" that he identified as the most important effect of the sexual revolution for liberal capitalism.

32. Bell, *Cultural Contradictions of Capitalism*, 251.

33. Katrina Forrester, *In the Shadow of Justice: Postwar Liberalism and the Remaking of Political Philosophy* (Princeton, NJ: Princeton University Press, 2019); John Rawls, *A Theory of Justice* (Cambridge, MA: Harvard University Press, 1971).

34. Bell, *Cultural Contradictions of Capitalism*, xxix.

35. Bell, *The Coming of Post-Industrial Society*, 456n111, 444.

36. Michael Lewis, *Liar's Poker: Rising Through the Wreckage on Wall Street* (New York: Norton, 1989). For a perceptive commentary, see Michael O'Malley, *Face Value: The Entwined Histories of Money and Race in America* (Chicago: University of Chicago Press, 2012), 197–214.

37. Bell, "The Future World Disorder," 224.

38. William L. Silber, *Volcker: The Triumph of Persistence* (New York: Bloomsbury Press, 2012), 178. Michael D. Bordo and Athanasios Orphanides, eds., *The Great Inflation: The Rebirth of Modern Central Banking* (Chicago: University of Chicago Press, 2013), 182, 226.

39. On Volcker's approval of Reagan's actions, see Paul Volcker, *Keeping at It: The Quest for Sound Money and Government* (New York: Public Affairs, 2018), 113.

40. Krippner, *Capitalizing on Crisis*, 16–22, 92, 138–141, 149–150.

41. Bell, *Cultural Contradictions of Capitalism*, 235.

42. Albert O. Hirschman, "The Principle of the Hiding Hand," *Public Interest*, no. 6 (Winter 1967), 10–23.

43. Bell, "The Future World Disorder," 227.

44. Bell, "The Future World Disorder," 227.

45. I am grateful to Paul Starr for a very helpful discussion of the point.

46. Krippner, *Capitalizing on Crisis*, 108–123. At the same time, it would be a mistake to deduce that inflation fighting was destined to be a loser

at the ballot box. See Stefan Eich and Adam Tooze, "The Great Inflation," in *Vorgeschichte der Gegenwart*, ed. Anselm Doering-Manteuffel, Lutz Raphael, and Thomas Schlemmer (Göttingen, Germany: Vandenhoeck & Ruprecht, 2016), 173–196.

47. Krippner, *Capitalizing on Crisis*, 141.
48. Krippner, *Capitalizing on Crisis*, 141.
49. Wolfgang Streeck, *Buying Time: The Delayed Crisis of Democratic Capitalism* (London: Verso, 2014). However, as Adam Tooze has put it in response to Streeck, if someone is buying time, who is selling it? Adam Tooze, "Who Is Afraid of Inflation? The Long-shadow of the 1970s," *Journal of Modern European History* 12, no. 1 (February 2014): 53–60.
50. Bell, "The Future World Disorder," 217.
51. Daniel Bell, *The Social Sciences Since the Second World War* (New Brunswick, NJ: Transaction Books, 1982); this was originally published in two parts in *The Great Ideas Today* series of the *Encyclopedia Britannica* in 1979 and 1980. See also Irving Kristol and Daniel Bell, eds., *Crisis in Economic Theory* (New York: Basic Books, 1981).
52. Bell, *The Social Sciences*, 73; Bell, "The Future World Disorder," 218.
53. Bell, "The World and the United States in 2013," 2n1.
54. Bell, "The World and the United States in 2013," 9.
55. Bell, "The World and the United States in 2013," 9.
56. Bell, "The World and the United States in 2013," 10.
57. Bell, "The World and the United States in 2013," 9.
58. Bell, "The World and the United States in 2013," 29.
59. Bell, "The World and the United States in 2013," 13–14.
60. Streeck, *Buying Time*.
61. Amir Sufi and Atif Mian, *House of Debt* (Chicago: University of Chicago Press, 2014).
62. Adam Tooze, *Crashed: How a Decade of Financial Crises Changed the World* (New York: Viking, 2018).
63. Mehrsa Baradaran, *How the Other Half Banks: Exclusion, Exploitation, and the Threat to Democracy* (Cambridge, MA: Harvard University Press, 2015).
64. "Household Debt and Credit Report," *New York Federal Reserve* (Q4 2020), https://www.newyorkfed.org/microeconomics/hhdc.html.
65. Bell, "The World and the United States in 2013," 31.
66. Bell, "The World and the United States in 2013," 31.

CONTRIBUTORS

JENNY ANDERSSON is Comité national de la recherche scientifique (CNRS) Research Professor at SciencesPo, and Professor of the History of Ideas and Science at Uppsala University in Sweden. She is the author of *The Future of the World: Futurology, Futurists, and the Struggle for the Post–Cold War Imagination.*

DAVID A. BELL is a historian of France and the Sidney and Ruth Lapidus Professor in the Era of North Atlantic Revolutions at Princeton University. His recent books include *Napoleon: A Concise Biography* and *Men on Horseback: The Power of Charisma in the Age of Revolution* He is the son of Daniel Bell.

STEVEN BRINT is Distinguished Professor of Sociology and Public Policy at the University of California, Riverside, and the director of the Colleges & Universities 2000 study. He is the author of four books, including *Two Cheers for Higher Education.*

STEFAN EICH is assistant professor of government at Georgetown University.

MICHAEL KAZIN is professor of history at Georgetown University and coeditor of *Dissent.* His seven books include *The Populist Persuasion: An American History; American Dreamers: How the Left Changed a Nation;* and *What It Took to Win: A History of the*

Democratic Party. He is also the editor-in-chief of *The Princeton Encyclopedia of American Political History*.

JAN-WERNER MÜLLER is Roger Williams Straus Professor of Social Sciences at Princeton University. His books include *Contesting Democracy*, a history of political thought in twentieth-century Europe; *What Is Populism?*, which has been translated into more than twenty languages; and, most recently, *Democracy Rules*.

MARGARET O'MARA is the Howard and Frances Keller Endowed Professor of History at the University of Washington and the author of several books, most recently *The Code: Silicon Valley and the Making of America*.

PAUL STARR is professor of sociology and public affairs at Princeton University and cofounder and coeditor of *The American Prospect*. He is the author of *The Social Transformation of American Medicine*; *The Creation of the Media*; *Freedom's Power: The History and Promise of Liberalism*; and, most recently, *Entrenchment: Wealth, Power, and the Constitution of Democratic Societies*.

FRED TURNER is the Henry and Norman Chandler Professor of Communication at Stanford University. His books include *From Counterculture to Cyberculture: Steward Brand, the Whole Earth Network, and the Rise of Digital Utopianism*, and *The Democratic Surround: Multimedia and American Liberalism from World War II to the Psychedelic Sixties*.

JULIAN E. ZELIZER is the Malcolm Stevenson Forbes Class of 1941 Professor of History at Princeton University, a CNN political analyst, and the author or editor of twenty-one books on American political history, including *The Fierce Urgency of Now: Lyndon Johnson, Congress, and the Battle for the Great Society*; *Fault Lines: A History of the U.S. Since 1974*; *Burning Down the House: Newt Gingrich, the Fall of a Speaker, and the Rise of the New Republican Party*; and, most recently, *Abraham Joshua Heschel: A Life of Radical Amazement*.

INDEX

AAC&U. *See* American Association
of Colleges & Universities
administrative pluralism, 241n75
Advanced Research Projects Agency
(ARPA), 184
Advanced Research Projects Agency
Network (ARPANET), 184
affordability, 230
Age of Surveillance Capitalism, The
(Zuboff), 285
alienation: certainty and, 233;
of Jewish immigrants, 11–12;
Marxism addressing, 65; writing
on, 65–67
ambiguities, 83, 134, 152, 161, 217–218
American Association of Colleges &
Universities (AAC&U), 234
American intellectuals, 10, 11
Americanism, 117
American Political Tradition, The
(Hofstadter), 118
American Prospect, The (magazine), 82
American socialism, 2, 8, 61, 67, 71, 95
American society, 256; Commission
on the Year 2000 anticipating,

15; communism outside of, 97;
cult of efficiency influencing,
66; *The Cultural Contradictions of
Capitalism* on, 18; intellectualism
in, 1, 11; radical right controlled
by, 128; socialism in, 12, 98;
Sombart on, 67–68; techno-
economic realm, 17
American system, 222
analytical distinctions, 53
analytical framework, 235–236,
267–268, 275
anarchists, 35, 92, 109n19
Andersson, Jenny, 46–47
anticommunism: with antifascism, 5;
distinctions in, 125; of McCarthy,
113
antiestablishmentarianism, 127
antifascism, 5
antiholism, 20, 79, 80
antiholistic social theory, 20
anti-intellectualism, 104, 113, 118,
268, 269
antipluralism, 148–149, 151
anti-Semitism, 10, 42, 114, 118, 127, 130

liberalism of fear, 72, 140, 145, 155n20
liberal politics, 3, 17, 67
Lindblom, Charles, 64
Lipset, Seymour Martin, 119–120
Lockheed, 200
long-term employment, 279
Luxembourg, Rosa, 96

Mably, Gabriel de Bonnot, 56
Macron, Emmanuel, 151–152
Making of a Counter Culture, The
  (Roszak), 272–273
Malcolm X, 270
Mannheim, Karl, 252
manufacturing, 164, 166, 171, 174–175;
  crisis in, 203; labor forces in,
  179; production impacting,
  176–177; techno-economic realm
  impacting, 280
marginalization, 229, 234; of ideology,
  14; meritocracy ignoring, 225–226;
  of minorities, 27n41. *See also*
  minorities
market society, 143, 155n27
Marx, Karl, 5, 7, 18, 43, 66–67, 107;
  Daniel Bell admiring, 93–94;
  double bind anticipated by, 294;
  Hegel and, 65; ideology impacted
  by, 67; Mills updating, 105. *See also*
  Marxism
Marxian Socialism in the United States
  (Bell, Daniel), 8, 21, 67–69, 71,
  94, 98
Marxism, and alienation, 65–66; and
  antiholism, 79; Bell's shift from,
  7; Harrington on, 93; as ideology,

73, 140; as model for Daniel Bell,
  67; modernization theory and,
  247; structural functionalism
  contrasted with, 18; theory of
  history of, 19
mass production, 70, 162, 268
mass society, 253, 260; social theory
  of, 70, 250; status anxieties in, 251
McCarthy, Joseph, 14;
  anticommunism of, 113; Coughlin
  contrasted with, 123; radical right
  crystallized by, 120; Right Wing
  Popular Front traveled by, 113
McCarthyism: against American
  socialism, 2; *The New American
  Right* on, 14; New Left and, 34;
  Parsons on, 119; as radical right,
  2; as right-wing extremism, 114;
  Viereck on, 118
McGee, Gale, 124
McKenna, Regis, 196
"Memoirs of a Trotskyist" (Kristol),
  63
meritocracy, 224–226, 271, 300
middle class, 11, 75, 115–116, 164, 170
Mills, C. Wright: Daniel Bell's
  relationship with, 70, 100–102;
  on end of ideology, 101; and New
  Left, 101; "Vulgar Sociology" on,
  102; and "young intelligentsia" as
  agents of change, 103
minorities. *See* racial minorities
modernism, 253–254, 269, 270–271;
  mass production sparking, 268;
  religion disrupted by, 78
modernization theory, 247

GPSR Authorized Representative: Easy Access System Europe, Mustamäe tee 50, 10621 Tallinn, Estonia, gpsr.requests@easproject.com

www.ingramcontent.com/pod-product-compliance
Lightning Source LLC
Chambersburg PA
CBHW021412050426
42334CB00068B/250